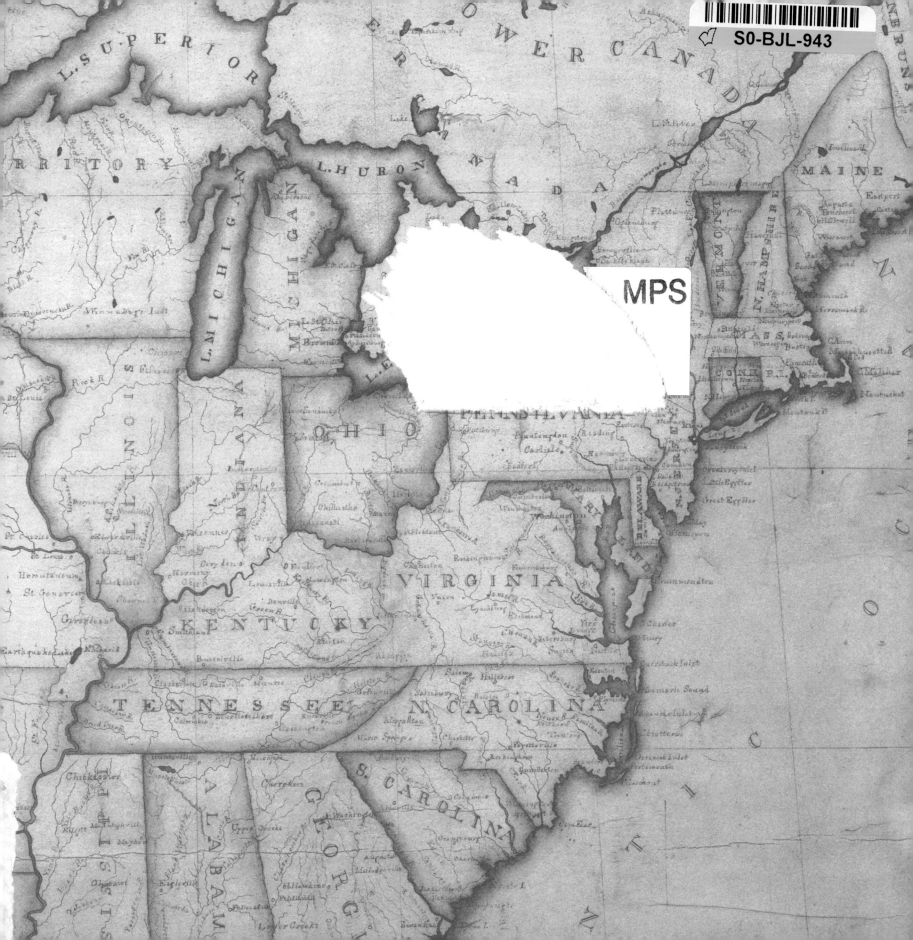

Samplers & Samplermakers

An American Schoolgirl Art 1700–1850

Sampler worked by Barbara Baner, 1812 (see entry 42)

Samplers & Samplermakers

An American Schoolgirl Art 1700–1850

Mary Jaene Edmonds

RIZZOLI, NEW YORK/LOS ANGELES COUNTY MUSEUM OF ART

Published in conjunction with the exhibition:

Samplers & Samplermakers
An American Schoolgirl Art 1700–1850

LOS ANGELES COUNTY MUSEUM OF ART
NOVEMBER 7, 1991–FEBRUARY 2, 1992

First published in the United States of America
in 1991 by Rizzoli International Publications, Inc.
300 Park Avenue South, New York, NY 10010

Photographs of samplers by Gene Ogami,
courtesy Los Angeles County Museum of Art
Photographs on pages 84 (left) by Chris Edmonds and 112 (left) by
Tony Senior

Unless otherwise noted, the samplers illustrated are in the collection of the
author

Library of Congress Cataloging-in-Publication Data
Edmonds, Mary Jaene.
    Samplers & Samplermakers: an American schoolgirl art, 1700–1850 /
Mary Jaene Edmonds.
        p.   cm.
    Published in conjunction with the exhibition held at Los Angeles
County Museum of Art Nov. 7, 1991–Feb. 2, 1992.
    Includes bibliographical references.
    ISBN 0-8478-1396-7
    1. Samplers—United States—History—18th Century.   2. Samplers—
United States—History—19th century.   I. Los Angeles County
Museum of Art. II. Title. III. Title: Samplers and samplermakers.
NK9112.E3   1991
746.39'73—dc20
                                                                    91-11425
                                                    CIP

Front jacket: sampler worked by Polly Phippen, 1783 (see entry 3)
Back jacket: detail of sampler worked by Jane Hanson, c. 1827 (see entry 40)
Endpapers: detail of map of the United States drawn by Jane Strong
(1814–1885), Hartford, Connecticut, 1827 (see page 11)

PRINTED AND BOUND IN JAPAN BY DAI NIPPON PRESS
DESIGNER: PAMELA FOGG
PRODUCTION AND DESIGN DIRECTOR: CHARLES DAVEY

To Betty Ring
for her constant encouragement, my most sincere and grateful thanks

Contents

Foreword

The meticulous craftsmanship and subtle beauty of these schoolgirl embroideries reveal the diversity and sophistication of this early American art form. Although it is popularly believed that samplermaking was a purely domestic pastime, samplers were not, in fact, sewn by young women at home, but were actually taught and made in schools. Thus a history of samplers becomes a study of the education of young women in colonial and post-Revolutionary America.

The Los Angeles County Museum of Art is pleased to present the exhibition *Samplers & Samplermakers: An American Schoolgirl Art 1700–1850* and this book as a milestone of research and scholarship in this largely neglected field. The generous promised gift of the Quaker material will enhance our Costume and Textile Department holdings in the area of American textiles, a subject that has become increasingly popular in the last decade.

Special thanks are due to Mary Jaene and Jim Edmonds, collectors and connoisseurs, who through dedication and patience have been able to form this outstanding collection of samplers. Mrs. Edmonds has been tireless in her quest for historic documentation relating to these pieces and her findings are both fascinating and revealing.

EARL A. POWELL III
DIRECTOR, LOS ANGELES COUNTY MUSEUM OF ART

Left: sampler worked by Mary Walton, England, 1650. Los Angeles County Museum of Art

Preface

It was long after I began collecting American sampler embroideries that I became convinced the young stitchers were taught the art of ornamental needlework in schools for girls. This was, for me, a stunning revelation as I had assumed that all forms of embroidery were taught within the home. It is now clear, however, that these exquisitely worked samplers were, indeed, stitched by young girls, not adults, under the watchful eye of a schoolmistress. It has also become increasingly apparent that this task was undertaken in private boarding or day schools for young girls and rarely, if ever, in a public institution or common school.

My purpose in writing this book was threefold: to portray sampler embroidery as indisputable evidence of colonial education for women in this country; to attempt to identify the often anonymous teacher and the location of her schoolroom; and to assist the reader in identifying specific patterns or design formats that will allow for classification of more schoolgirl embroideries and may, in time, lead to the discovery of additional early American schools for girls. It is my hope that this study will carry forward that which was published by the Rhode Island Historical Society in 1983, *Let Virtue Be a Guide to Thee: Needlework in the Education of Rhode Island Women, 1730–1830*, by Betty Ring.

Sampler embroideries—which are often inscribed with the name of their maker, the date, the age of the child, the name of the teacher who designed the format, and occasionally, the school in which they were embroidered—are only now being recognized as essential keys to the understanding of women's education in this country. Since, with few exceptions, early academic schooling for girls was not recorded, samplers can be seen as historic documents, verifying the existence of such schools. Most importantly, they reflect the first—and in some instances the only—exposure to formal education received by a young woman.

At first, samplers were used by schoolmistresses to train small children to stitch in order to mark initials on clothing and household linens. The students had mastered the alphabet through the use of the hornbook, and many could read passages of the Bible by the time they were sent to be educated. Those young women still attending school in their teens progressed on to more ornamental needlework instruction. Embroidery, in all its complexities, was the foremost accomplishment of a well-brought-up young woman.

The format of the sampler was entirely up to the schoolmistress—she developed the patterns for these delightful creations and then supervised their execution. The act of designing samplers became a creative outlet for her. She expressed her individuality by creating the format and embellishing the bands of lettering with flowery sprays, landscapes, and people in elaborate costumes of the period. Thus the schoolmistress assumed the role of folk artist and her exquisite designs for needlework on linen are a form of American folk art. The vast inventory of samplers that survive today attest to her remarkable abilities.

As education for girls became more widespread, sampler embroidery increased in popularity. Teachers were inclined to favor specific, recognizable motifs, and regional patterns began to emerge. For example, many of the samplers made around Boston in the eighteenth century feature green silk, hourglass-shaped bands and maple leaves. Samplers worked under the supervision of Sarah Fiske Stivours of Salem, Massachusetts, can be recognized by the crinkled silk floss worked in sunbursting rays of long-reaching stitches, intended to depict sky and clouds, as they do with a dazzling effect. Hannah Wise Rogers, the probable teacher and designer of the Canterbury, New Hampshire, samplers, made use of a plume-shaped leaf motif and handsomely crowned birds for samplers worked in her classroom. School records in the town indicate that Hannah's daughter, Lucy Rogers Foster, became a teacher in Canterbury, as did Lucy's daughter, Polly, who worked a sampler in 1787 (see fig. 8). In this way, students of embroidery classes, then, perpetuated a local tradition of samplermaking, using patterns and formats resembling those they had been taught.

Similar styles and motifs, therefore, allow for the grouping of

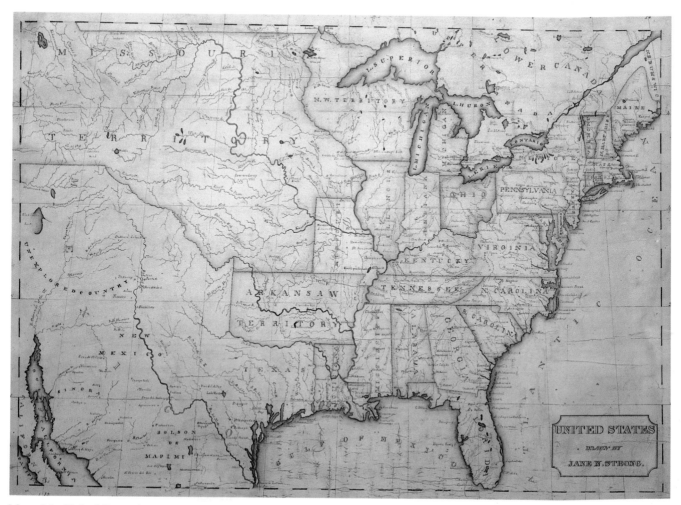

Map of the United States drawn by Jane Strong (1814–1885), Hartford, Connecticut, 1827

related pieces and their placement within a specific town or village. For example, if several samplers—about which little is known—are found to bear similar motifs, have identical shapes and thread colors, or display comparable methods of stitching, they can be assumed to have generated from the same region, perhaps even the same school. If one among them has been inscribed with the maker's name, a date, an age, or other vital information, this can be helpful in locating the entire group of samplermakers. Names can then be traced in the records of the Family History Library of the Church of Latter-Day Saints in Salt Lake City, Utah. More often than not, these records will contain documentation of the young women, along with complete genealogical histories. Evidence such as this has enabled me to ten-

tatively place the schoolmistress and the classroom in a given vicinity. Upon occasion, a teacher's name or initials are inscribed upon the linen ground. Then, armed with two or three samplermakers, the location, and the date, a serious search would begin in the local records. Of the twenty-six bodies or groups of sampler needlework represented in this book, each can be identified as originating within the sphere of influence of a particular teacher or region.

Researching women in early records can be a frustrating business, as they were generally overlooked by scriveners and not included in public documents. There are, however, exceptional women who kept detailed diaries recounting events in their lives that give an intimate view of the people and the town in which they lived. The diaries of the famed jurist Samuel Sewall and William Bentley of Massachusetts have also provided key names and places, as do the writings of other men of history.

Determined to document each sampler embroiderer, I pursued genealogical searches to determine where the samplermaker lived, the identity of her parents, their occupations, the location of her village and its significance. This often entailed traveling to the region in order to search local histories and land records, as well as wills, estate inventories, and unpublished papers in state and local libraries, historical societies, and courthouses. In some cases, I met with descendants of the samplermakers, who provided me with handwritten private papers. Landownership maps, sometimes inscribed with the surname of the property owner, provided locations of dwellings. Local newspapers of the period occasionally ran advertisements for schools or teaching vacancies, which helped to locate classrooms and sometimes outlined a teacher's curriculum. Church records, which note births and baptisms, were invaluable. By the second or third decade of the nineteenth century, city directories had increased in popularity and these yearly publications began to include the names and addresses of most, though not all, of the men and women comprising the general population within the town. Later, directories might list surnames in alphabetical order, along with an address and sometimes the occupation of the individual. In many instances, this information allowed for documentation of the headmistress—though not her teaching aides—and exact location of her often modest schoolroom.

Of the seventy-six girls whose work is studied in this book, fifty-four were actually located and identified. Approximately twenty of their schoolmistresses have also been identified; their names, however, were more difficult to document with any degree of accuracy. There are some teachers whose names are inscribed on the linen, while others fit into groups previously identified. There are also a few whose existence is based entirely on circumstantial evidence that I have outlined in the text.

The age of the samplermakers ranges from eight to twenty-eight; all of them were unmarried, which indicates that married women did not make samplers but directed their needleworking skills to more utilitarian purposes. One sampler was worked by a young woman twenty-six years of age, an indication that women attended school at a later age than previously suspected. Another, a widow known to have been keeping school, worked a sampler as a model for the classroom when she was twenty-eight. In the early years of sampler embroidery it was the daughter of the wealthy landowner who attended the most fashionable school, producing the most elaborate embroideries, while from the sec-ond decade of the nineteenth century on, needlework pieces were worked by a number of daughters of inn-keepers, merchants, and craftsmen.

Of the thirty-six who married, records reveal they married surprisingly late in life—between the ages of twenty-one and twenty-seven, with only one marrying at eighteen. While two samplermakers died after the birth of their first or second child, Elizabeth Cheever Henley, of Charlestown, Massachusetts, had twelve. Seven of the women remained single. One of the samplermakers, known for her ability as a business woman, was the financial advisor to her brothers in their successful banking enterprise; another became a highly respected writer of religious texts. One young woman attended the trial of John Brown in the courthouse of Charles Town in what is now West Virginia, her life later becoming torn by the battles of northern Virginia during the Civil War.

As material culture, then, samplers are lessons in social and geographic history rather than mere exercises in needle and thread. Most American samplers were made in New England and along the eastern seaboard where many of the first settlements were established. Samplers were also worked in the South, although widespread use of tutors appears to have eliminated a cohesive body of related schoolgirl embroideries. Needlework from the western part of the United States is quite rare, but examples from Arkansas and California are included in this book.

Until the Industrial Revolution and the invention of indelible ink, samplermaking flourished in this country. During the years immediately following 1840, this charming craft, in its most artistic form, virtually disappeared. The naive spirit of the art had vanished, replaced by a vast repository of unimaginative cross-stitched squares. But for over two hundred years, these beautiful sampler designs were carefully drawn by a host of quite remarkable pioneer women teachers whose daily task was to supervise the young women who stitched some of the most astonishingly ingenious examples of needlework ever produced in America. An enormous number of these schoolgirl samplers were preserved and survive today as testaments, unparalleled historic documents of the roots of education for women in America, a field that until recently has remained relatively unexplored.

MARY JAENE EDMONDS
LONG BEACH, CALIFORNIA

Introduction

THE INDUSTRY OF CHILDHOOD

Labour for lear[n]ing before thou art old
For lear[n]ing is better th[a]n silver and gold
For silver and gold will vanish away
But lear[n]ing is a jewel that will never decay

(Inscription on the sampler made by Fanny Drowne, 1797, age 12)

The history of samplermaking in this country is inextricably tied to the history of women's education, for samplers were made in classrooms and were often the first—and sometimes only—step in a young colonial woman's education.

Samplers—which are oblong pieces of linen embellished with patterns of embroidery worked in silk threads—were first brought to America from England and northern Europe, where they had been an established form of schoolgirl art for centuries. Textile historians believe that the first samplers, or *exemplars*, were made by young women during the Middle Ages, perhaps as a method of recording patterns for future reference.[1] Through the years the definition of a sampler has changed from that of a learning exercise in embroidery technique, signed and dated, to a finished work in its own right, intended for framing and display. Today, a sampler need not be signed or dated to merit the name.

There is ample evidence that children of both sexes were educated in nunneries in England as early as the tenth century; the embroideries of ecclesiastical furnishings for the church were created by nuns, as well as by professional embroiderers.[2] Teaching young girls to stitch, then, would have been a natural function of these early convent schools. Daughters of knightly families were also sent to be educated within the castle walls, where they were taught to spin, weave, and embroider under the watchful eye of the *chatelaine*. By the 1500s, the practice of samplermaking was widespread although scarcely any of these early examples have survived.[3]

Lace pattern design from Federico Vinciolo's *Les Singuliers et nouveaux pourtraicts*, Paris, 1587. Early lace pattern books remained a constant source of inspiration for schoolmistresses. This design, called "Ce Pelican," appeared two centuries after it was published as part of the central motif in the Dutch darning sampler shown on page 15.

seen in England at the close of the seventeenth century. The use of soft, pastel-colored embroidery threads places Winnifrid's sampler at about 1690, for within a decade these pale colors would fall from favor and give way to more garish and vibrant hues of red, green, and deep tones of indigo blue (Huish, *Samplers and Tapestry Embroideries*, 16, 28).

In flawlessly executed eyelet and satin stitches, Winnifrid has worked three alphabets, each lacking both the *J* and the *U*. It was customary at that time to use *I* for *J*, and *V* for *U*. She has stitched two maxims and has signed the embroidery. Unlike examples of sampler stitchery worked during the earlier years of the sixteenth century, which lacked either mottoes or signatures, the embroidered lettering on Winnifrid's sampler was introduced during a period of needlework history when samplermaking had evolved from simply a means of recording embroidery patterns to an exercise in needlework proficiency deemed worthy of display (Huish, 14). Traditional bands of narrow geometric patterns include a small measure of metal thread—sufficiently thin and flexible enough to be passed through the needle's eye—that can be detected in the third pattern row from the bottom. The scant use of this expensive sewing material reflects a diminishing enchantment with silver and silver-gilt embellishment, which was very much in evidence during the sixteenth century, a period now regarded as the golden age of embroidery (Colby, *Samplers, Yesterday and Today*, 151, 153).

Winnifrid Kennersley may have been a member of the Kennerley or Kennerleigh family who lived about five miles northwest of the village of Crediton in the parish of Devon, registered in 1645 by the Consistory Court of the Bishop of Exeter (Smith, *Genealogical Gazetteer of England*, 293).

SARAH OGDEN
English, 1792
Silk threads on linen (38 threads to the inch)
Satin, tent, and cross-stitches
13½ x 12 in. (33.3 x 30.4 cm)

Inscription: The Lord's Prayer
Sarah Ogden did this work in the year AD 1792

The pictorial sampler worked by Sarah Ogden in 1792 is inscribed with the Lord's Prayer in typical English fashion. English schoolmistresses were excessively fond of lengthy verses and biblical inscriptions, in an effort, one might suppose, to emphasize the lettering ability of the child. The ground fabric is a heavy, canvas-like linen, not found in American sampler embroidery of the same period.

A paper pattern drawn from a print or engraving must exist of this farmhouse, barn, and fenced pasture scene, for it has been found in the same arrangement on a sampler worked by Hannah Bennet in 1822 (collection, Rochester Museum and Science Center Historical Collections, Rochester, New York; see Rettew, Siener, and Wass, *Behold the Labour of My Tender Age, Children and Their Samplers, 1780–1850*, 49). Sarah Ogden's schoolmistress has added a peacock—an early English design—and farm animals, to further embellish her embroidery.

WINNIFRID KENNERSLEY
English, c. 1690
Silk and metal threads on linen
(44 threads to the inch)
Eyelet, satin, and cross-stitches
5½ x 8¾ in. (39.3 x 22.2 cm)

Inscription: *BLESSED.ARE.ThOSE.WhICh.GOD./ hAVE.ChOSE.AND.IN.hIM.PVT.ThEIR./TRVST.hE. WIL.APPEAR.TO.US.MOS/T.NEAR.WhEN.HeRS. DEPART.WE./MVST./WhEN.FRIENDS.ARE. GONE./AND.MONEY.SPENT.ThEN./LEARNING. IS.MOST.EXCE/LENT. WINNIFRID. KENNERSLEY. HER .WORK. AT. 8. YEARS. OVLD*

Undated samplers frequently offer subtle clues to the period and even the country in which they were worked. For example, the short length of Winnifrid Kennersley's embroidery reflects a sampler style

IIL (OR JJL)
Holland, 1799
Silk threads on linen (36 threads to the inch)
Weaving and darning patterns, and cross-stitches
16½ x 18 in. (41.9 x 45.7 cm)

Inscription: *IIL/ANNO/1799*

The weaving patterns of this darning sampler, worked by a young Dutch stitcher, were arranged in crosses, rectangles, and blocks of darning around a central sampler motif. The completed square is hemmed by a simple cross-stitched border. Close inspection reveals that two holes have been cut out of the linen at the topmost cross on the right. The samplermaker mended the two holes, employing different darning techniques. One of the holes is finely closed with row upon row of buttonhole stitches in linen thread, while the second is needle-woven with threads that appear to have been removed from a fragment of the linen ground.

The complicated, textured darns have been accomplished by employing two, or sometimes three, pastel-colored silk threads, as a method of highlighting the complex patterns. Both sides of the fabric are alike; the back of the sampler reveals a "reverse" damask effect. This sampler exhibits many of the same or strikingly similar patterns found on darning pieces throughout Europe. Recognizable weaves, such as web, diaper, twill, and damask, have been repeated with regularity, over and over, in the embroidery classes of Dutch and English schools. Such consistency suggests that particular weaving patterns in cloth were standard and, therefore, commonplace. Having completed a darning sampler, a child was well prepared to mend the domestic textiles found at home (Huish, *Samplers and Tapestry Embroideries*, 139).

The central motif—a mother bird feeding her fledglings—is of particular interest to sampler historians. It is taken from Federico Vinciolo's 1587 edition of the needlework pattern book, *Les Singuliers et nouveaux pourtraicts* (see page 13). This illustration of a pelican and her young, originally published in France, became a popular embroidery motif in Italy during the Renaissance. Rare pattern books such as this were traditionally shared among friends, and schoolmistresses, who pricked and pounced the designs until the pages fell out. The identical pattern appears on the earliest dated sampler yet to be identified, worked by Jane Bostocke, an English child, in 1598 (collection, Victoria and Albert Museum, London; see Ring, *Let Virtue Be a Guide to Thee*, 25).

With the invention of the printing press in the fifteenth century, books became increasingly available to the affluent. Lace patterns were published in volumes that were acquired by women of the emerging merchant class. The designs were easily translated into other forms of needlework, were copied and freely handed about. Teachers made use of the patterns, adjusted them to their needs, and included them in their curriculum.

Samplers, a primary tool of embroidery instruction, were a part of every teacher's repertoire from the Middle Ages until late into the nineteenth century. Early records reveal the names of only a handful of needlework teachers. According to the *Doomsday Book* (1085–86), Alwid, the Maiden of Buckinghamshire, was paid two hides of land in return for teaching embroidery to the daughter of Count Goderic.[4] Sometime before 1595, Miss Hannah Senior was engaged to teach the daughters of the Earl of Thomond the mysteries of the needle.[5] Actual boarding or day schools for girls in England were well established before 1635.[6]

In *The Dictionary of Needlework*, published in 1882, S. F. A. Caulfield and Blanche C. Saward stated that samplers came into prominence during the sixteenth and seventeenth centuries, the period we now designate as England's golden age of embroidery. No young lady's education during that time, they wrote, was considered complete until she had "embroidered in silks and gold thread a Sampler."[7] F. G. Payne described samplers as "a task for infant fingers," and recognized the form as a widespread cult with England as its real home.[8]

Prior to the 1590s, these embroideries were unsigned and undated. Northern European girls as young as eight or nine are believed to have worked the surviving examples, including those displaying complex needle-lace and needle-weaving techniques. This style of samplermaking imitated true lace-making, a much more difficult and complex craft. Embroidery bearing an early date often made use of finely worked satin stitches for alphabets and inscriptions, such as those found on the seventeenth-century English sampler worked by Winnifrid Kennersley (see page 14).

English samplers from the sixteenth and seventeenth centuries were long and narrow, and worked on linen that was cut in a thin strip across the width of the woven fabric from selvedge to selvedge. Mary Walton's sampler (see page 8) was originally embroidered on linen that was cut in this fashion. Samplers such as these were worked in patterned bands and were borderless.

America's earliest settlers brought this charming form of embroidery with them to the new land, for samplers made after their arrival in this country resemble those of Stuart England. The sampler worked by Loara Standish (collection, Pilgrim Hall Museum, Plymouth, Massachusetts), daughter of Miles Standish of Plymouth, is undated but is known to have been made before 1656. As was the fashion in England, her embroidery is long and is worked in silken bands across a narrow linen ground—evidence of dedication to the continuation of traditional forms of education for women in the new land.[9] In fact, British and colonial American schoolmistresses were inclined to use the same long, thin format until around the first quarter of the eighteenth century, when samplers became shorter and slightly wider. Teachers were by nature thrifty of their linen.

The instruction of schoolgirls in the art of embroidery in America spanned over two hundred years, beginning around 1650. The majority of the embroideries that survive today were worked in the first quarter of the nineteenth century. A variety of sampler styles were taught, including marking or alphabet samplers, pictorial samplers, mending and darning samplers (see page 15), and a small number of map samplers. Family record samplers were a particularly popular phenomenon in the newly formed United States. Combinations of these embroideries can also be found, some lavishly bordered, others unbordered. The more elaborate pictorial pieces on sheer linen or muslin were stitched by young women still attending school when they were in their twenties, as were the silk embroideries and silk mourning pictures. Fashionable trends in needlework, as in other facets of society, can be detected in sampler embroideries. For example, elaborate pictorial linen samplers and silk-on-silk embroideries were considered the height of fashion during the federal or neoclassical period.

It is evident that needlework schooling was the domain of the private, not the public, schoolmistress. In Boston, jurist Samuel Sewall noted in his diary that his young daughters had been placed in Dame Walker's school as early as 1687.[10] In America, dame schools for the instruction of the very young, as in England, sometimes offered elementary lessons in small, simple cross-stitched marking or alphabet samplers to both boys and girls. While few of these early schools for girls are noted in official records, contemporary newspapers provide evidence of their existence. Mistress Turfrey, for example, advertised that she kept a boarding school in Boston in 1706.[11] In the *Boston Newsletter* of March 27, 1729, Mrs. E. Atkinson announced that she would teach "Young Ladies all Sorts of Works."[12] By the middle of the eighteenth century, numerous teachers were informing the public of their intention to instruct plain sewing as well as a variety of complex forms of embroidery. In 1755, Elizabeth Hinche advertised that she could teach "plain Sewing, Irish stitch, Ten stich [sic], Sampler Work, Embroidery, and all other Sorts of Needle Work."[13] Advertisements of this kind assist in documenting fashionable trends and terminology in use at the time.

PHI(LLIS?) FRYER
English, 1808
Silk threads on gauze (54 threads to the inch)
Satin, chain, stem, and cross-stitches
20 x 17 in. (50.8 x 43.1 cm)

Inscription: *How happy is the blameless Vestals Lot/The World for getting by the World forgot/Eternal Sunshine of the spotless Mine/Each Prayer accepted and each Wish resign'd/Labor and Rest their equal Vigils keep/Obed'ent Slumbers which can wake and weep/Desires composed and Affections even/Tears which delight and Sighs that waft to Heav'n/Grace shines around her with serenest Beams/And whispering Angels prompt her golden Dreams/For her the Spouse prepares the Bridal Ring/For her white Virgins sweet Hymen als sing/For her th' unfading Rose of Eden blooms/And Wings of Seraphs shed divine Perfumes/To Sounds of Heav'nly Harps She dies away/And melts in Visions of eternal Day Phi Fryer/Aged 12 years 1808*

This stunningly beautiful sampler, worked by twelve year old Phi(llis) Fryer, reveals its country of origin by the delicate, flawless needlework so typical of English schoolgirl art. The extensive inscription—an English tradition—fills the center panel, which has been enclosed within a thin, varicolored grape and vine border.

The wide outer border has been worked with intricate flower and vase motifs, geometric in form, and exacting in execution; each side is a mirror image of the other. The red, cross-stitched building, placed at the top of the needlework, has minute windows, each with nine tiny panes. Detailed patterns such as these were probably drawn on a paper graph that could be thread-counted by the child.

It is in the meticulous stitching, the careful workmanship, supervised by demanding English schoolmistresses, that we may detect the difference between samplers worked in the United Kingdom and those with an American attribution. After comparing sewing materials, which differ to a degree, it is in the finely constructed stitches that the English child excelled.

In the years before the Revolution, colonial samplers began to differ entirely in style and format from their European counterparts. The linen grew more generous in width, although still rectangular in shape. Teachers designed samplers with fine borders, which became very fashionable. Within this lavish frame, naturalistic flowers and leaves began to appear in great abundance. Costumed figures and animals frolicked about landscapes that were further embellished with decorative vases and ornamental baskets. The formally patterned, exquisitely stitched British sampler had disappeared, leaving in its place the most delightful form of schoolgirl embroidery the world has ever seen.

Regional styles began to appear. Schoolmistresses in Essex County, Massachusetts, for example, fascinated with the new crinkled silk floss brought by shipmasters trading with China, designed extravagant, solidly worked borders to show off their expertise. Such elegance in samplermaking appears to have diminished in New England during the Revolution, only to spring forth after the war in even greater pictorial grandeur, particularly in the vicinity of Providence, Rhode Island, in the 1780s. Immigrant settlers, especially around Pennsylvania, retained their European needlework patterns and motifs making identification of their embroidery forms more easily recognizable. Pennsylvania-German immigrants clung to their traditional, small, scattered motifs. Samplers worked under their instruction are usually borderless. Those worked in schools kept by Quaker schoolmistresses are readily identifiable by their endearing floral sprays and distinctive alphabet lettering. These large, blocky letters, were probably conceived at Ackworth School in Yorkshire, England.[14] At least eleven samplers considered in this book reveal Quaker influence.

The first quarter of the nineteenth century brought forth surprisingly beautiful embroideries that were worked in the Susquehanna and Delaware river valleys, some of which came from the classrooms of Quaker teachers. Many of the most lavishly embellished samplers from this region are thought to be the product of the leading, most exclusive girls' schools in the community; thus samplers became symbols of status. Embroidery, for a time, was the mark of an aristocratic life style.

The most influential factor in determining the format of a sampler was the teacher's acceptance or adaptation of the local design tradition—one that had in the past gained the approval of the parents of schoolgirls in the community—for the success of a school might depend on a teacher's needlework expertise. If this style was to her liking, the teacher added a few touches of her own. This explains why samplers from the same vicinity are sometimes similar. Patterns developed by the teacher reflect not only her artistic ability, but influences recalled from childhood.

Vorschrift, 1787, Pennsylvania-German paper pattern showing traditional alphabet forms, trees, and geometric designs for thread-counting, 1787. Sotheby's, New York

MARGARET BETT
Creich, Scotland, c. 1825
Wool on linen (22 threads to the inch)
Eyelet and cross-stitches
16½ x 8 in. (41. 9 x 20.3 cm)

Inscription: *W HS DB HB M/AB PJB CB WB
MW/WS HT DB MW/Miss Mitchell Creich/
Margaret Bett Aged/10 Brunton School/AS*

Schoolmistress: Miss Mitchell

This sampler, worked by Margaret Bett, has been
inscribed with the name of the maker's teacher as
well as the school in which it was made: Brunton
School in the tiny hamlet of Creich in Scotland.

An example of the first embroidery attempted by
a young child, it is a charming sampler. Embroidered in sprightly colored woolen threads of violet,
red, green, and black on loosely woven homespun,
quite typical of Scottish samplers, the crooked, uneven cross-stitches reveal Margaret's limited needle
vocabulary. Wool is a textile rarely used in American needlework until the rage for Berlin work in
the 1840s (see page 21).

A long, narrow row of cross-stitches encloses line
upon line of initials, some of which are romantically
united by a heart. Many of the inscribed initials include the letter *B*, probably to honor members of
her family. Initials of this nature frequently embellish Scottish sampler embroideries (Swain, "Scottish Samplers Names and Places," 79). Possibly one
of those groups of initials joined with a heart are
those of her parents.

Margaret Swain, who has written extensively
on the historical needlework of Scotland, reveals
that it was customary for married women to maintain their maiden names, which would have been
used on legal documents, as well as on gravestones
(Swain, 79).

Pictorial patterns, such as the open-winged birds
on Margaret Bett's sampler can be found on early
British needlework (Colby, *Samplers*, 79), while the
striped tulips, so prominently displayed, appear on
many Pennsylvania samplers worked in the vicinity
of Chester County, Pennsylvania, including those
worked by Abigail Yarnall and Mary Lewis (see
figs. 58, 59). Design elements employed in the instruction of sampler embroidery were not necessarily limited to one place or country; motifs were commonly used by all schoolmistresses teaching the art
of samplermaking.

MARY ROBERTS
English, c. 1825
Wool with silk threads on linen
(34 threads to the inch)
Eyelet, chain, and cross-stitches
11 in. square (27.9 cm square)

Inscription: *Mary Roberts . Aged 10 yea/rs*

Through the use of bright colors and a clever
arrangement, this layered sampler design allows unrelated motifs to be interwoven into a stylish and
pleasing record of needlework patterns.

Worked in woolen threads and highlighted with
small amounts of silk, the embroidery motifs include crowns, butterflies, a large parrot, and most
charming of all, a man and a handsome young woman wearing a bonnet and carrying a parasol. Mary's
rendition of a ship suggests that early Dutch samplers may have influenced her schoolmistress.
These patterns are characteristic of samplers
worked in the United Kingdom during the first
quarter of the nineteenth century. Wool was not in
general use in American sampler embroidery at this
time (Colby, *Samplers*, 57, 77, 114, 182).

The popular British heraldic lion, here *passant*—
walking with its right paw raised—proves that ancient patterns retained their popularity among
schoolmistresses, appearing in schoolgirl embroidery until the fashion of samplermaking, in its traditional form, came to a close, around the middle of
the nineteenth century.

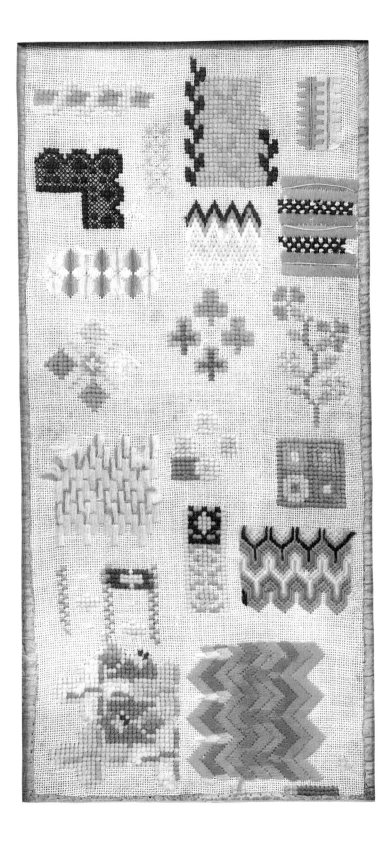

ANONYMOUS
Berlin wool work
English, c. 1870
Wool with silk threads on cotton or linen
(26 threads to the inch)
Tent, straight, satin, and cross-stitches
13 x 6½ in. (33 x 16.5 cm)

Berlin wool work, or Berlin work, is a style of embroidery that became fashionable during the second half of the nineteenth century. It was an excessively ornamental domestic craft made with brightly colored woolen threads. It was popular among young girls and women for at least half a century and is not considered a form of schoolgirl art.

Patterns similar to those seen here are known to date from a much earlier time. For example, Averil Colby illustrates a British sampler worked by Elizabeth Branch in 1670, which displays closely related geometric motifs (Colby, *Samplers*, 193). Embroideries featuring related designs were popular in America, making the origin of this piece somewhat questionable, although it was probably worked in England. Edged with a gathered, or quilled, blue silk ribbon, the partially worked motifs served as a reference, or a "sampler," for the needleworker.

Hand-colored paper patterns were introduced by a Berlin printseller named Wittich around 1810. His designs, intended to be worked in silks, were soon found by embroiderers to be readily adaptable to the new soft wools; they then proceeded to lavishly embellish their work with beads and other ornamentation. By 1820, the needlework fad was known as "Berlin work." Colored paper patterns and designs painted directly on canvas replaced linen in popularity. In a short time, large-sized canvases, garishly colored wool, and cross-stitches became the rage of needleworkers of all ages (Caulfield and Saward, *The Dictionary of Needlework*, 28).

Embroiderers have always been fascinated with the mathematical nature of specific overlapping (or bumpy) stitches that create a textural surface. When groups of these stitches are arranged in a pleasing design, the result brings forth a high and low effect as light plays across the embroidered fabric. More interesting than copying preconceived patterns, the resulting geometry, formed by fitting stitch against stitch, had great appeal for the imaginative nineteenth-century embroiderer. Variety within the chosen design could be achieved through changes in the size of the woven ground, the number of threads the stitch encompassed, and the vast selection of colors, as well as textures, in the embroidery thread itself. Freedom of selection has always attracted the serious needleworker (Edmonds, *Geometric Designs in Needlepoint*, 22–29).

Whether a sampler resembled the formal, traditional English sampler design or reflected a more relaxed, decidedly folksy format, the young child was merely the stitcher. She did not add or subtract a motif, or turn her hand to an inscription without the express permission of her schoolmistress.

With the emergence of a merchant class in the early nineteenth century, education for women flourished, more as a consequence of social pressures, however, than educational reform. More samplers were worked during this period than at any other time in our history. While it was common practice for the wealthy to send their young daughters away to boarding schools, either for a term during the summer, or for a longer period of time, the reasons for doing so seem to have been less educational than social. Parents were still especially anxious for their girls to become well-mannered, accomplished young ladies. An anonymous Philadelphia woman at the turn of the century wrote to her daughter with delight, "I received a letter from Mrs. Bromley, in which she commends you for the sweetness of your temper, and your great improvement in the needle. To say that I was glad on this occasion, is flat and unmeaning: I was overjoyed."[15]

Public schools also became more plentiful after 1800; teachers were hired and classes in academic subjects were offered to all the children of the town. Evidence of these schools and their various branches of instruction are recorded in town histories written in the 1880s and 1890s by local historians. They are also sometimes mentioned in newspaper articles. Needlework, however, would not have been part of the curriculum of these public schools, although various forms of needlework instruction and other "polite accomplishments," as noted in newspaper advertisements, continued to be provided at private institutions well past the middle of the century.

As the popularity of samplermaking increased dramatically in America during the first years of the nineteenth century, a change in the quality of the craft also became apparent. In her book, *The History of Embroidery: Sampler Making 1540–1940*, Joan Edwards notes that when examining sixteenth- and seventeenth-century samplers, more than thirty-six varieties of stitches can be recognized, many of them difficult to master. But, when she studied samplers worked after 1800, only about twenty, rather commonplace stitches were used, with tent, eyelet, satin, stem, and cross-stitches preferred. In the samplers discussed in this book, too, a noticeable transition can also be detected from more complicated stitchery in the early pieces, tending to the less complex toward the end of the first quarter of the nineteenth century. Work accomplished after 1840, with few exceptions, makes excessive use of the prevailing cross-stitch, which explains why this simple crossing of threads has often been termed the "sampler stitch."[16]

After 1850, samplermaking rapidly declined. This can be attributed to several factors. As education for women became more comprehensive, academic subjects were stressed over "the gentle arts"; while the fine arts were still taught in schools, painting and drawing gained prominence over needlework, as can be seen in later pictorial samplers, which combined both painting and needlework.

During the Industrial Revolution, the marking of clothing and other domestic textiles with cross-stitched threads became obsolete due to the availability of indelible inks. Additionally, trends in needlework changed. In America and Europe women of all levels of society began to stitch in the newest fashion, with chemically dyed woolen yarns on a heavy linen canvas. Berlin wool work had become the rage (see page 21). During the Victorian and Edwardian periods in England, canvas work, or needlepoint as we call it today, became the primary diversion of a woman of leisure. Fascinated with the newest fad, American women, too, embellished their furniture, mantelpieces, and doorways with yards of tent-stitched tapestries of canvas and wool. The schoolgirl art of samplermaking had virtually disappeared.

In America—as early as the 1740s when the most imaginative pictorial needlework appeared, and over a period of one hundred years thereafter—the schoolmistress, hand in hand with the schoolgirls under her supervision, created the most extraordinary and certainly the most amazingly beautiful embroidered sampler art in the history of the western world.

NOTES

1. Mrs. Bury Palliser, *History of Lace*, eds., M. Jourdain and Alice Dryden (reprint, New York, NY: Dover, 1984), 8.
2. For further information on the education of young girls during the Middle Ages, see Eileen Power, *Medieval English Nunneries* (Cambridge: Cambridge University Press, 1922).
3. Betty Ring, *Let Virtue Be a Guide to Thee: Needlework in the Education of Rhode Island Women, 1730–1830* (Providence, RI: Rhode Island Historical Society, 1983), 27.
4. Rozsika Parker, *The Subversive Stitch* (London: The Women's Press, 1984), 44. According to Noah Webster's *American Dictionary of the English Language*, 1828, a hide of land is described as "a certain portion of land, the quantity of which however is not well ascertained. Some authors consider it as the quantity that could be tilled with one plow; others as much as would maintain a family. Some suppose it to be 60, some 80 and others 100 acres."
5. Palliser, *History of Lace*, 12.
6. Dorothy Gardiner, *English Girlhood at School: a Study of Women's Education through Twelve Centuries* (London: Oxford University Press, 1929), 211.
7. S. F. A. Caulfield and Blanche C. Saward, *The Dictionary of Needlework* (London: L. Upcott Gill, 1882), 433.
8. F. G. Payne, *Guide to the Collection of Samplers and Embroideries* (Cardiff, Wales: National Museum of Wales, 1939), 22, 23.
9. Ring, *Let Virtue be a Guide to Thee*, 31.
10. M. Halsey Thomas, ed., *The Diary of Samuel Sewall: 1674–1729*, vol. 1 (New York, NY: Farrar, Straus and Giroux, n.d.), 33.
11. Glee Krueger, *New England Samplers to 1840* (Sturbridge, MA: Old Sturbridge Village, 1978), 156.
12. George Francis Dow, *The Arts and Crafts in New England: 1704–1775: Gleanings from Boston Newspapers* (Topsfield, MA: The Wayside Press, 1927), 273.
13. Ibid., 274.
14. Betty Ring, "Samplers and Pictorial Needlework at the Chester County Historical Society," *Antiques* (December 1984): 1425.
15. *The Polite Lady; or, A Course of Female Education in a Series of Letters from a Mother to Her Daughter* (Philadelphia, PA: printed for Matthew Carey, 1798), 41.
16. Joan Edwards, *The History of Embroidery*, vol. 5, *Sampler Making: 1540–1940* (Guildford, England: Bayford Books, 1983), 5.

L. DESPA
Saucy, France, 1874
Cotton threads on canvas, and linen
(56 threads to the inch), netting, paper, and silk ribbon
Fagoting, feather, buttonhole, tambour, satin, padded satin, crochet, and cross-stitches, machine and hand sewing
19 square in. (48.2 square cm)

Inscription: *Ecole Communale De Saucy/1874/ L. Despa/ Souvenir*

For a century, from around 1830 until well into the 1930s, sample models of plain sewing were required of girls attending homemaking classes in both private and common, or public schools, in America and in Europe. Worked by L. Despa, who was a student at the Ecole Communale (common school) in Saucy, France, this imaginative example of practical sewing techniques includes pleating, buttonhole making, drawn thread work, mending, and needle-lace, as well as the padded satin initials of the maker. Each of the four corners has been ornamented with needlework accomplishments worked on a ground of netting. Backed by lime-green tissue, outlined in burgundy ribbons of silk, they include examples of cutwork, tambour, tape or braid lace (described in Caulfield and Saward, *The Dictionary of Needlework*, as consisting of plain or ornamental braids, or tapes, arranged to form a pattern, connected together with plain open mesh grounds, and filled with needle-laces; today tape- or braid-lace may be compared to Battenberg lace, but that term was not in common use when this book was published), and appliqué.

All of these examples, save the mending patch, have been applied to the linen with the uneven stitching of a hand-operated sewing machine. Essential to a young woman's education at the time, the newly popular sewing machine was operated by a small handle attached to the flywheel. Turning the handle at an uneven speed resulted in a variation of the size of the stitches.

Inserted into the center of the muslin is a red, cross-stitched sampler, an exercise that decreased in popularity after 1850. Replaced by the rage for Berlin work, samplermaking was reduced to these simple forms of needlework that continued to be stitched until shortly after the turn of the twentieth century.

Eighteenth Century

1. ELIZABETH CHEEVER (1723/24–1762)
Boston, Massachusetts, 1736
Silk and twisted silk threads on linen
(30 threads to the inch)
Slanted Gobelin, satin, couched satin, outline, eyelet, flame, long-armed cross-, and cross-stitches
14½ x 9½ in. (36.8 x 24.1 cm)

Inscription: *ELIZabetH CheeveR Made/ThIS*
SamppLER In The 13/yeaR of her/Age 1736

Boston Harbor, woodcut by Paul Revere, 1768. Library of Congress, Washington, D.C.

Education in Puritan New England was not the exclusive prerogative of boys. As early as 1687, young colonial girls were attending school in Boston, for on January 7 of that year Samuel Sewall, the noted American judge and diarist, recorded in his diary: "This day Dame Walker is taken so ill that she sends home my Daughters, not being able to teach them."[1] By the first years of the eighteenth century, school advertisements began to appear in Boston newspapers announcing the instruction of various forms of needlework. One of the earliest to proclaim her talent as a teacher in this field was Mary Turfrey in 1706.[2] By 1738, the number of teachers and needlework classrooms had grown at a prodigious rate, indicating that ornamental embroidery had become increasingly fashionable. The number of surviving examples of samplers known to have been worked in Boston around this time attests to their popularity.[3]

Many dressmakers and schoolmistresses, in an effort to supplement their income, advertised that they would create all sorts of designs for embroidery. Such evidence indicates that a variety of select patterns was available for purchase by those whose need for instruction was minimal. These individual designs were a boon to the accomplished embroiderer as well as to the unskilled sampler instructress, for her youthful pupils would in time graduate to more complex exercises in the art of embroidery. Fabrics, other than linen, upon which the designs were drawn included muslin, silk, satin, and canvas.[4]

There exists today a distinctive group of American embroideries that were embroidered by schoolchildren during the eighteenth century in and around Boston and along the shoreline north to Maine, which was once a part of the Commonwealth of Massachusetts. This unique group is patterned on the English sampler of the Stuart period (1603–1688; see page 8), which was slender and borderless and stitched in relatively narrow bands of geometric motifs extending rather uneventfully across the linen.

The samplers belonging to this group can be identified by a row of hourglass hexagonal motifs, as seen on the embroidery of Susannah Richardson (fig. 2). In addition, these samplers feature other characteristics that place them on the American side of the Atlantic. A small maple leaf design can frequently be found, occasionally arranged in serpentine reversing order in a vine-like decoration. Distinctive birds in profile are usually perched on sparsely branched trees. In almost every instance the eyelet stitch is evident either in one linear strip or worked to form an alphabet. Many of the works in this Boston-area group also include the figures of Adam and Eve, the apple tree, and the serpent; they are known as the "Adam and Eve samplers." Together with a selection of counted thread patterns, these stitched designs help to identify this significant body of colonial sampler embroidery.

Elizabeth's sampler belongs to this important body of schoolgirl work, which is believed to have flourished in the Boston area from 1729 to 1801. The unfinished, solidly stitched section at the bottom of her sampler would, in the years to come, develop into the bouncing grassy mounds that may be seen on a number of needlework pieces shown in this book, including the sampler worked by Mehitable Foster of Canterbury, New Hampshire (fig. 8), and the anonymous sampler worked in Boxford, Massachusetts (fig. 14).[5]

Probably educated in Boston, Elizabeth Cheever was born on New Year's Eve, 1723, the daughter of Ezekiel Cheever and Elizabeth Jenner of Charlestown, Massachusetts. Records indicate that Ezekiel Cheever was a very successful sea captain. Four children were born before the death of his wife in 1728; Elizabeth was the third.[6] She was eighteen when, on October 19, 1741, she married Samuel Henley, a ship captain like her father, who was to earn great wealth and prestige during his lifetime. They became

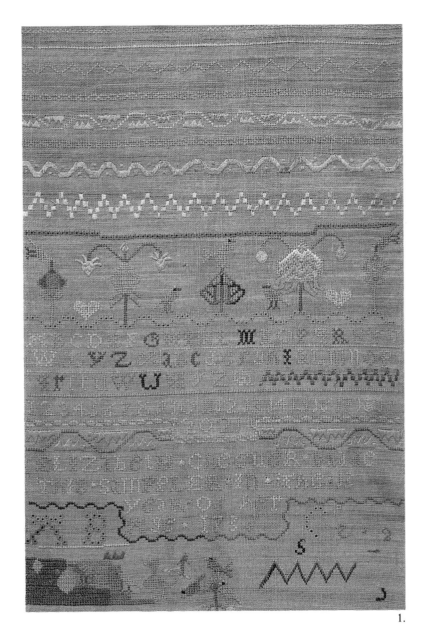

1.

NOTES:

1. M. Halsey Thomas, ed., *The Diary of Samuel Sewall: 1674–1729*, vol. 1 (New York, NY: Farrar, Straus and Giroux, n.d.), 139.

2. Glee Krueger, *New England Samplers to 1840* (Sturbridge, MA: Old Sturbridge Village, 1978), 156.

3. Betty Ring, *American Needlework Treasures* (New York, NY: ⁀ itton, 1987), 1, 2.

4. George ᴜncis Dow, *The Arts and Crafts in New England: 1704–1775* (Topsfield, MA: Wayside Press, 1927), 267, 274.

Copied from engravings and print sources, the elegant pictorial examples of canvas embroidery, which we now call needlepoint, are frequently termed "The Fishing Lady Pictures"—referring to a costumed figure of a woman seated in a sylvan glade with a fishing pole in her hand. This figure is thought to have been copied from antique playing cards. Examples of this embroidered art may be seen in two articles written by Nancy Graves Cabot in *Antiques*, "Engravings and Embroideries," July 1941, and "The Fishing Lady and Boston Common," December 1941.

5. Betty Ring, "Legacy of Samplers," in *1979 Antiques Show, Hospital of the University of Pennsylvania, Philadelphia* (Philadelphia, PA: Hospital of the University of Pennsylvania, 1979), 42.

6. Thomas Bellows Wyman, *The Genealogies and Estates of Charlestown, Massachusetts: 1629–1818* (reprint, Somersworth, MA: New England History Press, 1982), 209.

7. Ibid., 209, 493.

8. Ibid., 494.

the parents of twelve children before Elizabeth died following the birth of her last daughter, Sarah, early in 1762.[7]

When Samuel Henley died in 1789 the inventory of his estate amounted to 10,566 pounds sterling—an enormous sum. On a nineteenth-century map of Boston, slightly south of Bunker Hill in Charlestown, is a short and narrow street known by the name of Henley. Close to the Naval Basin, it is now crowded with factories, but it once embraced the elegant mansion that belonged to Samuel and Elizabeth Cheever Henley.[8]

2. SUSANNAH RICHARDSON (b. 1755)

Boston, Massachusetts, 1764
Silk threads on linen (44 threads to the inch)
Satin, eyelet, bullion, long-armed cross-, and cross-stitches with French knots
16¾ x 10¾ in. (42.5 x 27.3 cm)

Inscription: *Next.unto.God.Dear.Parents.I
Address.My./self.to.you.in.Humble.Thenkfulness.For.all/
your.care.and.Charge.on.Me.Bestowd.the./Means.of.
Learning.unto.Me.allowd.go.on./I.Pray.and.Let.Me.
Still.Persue.These.Golden./Arts.The.Vulgar.never.new.
Susannah.Richardson.Ended.This.Samplar.In/
The.Ninth.Year.Of.Her.Age.November.The./
Twenty.Second.1764*

Susannah Richardson's finely worked sampler, dated 1764, is representative of one of the earliest recognized groups of eighteenth-century American sampler embroideries. These distinctive pieces were worked in the vicinity of Boston as early as 1729.[1] Elizabeth Cheever (fig. 1) made her related sampler in 1736, nearly three decades earlier.

Specific patterns typical of this Boston group are present in this unbordered, banded sampler. The maple leaf motif, for example, has been used extensively, while the characteristic hexagonal band pattern has been depicted, as it often is, in threads of deep green silk, and the favored eyelet stitch forms one of the alphabet rows. By 1764, when the design for this piece was conceived, a pictorial garden along the base of the sampler had become the prevailing style.

Susannah has worked a naturalistic scene, relaxed and decidedly folksy. Quite unexpectedly, a delightful black and white cow has wandered into the landscape. This charming element is nearly obscured by the grassy mounds in the foreground, which are deeply embedded with blossoms.

As colonial samplers became more Americanized, Boston schoolmistresses veered away from the formal, precise needlework taught by their British counterparts, and schoolgirl embroideries in New England evolved into pictorial scenes of great imagination and charm. Borders became wider and more elaborate. The sampler worked by Susannah Richardson, then, is a reflection of a regional pattern in transition. Still English in style, it is borderless, and the alphabets and sawtooth stitches are worked in bands. Susannah has also inscribed on it a traditional pious verse. Yet at the same time, she has added to the work a lively pastoral scene, inhabited by frisky cattle.

Susannah, daughter of Jonathan Richardson and Mary Woodward Richardson, was born December 12, 1755, in Newton, Massachusetts, a small settlement to the west of Boston. She was one of a family of ten children.[2] The family eventually moved to Mohawk, New York, in the valley of the Mohawk River.[3]

NOTES:

1. Sotheby's, New York, catalogue, *Fine American Furniture, Folk Art, Silver, and China Trade Paintings,* 5736, June 23, 1988, lot 320.
2. John Adams Vinton, *The Richardson Memorial* (Portland, ME: Brown Thurston and Company, 1876), 229.
3. Ibid., 229. While evidence suggests that the family moved to Whitestown, New York, in 1768, Vinton questions the reliability of his source for this, stating that it was sometime after June 1784 that the first "white settlers" arrived in that place "only lately having been relieved from the inroads of savage Indians."
From the *Federal Census, New York State,* 1800, Susannah Richardson's brothers are known to have been established in Herkimer and Otsego counties nearby. See also *Federal Census, New York State,* 1790.

2.

3. POLLY PHIPPEN (1770–1812)
Salem, Massachusetts, 1783
Silk and twisted silk threads with crinkled silk floss
on linen (22 threads to the inch)
Bullion, satin, couched and uncouched satin, outline, eyelet, and cross-stitches with French knots,
and hem-stitching
21 in. square (53.3 cm square)

Inscription: *NO TIS IN VAIN TO SEEK
FOR/BLISS FOR BLISS CAN NEER BE/FOUND
TILL WE ARRIVE WHERE/JESUS IS AND
TREAD ON HEAVNLY/GROUND. THERES
NOTHING/ROUND THESE PAINTED SKIES
NOR/ROUND THE DUSTY CLOD NOTHING/ MY
SOUL THAT WORTH THY JOY/OR LOVELY AS
THY GOD
Polly Phippen/HER SAMPLER. 17/WROUGHT
1783. IN/THE 14.YEAR.OF/HER AGE*

Schoolmistress: Sarah Fiske Stivours
(1742–1819)

4. NABY DANE (1777–1834)
Salem, Massachusetts, 1789
Silk and twisted silk threads with crinkled
silk floss on linen (22 threads to the inch)
Eyelet, satin, outline, chain, and cross-stitches
16 x 12 in. (40.6 x 30.4 cm)

Inscription: *Naby Dane Her Sam/pler Wrought
June/The 27 1789 Bo/rn July The 19 1777
Next Unto God Dear/Parents I Address M/ySelf
To you In Hu/mble Thankfulness/For All your
Care/And Charge On me*

Schoolmistress: Sarah Fiske Stivours
(1742–1819)

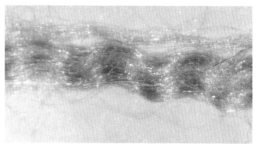

Magnification of the crinkled silk floss favored by Essex
County schoolteachers during the last years of the eighteenth century

In the well-established, affluent communities of post–Revolutionary New England, samplers gradually became larger and
more sumptuous than their British counterparts, displaying an
extravagant use of material. Often highly pictorial and bordered
with an impressive frame of needlework patterns, these schoolgirl
embroideries no longer emphasized the modest alphabet seen so
often during the early years of the eighteenth century.

Toward the end of the eighteenth century, as a consequence of
trade with China, samplers worked under the supervision of
schoolmistresses in the vicinity of Essex County, Massachusetts,
were lavishly embellished with an unusual type of crinkled silk
floss (see left). These precious skeins of silk were cautiously un-
raveled into manageable strands and then worked in long, uncouched stitches over the entire unembroidered portion of the
border, framing the samplers with brilliant colors and a thick, lustrous sheen. This technique became an established tradition in
the vicinity of Salem.[1]

Polly Phippen worked her splendid sampler in 1783 at the
school kept by Sarah Fiske Stivours of Salem. As with most female teachers in the colonies, Sarah Stivours is not recorded in
the history of this early Massachusetts settlement, although at
least fifteen samplers have been attributed to her instruction.[2]
While little is known about her school, it remains one of the earliest regional schools for young women yet to be recognized in
this country because of a number of embroidered samplers bearing her name. A comparison of embroideries known to have been
worked under her supervision allows us to identify others by similarity of style, technique, and specific patterns stitched upon the
linen ground.[3]

Often distinguished by a wide border edged with hem-stitching and sawtooth ribs, the samplers believed to be the product of
her tutelage reflect more than one style. The first and most commonly recognized format appears on the sampler worked by Polly Phippen (fig. 3), while another more pictorial variation may be
seen on the example stitched by Naby Dane in Salem in 1789
(fig. 4). The Phippen sampler employs long, diagonally worked
stitches of white, blue, and berry in two wide bands, one along
the top and another representing the sky across the bottom layer.
Her stiff figures, puffy birds, and animals are of crinkled silk floss,
and the characteristic flower-strewn border includes clusters of
detached stems of small, round cherries worked in eyelet stitches. A delicate arbor placed near the top of both samplers is a favored motif of the Stivours school. In some instances, samplers
depict distinctively shaped urns, complete with bouquets tied
with thin ribbon bows, placed diagonally in each of the corners.[4]

The sampler worked by Naby Dane in 1789 is more pictorial in

Polly Phippen's home in Salem, built by her father, Joshua, in 1782. Essex Institute, Salem

design. Black inked lines drawn as a guide for the samplermaker are still noticeable in the border that is a perfect duplicate of the one worked on the Phippen sampler. Long satin stitches of crinkled floss have been used to depict the domed building and the elaborately costumed figures. The sky, portrayed more naturally here in scallops of blue and white silk, the wide sawtooth edges, the arbor of floral sprays, and the cherry twigs assure us that Naby unquestionably stitched this sampler in the school of the accomplished Sarah Stivours.

POLLY PHIPPEN

The daughter of Joshua Phippen and Hannah Sibley Phippen, Polly was baptised Hannah—or, perhaps, Hannah Mary—Phippen, on June 3, 1770.[5] In 1782, her father, an orphan who became a successful merchant, built a three-story mansion on Hardy Street in Salem that still stands today (see above). He was considered a kind, generous man who "daily had seated at his table between twenty and twenty-five persons."[6]

After the death of his wife in 1801, Joshua married Ursula Symonds, widow of Jonathan Symonds, who for over thirty years kept a school for girls in her home in North Salem.[7]

Polly married Captain Benjamin Babbidge (b. 1768) in 1793. They had two children. His grandmother, Susanna Beckett Babbidge, kept a school for girls in Salem from 1750 to 1800, where "she taught reading and sewing for domestic purposes." His aunt, Lydia Babbidge, daughter of Susanna, also offered classes of "higher school for young Misses only."[8]

After twenty years of marriage, the Babbidge family experienced grave financial losses. Master of the brig *Nancy*, Benjamin was lost at sea in 1811. Polly Phippen Babbidge died in March 1812 of "distress of mind ended in consumption." She was forty-one years old.[9]

NABY DANE

Naby Dane has inscribed the date of her birth on her sampler: July 19, 1777. She was the daughter of Captain Joseph Dane and Mary Welcome (Wellman), who were married in Danvers, Massachusetts, on January 12, 1777, but did not long remain together. As family genealogists were notoriously reluctant to discuss family problems, the lack of information about the young couple implies that they may never have lived together as man and wife. According to *The Wellman Genealogy*, Joseph Dane died soon before 1814, yet when Naby was baptised on March 12, 1786, she was shown to be the "daughter of the widow Mary Dane." Mother and child may have made their home with her mother, Mary Henderson Wellman, for in 1785, William Bentley noted in his diary, "Widow Welman has seven children living in her family, five of them girls."[10]

In 1803, Naby Dane married her first cousin, Captain Joseph Phippen (b. 1779). They had five children. In 1813, Joseph sailed aboard the sloop *Wasp* and was lost at sea; the ship is believed to have been a victim of a fierce hurricane in 1814.[11] Naby Dane Phippen died on April 1, 1834.[12]

SARAH FISKE STIVOURS

The schoolmistress of these two young women was Sarah Fiske Stivours (1742–1819), the daughter of Reverend Samuel Fiske and Anna Gerrish, and one of five children. In 1766, her only surviving brother, John, married Lydia Phippen, first cousin to Polly Phippen and Joseph Phippen (who was later to become Naby Dane's husband), firmly uniting teacher to pupils through family ties.[13]

Sarah Fiske married Jacob Stivers (Stivours), a Dutch baker, in 1771. She became an exceptional embroidery teacher and kept a school for girls in Salem from at least 1778 to 1798.[14]

Her schoolroom may have been located "in Essex street above Elm, opposite the pumps at Neptune and Vine," where she is known to have been living when she died about the age of seventy-six.[15]

NOTES:

1. Ring, *American Needlework Treasures*, 8.
2. Krueger, *New England Samplers*, 178. See also Ring, "Legacy of Samplers," 41.
3. Ring, *American Needlework Treasures*, 9.
4. Ethel Stanwood Bolton and Eva Johnston Coe, *American Samplers* (Boston, MA: Massachusetts Society of the Colonial Dames of America, 1921), opp. 129, 166. The samplers worked by Lydia Stocker, 1798, and Content Phillips are now being attributed to Sarah Stivours's school. See also Ring, *American Needlework Treasures*, 9. The location of the Stocker sampler is unknown; see Bolton and Coe, *American Samplers*, opp. 129. The Phillips sampler is in the collection of the Cooper-Hewitt Museum of Design (Smithsonian Institution), New York, NY.
5. *Vital Records of Salem, Massachusetts, to the End of the Year 1849*, vol. 1 (Salem, MA: Essex Institute, 1916), 166. See also Sidney Perley, *The History of Salem, Massachusetts*, vol. 2 (Salem, MA: published by the author, 1926), 329.
6. George D. Phippen, *A Genealogy and History of the Descendants of David Phippen also Fitzpen* (Salem, MA, Essex Institute Historical Collections, 1848), 183–192.
7. Phippen, *Genealogy and History*, 189.
8. Perley, *History of Salem*, vol. 2: 314, 315. See also *Vital Records of Salem*, vols. 1: 58 and 4: 190. The school kept by Susanna Babbidge and her daughter, Lydia Babbidge, is discussed in Krueger's *New England Samplers*, 177, 178.
9. *The Diary of William Bentley, D.D.*, vol. 18 (Salem, MA, Essex Institute Historical Collections, 1881), 217.
10. *Vital Records of Salem*, vols. 1: 231 and 3: 275. See also Rev. Joshua W. Wellman, *Descendants of Thomas Wellman of Lynn, Massachusetts* (Boston, MA: Arthur Holbrook Wellman, 1918), 167, 168.
11. *Vital Records of Salem*, vols. 3: 275 and 6: 137, 138. See also Wellman, *Descendants*, 168, and William Armstrong Fairburn, *Merchant Sail*, vol. 2 (Center Lovell, ME: Fairburn Marine Educational Foundation, 1945–1955), 790, 791.
12. *Vital Records of Salem*, vol. 6: 138.
13. Frederick Clifton Pierce, *Fiske and Fisk Family* (Chicago: published by the author, 1896), 80, 81, 82.
14. Pierce, *Fiske and Fisk Family*, 82. See also *Vital Records of Salem*, vol. 4: 351. See also Ring, *American Needlework Treasures*, 8.
15. *Bentley Diary*, vol. 19: 179. See also *Vital Records of Salem*, vol. 6: 251.

4.

5.

5. NABBY GOSS (1783–1842)
Salem, Massachusetts, 1796
Twisted silk threads and crinkled silk floss on linen
(24 threads to the inch)
Eyelet, satin, and cross-stitches
14 x 12½ in. (35.5 x 31.7 cm)

Inscription: *Salem/Massachusetts State County of
Essex 1796/ Nabby Goss Salem*
Inscribed on back panel in pencil and ink: *Sa
Gossa of Spain/Nabby Goss Salem 1796/C. Priscilla
Low Cutts/Annie Cutts Newhall/Abby Lee
Newhall/Sa Gossa/Louis A. Wentworth/
1932/1796/136 years/Property of Abby Newhall
Wentworth/Great, great, Grandmother to Louis and
Edwin Wentworth*

U nlike other schoolgirl embroideries attributed to Essex
County, Massachusetts, this unbordered sampler represents a style not previously known to needlework historians. Inscribed on the sampler linen and the backboard is solid evidence, however, that the sampler was worked in Salem, although
the teacher who designed the format still remains a mystery.

As was the custom at the time, crinkled silk floss is the predominant embroidery thread of this sampler. Federal-style
draperies with fat cross-stitched tassels dip in measured swags
across the linen, but the ornate, naturalistic border fashionable at
the time (see figs. 3, 4) is conspicuously absent. A layered format
has been integrated into the design, allowing unrelated patterns
to be introduced. Shallow, footed urns decorated with geometric
patterns form an atrium cluttered with greenery and birds. The
center vase motif creates a platform for the improbable figure of a
lion with a splendidly regal crown, reminiscent of animal designs
in early lace pattern books.[1]

In the wide, lower band, a forest of tree and leaf shapes surrounds two elegantly costumed women, who face each other and
together hold a branched, floral spray. Although these figures bear
a faint resemblance to those worked by Naby Dane (fig. 4), they
are the only design element within the Goss sampler that can be
compared to those found in other known Essex County embroideries. Perhaps the discovery of similar samplers will eventually
reveal the identity of this schoolmistress.[2]

Nabby (Abigail) Goss was probably the daughter of Thomas
Goss (La Gossa of Spain) and his wife, Abigail.[3] It is likely that
Nabby was born in Spain in 1783 and was thus about thirteen
when she worked her sampler.[4] She married Thomas Low in
1808.[5] They had one daughter, Priscilla L. Cutts.[6] Abigail Goss
Low died in 1842, when she was fifty-nine.[7]

NOTES:

1. Federico Vinciolo, *Renaissance Patterns for Lace
and Embroidery*, 1587 (reprint, New York, NY:
Dover, 1971), 83.
2. Krueger, *New England Samplers*, 177, 178, 179.
There are countless schoolmistresses known to
have taught embroidery in Salem around the time
this sampler was worked, and many more still to be
documented. For the present, the most obvious selection would be the school kept by Susanna Babbidge and her daughter, Lydia. Further evidence
must be uncovered, however, before any attribution
may be made. No genealogical information has surfaced that would suggest a relationship between
Nabby and a teacher in Salem.
3. *Vital Records of Salem*, vol. 5: 289. See also *Federal
Census, Salem, Massachusetts*, 1820.
4. Francis, Nabby Goss's brother, is recorded as being the son of Thomas Goss, a Spaniard and a
mariner. Records also state that he was brought to
Salem as a young child. See *Essex Institute, Historical
Collections*, vol. 19 (Salem, MA: Essex Institute,
1882), 98.
   Presumably, Thomas Goss arrived in Salem
around 1790, for he was "warned out" of town for
unknown reasons in 1791, although he did not
leave. See *Essex Institute, Historical Collections*, vol.
43: 346.
5. *Marriage Records, Salem, Massachusetts*, vol. 4: 157.
6. Backboard of the sampler. Research verifies the
genealogical inscription on the sampler.
7. *Vital Records of Salem*, vol. 5: 408.

6. HANNAH S. WOLCOTT (1785–1843)
Massachusetts, c. 1800
Silk threads and human hair on linen
(20 threads to the inch)
Satin, outline, tent, eyelet, Bargello, stem, buttonhole, and cross-stitches with French knots
15½ x 13 in. (39.3 x 33 cm)

Inscription: *Hannah S Wolcott/On Music/Music the
fiercest grief can charm/And fates severest rage
disarm/Music can soften pain to ease/And make despair
and madness please*

6.

Hannah Sewall Wolcott's great-grandfather, Samuel Sewall, a member of the New England Council and a distinguished judge, was dedicated to equal education of the sexes. In 1687, his young daughters were in regular attendance at a school in Boston kept by Dame Walker.[1] This early established tradition of education for women was clearly upheld by future generations of the Sewall-Wolcott family.

Hannah Wolcott was attending school in her early teens when she embroidered this exquisitely worked sampler. With its broad, colorful border of bowknots and leafy swags, it displays great sophistication in design and execution. Samplers embellished with this identical border pattern have been attributed to the Boston area, although an identifiable group has yet to be established. This suggests that these tasteful motifs appealed to many embroidery mistresses in the region, who then adapted the design for their particular classroom needs.

The figure of a woman has been finely embroidered within a serene bower, surrounded by naturalistic roses of unusually large proportion. The sky above is adorned with birds. Grassy Bargello stitches in shimmering tones of sea green have been worked across the base of the sampler. The central figure is garbed in a fashionable dress that still retains its original, rich aqua color. A pristine white fichu, finely worked in buttonhole stitches, frames her face. Black threads outline the lute she holds in her lap, emphasizing the importance of music to the samplermaker. Surprisingly, we find that the figure's long brown hair is made of real hair.

Wolcott's sampler format includes a verse in praise of music, a subject of study at which she must have excelled. Liberal use of the long *s* is evident in the embroidered inscriptions, an archaic tradition soon to lose favor with schoolmistresses and samplermakers alike. It would appear, however, that scarcely a thought was given to the placement of her signature until the needlework was declared complete, for it has been awkwardly inserted high within the decorative border. Her age and the date of the sampler remain undisclosed.

One of six children born to Hannah Sewall (daughter of Captain Henry Sewall and Ann White) and Edward Kitchen Wolcott of Brookline, Massachusetts, Hannah S. Wolcott was baptised in 1785.[2]

Hannah S. Wolcott married John Folsom, a merchant in Boston, April 30, 1814. They had one son, Samuel.[3] Six years later, possibly widowed, she was living in Brookline.[4] Hannah Wolcott Folsom is probably the same Hannah who died in Lowell, Massachusetts, on October 24, 1843.[5] She is buried in the Wolcott family tomb in the Walnut Street Cemetery, Brookline.[6]

Hannah's younger sister Elizabeth worked an elegant silk mourning embroidery in 1808. The Wolcott girls undoubtedly attended the same fashionable school for girls near Longwood, the family estate in Brookline, Massachusetts.[7]

NOTES:

1. Thomas, ed., *Diary of Samuel Sewall, 1674–1729,* vol. 1: 139.
2. Chandler Wolcott, *Wolcott Genealogy: The Family of Henry Wolcott* (Rochester, NY: Genesee Press, 1912), 127.
3. Ibid.
4. *Federal Census, Brookline, Massachusetts,* 1820.
5. *Death Records, Massachusetts,* 1843–1844, vol. 35, no. 216.
6. Harriet Alma Cummings, comp., *Burials and Inscriptions in the Walnut Street Cemetery of Brookline, Massachusetts* (Brookline, MA: Brookline Historical Society, 1920), 130, 132, 133. The date of death for Hannah S. Wolcott is incorrectly given as between 1900 and 1913.
7. Elizabeth Wolcott's sampler is in the collection of Betty Ring; see Ring, *American Needlework Treasures,* 64. See also John Gould Curtis, *History of the Town of Brookline, Massachusetts* (Boston, MA, and New York, NY: Houghton Mifflin Company, 1933), 93, 94, 95.

7. MARY [CANNEY]
Southeastern New Hampshire, 1772
Silk and wool threads on linen
(28 threads to the inch)
Back, double-running, knit, chain, satin, slanted
Gobelin, eyelet, straight, split, and cross-stitches
15½ x 9½ in. (39.39 x 24.15 cm)

Inscription: *Mary* [name removed] *HER/WORK
AGD* [number removed] */June.6.1772*

Sensitive to political unrest within the colonies, many New England schoolmistresses echoed the defiance of the times by incorporating a new spirit of freedom into their work. They began designing more imaginative, energetic patterns for their embroidery classes. Having more or less discarded traditional British forms, they experimented with new techniques but, not to be too daring, endowed their artistic patterns with regional characteristics found on local samplers.

This enchanting sampler worked by Mary Canney in 1772 combines both new and regional design elements. It depicts a delightfully hefty Adam and Eve worked in vertical rows of diagonal stitchery. Present are the familiar apple tree, with globes of russet-colored fruit, and a stalwart serpent vividly worked in stripes of teal blue and cream. Crowns of royalty, often appearing on colonial stitchery, have been worked on either side of the tree.

During the 1740s and 1750s, countless depictions of Adam and Eve with the serpent and Tree of Knowledge appeared on samplers worked in and around Boston.[1] Rarely out of favor, these figures are still found on modern stitchery, but their popularity on colonial sampler embroidery waned as more innovative designs became fashionable. Although Mary's figures are similar in shape and stitching technique to those worked on an anonymous piece dated 1744,[2] this Adam and Eve sampler bears only faint resemblance to those worked near the shores of Boston Bay a generation before and may have been stitched in New Hampshire.

Mary's anonymous schoolmistress designed her sampler with a three-sided border of trifoliate leaves. The reversing vines grow from a pair of footed, double-handled vases, which are decorated to resemble fine porcelain. Splendid blue birds rest on vine-twigs near the upper corners of the frame. This may be one of the first uses of this impressive vase and vine design; a decade later it appears on samplers in extravagantly needleworked border patterns. At present, three examples of the adaptation of this stylish design come to mind: samplers worked in the 1780s at the preeminent school kept by Mary Balch in Providence, Rhode Island;[3] samplers by Mehitable Foster (fig. 8) and the Canterbury, New Hampshire, group; and a sampler worked in 1800 by Elizabeth Cutts of Berwick, Maine.[4]

The use of a darkly colored thread to outline the predominant leaf designs on the apple tree and those within the space of the border is an artistic technique frequently employed in New Hampshire samplerwork. It served to emphasize specific shapes, propelling the eye to selected fields in the design. The decorative basket that appears center top, for example, was a favorite motif of the Canterbury schoolmistress, Hannah Wise Rogers (see fig. 8), from Ipswich, Masssachusetts.

The delicate corner motifs, reaching diagonally into the needleworked picture, are reminiscent of seventeenth-century English sampler patterns worked in a double-running stitch, such as those illustrated in Averil Colby's *Samplers*.[5] Considered in its entirety, Mary's sampler is a reflection of the changing trends that appeared in schoolgirl embroidery in southeastern New Hampshire and along the north shore of Massachusetts during the turbulent 1770s: the schoolmistress imported proven figurative forms from the Boston area, where she may have attended school; she then embellished the pictorial panel with a regional flourish and added an innovative border of her own design.

The samplermaker, identified by descendants as Mary Canney, cannot be traced.[6] She may have lived in Dover, New Hampshire, situated across the Great Bay from Portsmouth, where public schooling for girls began as early as 1773.[7] A private school for girls, where "any sort of Needlework" was taught, was advertised by Mary Homans in a 1772 issue of the *New Hampshire Gazette*.[8]

While it is not out of the ordinary for embroidered numbers indicating dates or ages to be missing from samplers, it is most uncommon to discover that a surname has been removed, as is the case with this sampler. Unfortunately, the reason for this drastic measure has not yet been discovered.

Information accompanying the sampler points out that it was handed down in the family in this order: Ichabod Canney (1774–1854); Mary Canney Waldron (1804–1891), daughter; Richard Waldron (1832–1900), son; William Perry.[9] Ichabod Canney was the son of Moses[10] and Mary Canney of Dover, New Hampshire.[11] In 1799, Moses remarried.[12] Although she has not been specifically identified, the samplermaker was probably Ichabod's mother, Mary, who died sometime before 1799.

By counting the barren strands of the linen ground, Mary's maiden name would appear to have comprised only four diminutive, cross-stitched letters (possibly "Cany," a variation of Canney), but, along with the numbers that revealed her age, those threads were removed long ago.

NOTES:

1. See the samplers of Mariah Deavenport, 1741 (collection, Windham Library, NH), and Mary Parker, 1741 (private collection), in Bolton and Coe, *American Samplers*, opp. 38, 41, 67.
2. Sotheby's, New York, catalogue, *Important Frakturs, Embroidered Pictures, Theorem Paintings, and Cutwork Pictures: from the Collection of Edgar William and Bernice Chrysler Garbisch*, January 23 and 24, 1974, lot 200.
3. Betty Ring, *Let Virtue Be a Guide to Thee* (Providence, RI: Rhode Island Historical Society, 1983), 119, 121, 125.
4. The Cutts sampler is in a private collection; see Glee Krueger, *A Gallery of American Samplers* (New York, NY: E. P. Dutton/Museum of American Folk Art, 1978), 36.
5. Averil Colby, *Samplers* (London: B.T. Batsford, 1964), 72, 162.
6. *International Genealogical Index*, 1988, lists a Mary Canney, born August 3, 1758, daughter of John Canney and Love Tebbetts of Dover Township, Strafford County, New Hampshire. Other records indicate that the Canney and Waldron families frequently intermarried. It is thus possible to surmise that Mary Canney could have married Moses Canney of Dover. She would then have been fourteen years old when working the sampler and nineteen when Ichabod was born. The surname removed from the sampler linen could have been "Cany," as documents reveal the spelling varied from Cenny or Canny to Kenny and Canney.
7. Thomas Woody, *A History of Women's Education in the United States*, vol. 1 (New York, NY: Octagon Books, 1974), 144.
8. Krueger, *New England Samplers*, 193.
9. Christie's, New York, catalogue, *Highly Important American Furniture, Silver, Folk and Decorative Arts*, October 21, 1989, lot 166.
10. *International Genealogical Index*, 1988.
11. Ibid. See also *Deed Book, Strafford County, New Hampshire*, vol. 108: 59.
12. *International Genealogical Index*, 1988. See also *Deed Book, Strafford County, New Hampshire*, vol. 47: 201.

7.

8. MEHITABLE FOSTER (1771–1803)

Canterbury, New Hampshire, 1786
Silk, twisted silk threads, and silk floss on linen
(22 threads to the inch)
Tent, satin, long and short, outline, eyelet, chain,
herringbone, bullion, and cross-stitches
17½ x 14½ in. (44.3 x 36.7 cm)

Inscription: *Mehitable Fosters sampler wrought/in the
Fifteenth year of her age/A.D. 1786*

Schoolmistress: probably Hannah Wise Rogers
(b. 1719)

Samplers worked in Merrimack County, New Hampshire, around the adjoining villages of Canterbury, Sanbornton, and Northfield, have long been appreciated by collectors for their skillfully worked, instantly recognizable format. Exclusive to this rural settlement, this embroidery design was conceived by an imaginative schoolmistress who favored a bordering frame of exquisitely patterned vases—resembling Chinese porcelain—overflowing with distinctive, double-plumed foliage and brightly colored flowers. Paired birds pose beside an elegantly adorned urn, displaying the characteristically scalloped, heavily veined leaves. The sampler worked by Mehitable Foster in 1786 represents the earliest example of this remarkable and important group. First appearing in the last decades of the eighteenth century, this distinguished pattern endured for at least forty-four years, until Mary K. Osgood[1] worked her sampler in 1830, when schoolgirl embroideries were on the wane. At least seventeen stylistically related samplers make up this group.

This schoolmistress required her meticulously embroidered decorative motifs to be embellished with an outline of black silk threads. The clever device serves to enliven the subtle tones of the sampler palette, as well as to accentuate the various and interesting shapes within the design. The princely birds on this sampler have been adorned with crowns of silver metallic thread. As with many of the surviving samplers from this group, a pale blue sawtooth border surrounds the interior rectangle of alphabets, a reversing strawberry band, the signature, and the date.

The tall trees, extending from the pictorial garden upward into the border, are distinctive in shape and each have six horizontal branches. These cross-stitched trees were sometimes replaced with a more formal style, tapering and stately with upreaching points. In 1806, however, Anna Lyford[2] worked two airy, feathery trees on her unfinished sampler, suggesting that variations may have occurred under the supervision of another teacher.

HANNAH WISE ROGERS

Who was the long sought-after schoolmistress of eighteenth-century Canterbury? Who originated this exquisite needlework pattern that spread throughout the county? The answer may lie in the colonial village of Ipswich, Massachusetts, in the person of Hannah Wise Rogers.

Hannah Wise was born in Ipswich, Essex County, Massachusetts, in 1719, the daughter of Ammi Ruhami Wise. She married Samuel Rogers, an Ipswich physician. A great deal has been written about this Massachusetts family, which included Samuel Rogers's father, John, once president of Harvard College.[3]

Samplers depicting embroidery patterns similar to those from Canterbury are known to have been favored by schoolmistresses teaching in Essex County and in the villages along the shoreline north of Boston. For example, the vase worked on the Boxford sampler (fig. 14) is suggestive of Canterbury, as is the vase and vine border of Mary Canney's 1774 sampler (fig. 7). It is possible, then, to assume that these young Canterbury women attended embroidery classes taught by Hannah Rogers, for she is known to have kept a school for girls in Ipswich from 1774 to 1784. In a history of the town, the Reverend Augustine Caldwell is quoted, sometime around 1784, as saying, "Madam Rogers kept a school for young ladies that was in great repute."[4]

By the time Mehitable Foster worked this sampler, however, Hannah Rogers was no longer teaching in Ipswich. This presented a dilemma until genealogical studies revealed that the schoolmistress and samplermaker were related by marriage.

Along with her cousins, Polly (or Mary) Foster, whose sampler is dated 1787,[5] and Hannah Foster, who worked an identical sampler in 1796,[6] Mehitable lived in a village originally known as Hackleborough. The town historian described it as "a Foster settlement, a Foster neighborhood."[7] Hannah Rogers was a great-aunt to Mehitable and grandmother to cousins Polly and Hannah.

By following the thread of Hannah Rogers's life we can piece together a wealth of circumstantial evidence that substantiates this theory. When Samuel Rogers died in 1772, Hannah was obliged to sell half of her home to cover her husband's debts. In 1774, she began teaching the girls of Ipswich in her diminished living quarters. It is unlikely that she kept a boarding school.

In October 1784, Hannah was forced to sell what remained of her home. At this time, she may have moved to Canterbury to be near her daughters (Mehitable's aunts), for the census records for 1790 seem to confirm that Hannah became a member of the household of Abiel and Mary Foster.

The samplers made by Mehitable Foster in 1786, her cousin Polly Foster in 1787, and Appha Woodman in 1787[8] suggest that a

8.

school for girls had been started in Canterbury, but subtle changes in the stylistic patterns of Canterbury samplers imply that Hannah died around 1799.[9] There is a refinement and delicacy to the early pieces that is lacking in those worked after 1800.

It is not difficult to detect the minor changes that occurred in this elegant embroidery pattern. Most of the eighteenth-century pieces give prominence to a wide strawberry band within an enclosed rectangle of alphabet forms, while many of the nineteenth-century ones do not (although in 1826, Harriet Peverly worked such a reversing band on her embroidery[10]). Tree shapes on the later samplers vary, and many examples are borderless.

We can only surmise that Hannah Rogers's original pattern became the forerunner of a sampler design that remained in vogue in the region until at least 1833, when Apphia Amanda Young finished hers.[11]

Evidence recently unearthed reveals that both Lucy Rogers Foster (daughter to Hannah Rogers) and her daughter, sampler-maker Polly Foster, became schoolmistresses in the district, or common, schools, as did numerous Foster women. But there is no record of embroidery worked under their supervision.[12] Needlework, it appears, was primarily the domain of the private schoolmistress, as taxpayers were suitably cautious of their expenditures.

MEHITABLE FOSTER

Mehitable Foster, the daughter of Asa Foster and Hannah Symons, was born on November 19, 1771. She married Benjamin Kimball, a hatter, in March of 1798. They lived in Concord, New Hampshire, in an impressive five-bay frame mansion that remains there today. Mehitable Foster Kimball died on September 23, 1803, after the birth of four sons in five years of marriage. She was only thirty-two.[13]

NOTES:

1. The Osgood sampler is in a private collection; see *The Encyclopedia of Collectibles* (Alexandria, VA: Time-Life Books, 1980), R–S, opp. 88.
2. The Lyford sampler is in the collection of the Museum of the Daughters of the American Revolution, Washington, D.C.; see Elisabeth Donaghy Garrett, *The Arts of Independence* (Washington, D.C.: The National Society, Daughters of the American Revolution, 1985), 80.
3. Joseph B. Felt, *A History of Ipswich, Essex, and Hamilton* (Cambridge, MA: Charles Folsom, 1834), 234, 235, 236. See also *Vital Records of Ipswich, Massachusetts, to the End of the Year 1849*, vol. 3 (Salem,

MA: Essex Institute, 1919) and *Records of the First Congregational Church of Ipswich*. This information was documented for me by the librarians of the Public Library of Ipswich, to whom I am indebted.

For more information on the status of the Rogerses of Ipswich, see Laurel Thatcher Ulrich, *Good Wives, Image, and Reality in the Lives of Women in Northern New England: 1650–1750* (New York, NY: Alfred A. Knopf, 1982), 57, 58.
4. Franklin Waters Thomas, *Ipswich in the Massachusetts Bay Colony*, vol. 2 (Ipswich, MA: Ipswich Historical Society, 1905), 454.
5. Polly Foster's sampler is in the collection of the New Hampshire Historical Society, Concord; see Krueger, *New England Samplers*, fig. 59.
6. Hannah Foster's sampler is in the collection of the New Hampshire Historical Society, Concord; see Krueger, *New England Samplers*, fig. 60.
7. James Otis Lyford, *History of the Town of Canterbury, New Hampshire: 1727–1912* (Concord, NH: Rumford Press, 1912), vols. 1: 430, 431 and 2: 134, 135.
8. The location of the Woodman sampler is unknown; see Krueger, *New England Samplers*, fig. 61, and Bolton and Coe, *American Samplers*, opp. 364.
9. *Vital Records of Ipswich*, vol. 2: 662. See also *Deed Book, Essex County*, vol. 135: 262, 263. According to this document, dated May 24, 1775, Hannah's share of the house measured "from the center of the kitchen and through the center of the chimney of the fore doors to a stake on the road." See also *Deed Book, Essex County*, vol. 145: 50, 51. *Federal Census, Canterbury, New Hampshire*, 1790, lists six females living in Abiel Foster's household. Mary and Abiel had only three daughters—two were Mary's stepdaughters and one her own—leaving two women unaccounted for. An early map of the district indicates that the Foster brothers lived within walking distance of one another. See also Lyford, *History of Canterbury*, vol. 1: 425–439; map, 433.
10. The Peverly sampler is in a private collection; see Krueger, *New England Samplers*, fig. 62.
11. The Young sampler is in a private collection; see *Lessons Stitched in Silk: Samplers from Canterbury Region of New Hampshire*, catalogue (Hanover, NH: Dartmouth College Hood Museum of Art, 1990),
10. This recent exhibition allowed for comparison of thirty-three related samplers.
12. Theodore Foulk, "The Mustache Mystery: a Canterbury Tale," *Maine Antiques Digest* (April 1990): 1B.
13. Lyford, *History of Canterbury*, vol. 2: 134. See also Grace P. Amsden, *A Capitol for New Hampshire* (unpublished; New Hampshire Historical Society, Concord), 12, 13.

9. LUCY COIT (1773–1845)
Norwich, Connecticut, 1785
Silk threads on linen (50 threads to the inch)
Queen, rice, eyelet, straight, and cross-stitches
12 x 9 in. (30.4 x 22.8 cm)

Inscription: *Virtues our Safeguard and our*
guiding Star/That stirs up Reason when our Senses
err/Open thy mou/th judge righ/teously and/plead the
cau/se of the poor/and needy
Lucy Coit/her Sampler/Wrought at/the age of 12 year
Norwich/Novr.17.1785

10. MARTHA AVERY (1773–1800)
Norwich, Connecticut, 1786
Silk threads on linen (24 threads to the inch)
Eyelet, queen, tent, and cross-stitches
15½ x 12½ in. (39.39 x 31.77 cm)

Inscription: *She maketh her cove/ring of tapestry*
her/clothing is silk and/purple ProvXXXI 22
Martha Avery her/Sampler wrought at/the age of 13
Norw/ich September 1786

A view of Norwich and the Thames River, c. 1850, engraving attributed to M. Osborn and W. Coit, probably Lucy Coit's brother. Library of Congress, Washington, D.C.

By the eighteenth century, the township of Norwich, Connecticut, was comprised of adjoining settlements, or societies, which looped in a curve from the Yantic River Falls in the west, along the lakelet called the Cove, around in a slim band below the hills where the Shetucket River flows into the Thames, and east to the Quinebaug—a distance of some six miles. Prominent citizens built their houses facing the village green, but shipmasters preferred spacious tracts of land on the bluff in Chelsea Society where their property spread down in a swag of meadowland that met the Shetucket shore.

This arrangement offered a splendid view of the joining rivers and afforded each captain an opportunity to keep watch on his ship. Participating in the exceedingly lucrative triangular West Indies trade of slaves, rum, and sugar, they sailed to Demerara on the coast of South America, England, and the Continent, ending back in the safe, protective waters of the Cove.[1]

In the decades before the Revolution, life in Norwich was gracious and easy. Goods were imported, and fashions for the higher circles bordered on the extravagant. Norwich residents treasured their British heritage and exalted English culture. As the struggle for liberty approached, however, all imported ornaments were discarded and women appeared in society in simple costumes of brown homespun cloth and checked handkerchiefs.[2]

Shipping, a major commercial enterprise, became increasingly hazardous. Norwich shipmasters braved the blockades and indulged in reckless privateering. Wealth and reputation followed a successful voyage, and a merchant aristocracy soon emerged.[3]

The first village, or common, school was planned for the children of Norwich in 1677. By 1745, the exact location of each of the town schools had been decided and the length of each session determined, even to the number of months and days. The town fathers, after much consideration, gave girls permission to attend the district school "early in the morning before the boys arrived and after they had gone home in the evening."[4] If the schoolteacher were a woman, her pay was to be "but half that of the master" but the "time was to be doubled."[5] By 1782, a common school for both boys and girls was constructed with a high wooden belfry above a gambrel roof at the bequest of Dr. Daniel Lathrop.[6]

However, it was in the fashionable private academy that embroidery and the art of the needle prevailed. The daily arrival of ships brought many talented young women seeking posts as schoolmistresses to the daughters of the newly established gentry. Many of these daughters were routinely sent to Boston boarding schools. Early historians have sadly neglected to record the names of Norwich schoolmistresses, but there is evidence that

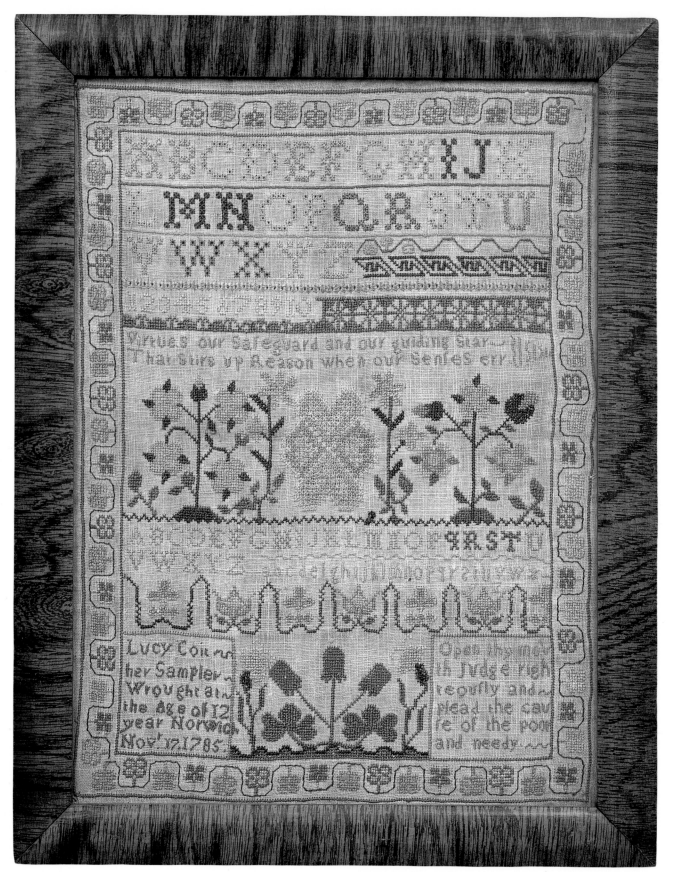

9.

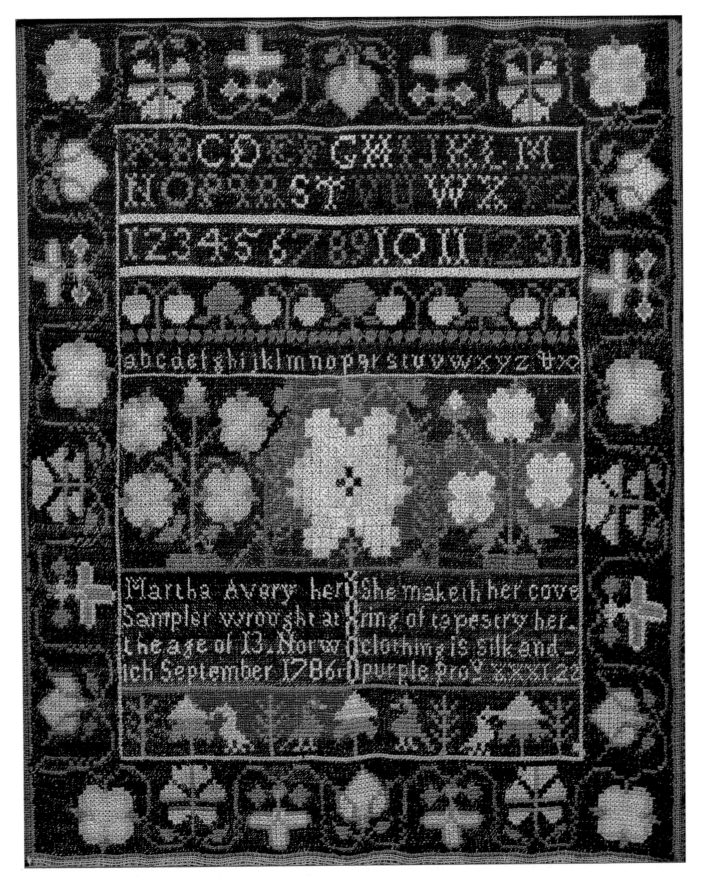

10.

"Miss Sally Smith," who taught at the Landing, and "Miss Molly Grover of the Town-plot" were remembered with fondness by the young schoolgirls of the town.[7]

An imaginative schoolmaster advertised in the *Chelsea Courier*, March 15, 1797, dangling prizes of "no less than a Silver or Gold Medal" before the eyes of the girls of Norwich. And from November 11 to the middle of December 1799, the *Courier* ran an advertisement for "Mrs. Brooks, from London" who would offer courses in "Plain Work, Marking, Tambour, Embroidery & Dresden, along with Fillegree, Paint Work, and Maps."[8] Lydia Huntley Sigourney, in *Letters to My Pupils*, writes about attending school in Norwich at the age of four, then later being enrolled in an embroidery school where she was tutored in ornamental needlework with "precision and elegance."[9]

Exquisite schoolgirl embroideries, samplers as well as canvaswork pictures, of splendid composition and execution, were worked in the vicinity of Norwich. Antiquarians in the field of textile arts have often debated the source of instruction in this design center, where such exceptional pieces were developed. Newspapers of the period add little to our knowledge, leaving us to assume that the teachers were well-known figures in the community with no need to publicize their superior accomplishments.[10]

The samplers of Martha Avery and Lucy Coit are recognizably similar in form and style, and both incorporate the town name of "Norwich," allowing unquestionable attribution to the same instructress. On Lucy's sampler, for example, a strawberry plant separates signature, biblical quotations, and aphorisms. While Martha Avery does not use this same formula, giving ample space instead to her delicate inscriptions, both embroideries display alphabet rows completed with similar geometric motifs. Most important, each sampler is adorned with a four-heart motif, worked in shaded tones of beige; the hearts are all joined together at their heartpoints to form a stunningly graphic design.

Martha Avery has ambitiously cross-stitched the entire background of the linen in black silk thread; hers is one of a group of at least five related samplers with embroidered grounds that fool the eye into believing they are worked on colored fabrics.[11] Of the two, however, it was Lucy Coit who controlled her needle with a particularly skillful hand.

Their elusive schoolmistress taught the daughters of wealthy Norwich citizens for at least twenty years beginning about 1764. But the stylish patterns that she designed lived on well into the nineteenth century on at least one surviving example: a sampler worked by Phebe Esther Copp of Stonington. Dated 1822, it displays many of the earlier characteristic motifs. It seems, therefore, that this tradition continued as a regional pattern well after these endearing samplers were made and this influential schoolmistress had departed the scene.[12]

Martha Avery was born on August 22, 1733, in Preston or East Society, the second of eight children to James Avery and Martha Smith.[13] Lucy Coit, ninth and last child of William Coit and Sarah Lathrop, was born on September 9, 1773, directly across the Shetucket River by way of a narrow wooden horse bridge. Late in 1780, William married Elizabeth Palmes Coit.[14] Thus the two young girls probably spent much time together scanning the sailing vessels anchored at their doorway, for both fathers were involved in shipping.

Judging by the dates stitched on their samplers, the girls were attending school during the winter of 1785 and September 1786. Lucy finished her embroidery almost a year before Martha. Little else is known of their childhood years.

Martha Avery married Moses Benjamin (b. 1774), a ship captain, in 1798. They lived for a time in a house on Back Street in Chelsea. Their first son was born in 1798; but after their second child was born in 1800, Martha failed to recover. Although Moses purchased an elegant house at 23 Washington Street, it is doubtful that Martha ever enjoyed the lovely five-bay mansion, for she died on September 12, 1800. Both sons died without issue in Demerara.[15]

Lucy Coit remained unmarried, probably devoting most of her days to the execution of the needlework at which she was so highly skilled. She died in January 1845, leaving a considerable estate valued at $922.[16]

NOTES:

1. Frances Manwaring Caulkins, *History of Norwich, Connecticut* (Norwich, CT: Pequot Press, 1976), 356, 406.

2. Ibid., 482.

3. Ibid., 333–335.

4. Woody, *History of Women's Education*, vol. 1: 92.

5. Caulkins, *History of Norwich*, 275. See also Mary E. Perkins, *Old Houses of the Ancient Town of Norwich, 1660–1800*, vol. 2 (Norwich, CT, 1895), 375.

6. Joan Nafie, *To the Beat of a Drum* (Norwich, CT: Old Town Press, 1975), map between 91–92. See also Marian K. O'Keefe and Catherine Smith Doroshevich, *Norwich Historic Homes and Families*, (Stonington, CT: Pequot Press, 1967), 19.

7. Caulkins, *History of Norwich*, 541, 542.

8. Ibid, 542.

9. L. H. Sigourney, *Letters to My Pupils* (2nd ed., New York, NY: Robert Carter & Brothers, 1853), 153.

10. The anonymously worked "Chandler Wedding Tapestry" (private collection) is usually given simply a New England attribution, but many textile historians believe it to be a Norwich, Connecticut, piece. See Mirra Bank, *Anonymous Was a Woman* (New York, NY: St. Martin's Press, 1979), 68. Closely related to this tapestry is a sampler worked by Margret Calef of Middletown, Connecticut (private collection), who may have attended school in Norwich;. see Bolton and Coe, *American Samplers*, opp. 66.

11. Ring, *American Needlework Treasures*, 22. Ilustrated are the samplers of Elizabeth Lord, 1764 (collection, Betty Ring), and her sister, Naby Lord, 1765 (collection, Betty Ring). Both samplers have solidly embroidered backgrounds.

In 1765, Esther Copp worked her related sampler (collection, National Museum of History and Technology, Smithsonian Institution, Washington, D.C.); see Grace Rogers Cooper, *The Copp Family Textiles* (Washington, D.C.: Smithsonian Institution Press, 1971), 11. See also Nabby Fitch's sampler, 1766 (private collection), in Susan Burrows Swan, "Appreciating American Samplers: Part 2," *Early American Life* (April 1984): 45. This sampler has been embroidered with varying shades of blue-dyed threads, probably of indigo, giving it a patch-worked appearance.

The gem-like sampler worked by eleven-year-old Ruth Huntington, 1787 (location unknown), was stitched in a rectangular shape, but the ground has been covered with cross-stitches.

12. Phebe Esther Copp's sampler is in the collection of the National Museum of History and Technology (Smithsonian Institution), Washington, D.C.; see Cooper, *Copp Family Textiles*, 12.

13. Elroy McKendree Avery and Catharine Hitchcock (Tilden) Avery, *The Groton Avery Clan*, vol. 1 (Cleveland, OH: 1912), 229.

14. F. W. Chapman, *The Coit Family* (Hartford, CT: Chase, Lockwood and Brainard, 1874), 62, 63. See also Perkins, *Old Houses of Norwich*, vol. 2: 162.

15. Avery and Avery, *Avery Clan*, 364. See also *Norwich Land Records*, vol. 31: 340, and Nafie, *To the Beat of a Drum*, opp. 68.

16. Chapman, *Coit Family*, 63. See also *Town of Norwich Estate Records of Lucy Coit*, administered by her brother-in-law, Joseph Williams.

11. ELIZABETH DAY HALL (1772–1858)
Wallingford, Connecticut, 1791
Silk threads on linen (24 threads to the inch)
Chain, outline, tent, and cross-stitches
10½ x 9½ in. (26.6 x 24.1 cm)

Inscription: *You that enjoy the bloom of youth let virtue/be your guide let learning be your chief/delight and modesty your pride*
Elizabeth Day Hall

11.

As early as 1695, the town of Wallingford, Connecticut, authorized the school committee to employ a woman to teach in the summertime. The first female teacher recorded in the area, she was expected to accommodate her students—both boys and girls—in private quarters, for no funds had been set aside to build a school. Ironically, at a time when little emphasis was placed on women's education, female teachers were being considered as qualified professionals, even in this small colonial village edging on Long Island Sound.[1]

By the middle of the eighteenth century, it was accepted that the duty of the private-school teacher was to teach girls "to behave, to ply the needle through all the mysteries of hemming, overhand, stitching and darning, up to sampler."[2] Students were expected to learn the alphabet, read the Psalter, and be familiar with the spelling book.[3]

In 1791, when she was nineteen, Elizabeth Day Hall worked this diminutive, unbordered sampler in an exceedingly uncommon style. Entirely embroidered in tent stitches, the pictorial scene is placed at the top of the sampler. The charming miniature townscape includes a splendid turquoise bird of enormous proportions and a beguiling variety of flowers. A deep red neoclassical curtain, swagged with fringed cording, has been invitingly draped to reveal the charming tableau. Draperies such as these were a popular addition to portraits painted during the Federal period.

The naif format of Elizabeth's sampler, while not characteristic of the lavishly stitched schoolgirl embroideries, such as that worked by Mary Ann Goodrich (fig. 37), nevertheless exudes an engaging charm. Elizabeth may have attended an embroidery school in Wallingford or been sent to a boarding school in New Haven, where schools for the daughters of the well-to-do were more plentiful.[4]

Elizabeth Day Hall, born March 14, 1772, was the second child born to Hezekiah Hall and Elizabeth Merriman. One of nine children, only one a boy, she had sisters with the Puritan names of Content, Thankful, and Hopeful.[5]

Between the years 1791, when her sampler was worked, and 1797, when her first child was born, Elizabeth married Captain David Merriman Cook, who was by trade a farmer, shoemaker, and frequently a member of the state legislature. Parents to four children, they lived in a large house on a rise of land facing south on a country road near the old Pond Hill in Wallingford. Elizabeth died on December 1, 1858, and is buried in the Center Street Cemetery.[6]

The original wooden backboard on the sampler bears this faint handwritten inscription: "Worked by Miss Elizabeth Day Hall/in 1791— Aunt of J R Hitchcock."

NOTES:

1. Charles Henry Stanley Davis, *History of Wallingford, Connecticut* (Meriden, CT: published by the author, 1870), 311.
2. Ibid., 317.
3. Ibid. *Dilworth's Spelling Book* had been well received in Wallingford and was much used in Connecticut from its inception in 1743. He subsequently published the *Schoolmaster's Assistant*, a book on arithmetic.
4. Krueger, *New England Samplers*, 144, 145.

5. Donald Lines Jacobus. comp., *Families of Ancient New Haven* (Rome, NY: Clarence D. Smith, 1923), 449, 716. See also Rev. David B. Hall, *The Halls of New England* (Albany, NY: published by the author, 1883), 110.

6. Jacobus, *Families of Ancient New Haven*, 449. See also Davis, *History of Wallingford*, 696. The location of the house is marked on an early landownership map. Although the cemetery is crowded with members of the distinguished Hall family, I was unable to find Elizabeth's gravesite.

12. FANNY DROWNE (b. 1786)
Probably Rhode Island, 1797
Silk threads on linen (14 threads to the inch)
Eyelet and cross-stitches
24½ x 7¾ in. (62.25 x 19.68 cm)

Inscription: *Fanny Drowne work this/sampplar in the year of our/Lord 1797 aged 12*
Labour for Learing before/thou art old/For Learing is better then/Silver and gold/For silver and gold will vanish/away/But Learing is a jewel that will never decay

12.

This sampler worked by Fanny Drowne is reminiscent of a style prevalent in North America during the colonial period. Simple in design, the long, thin embroidery has been edged with a border so unobtrusive as to be unnoticeable.

Fanny Drowne's schoolmistress may have been a recent arrival from England, for this sampler follows a traditional English pattern. The 1790s were a time of great experimentation in classrooms of post–Revolutionary America, particularly New England. Samplers appeared with wide flowery borders, fancy vases filled with colorful, exotic blossoms, and stylish figures parading across yards of embroidered linen. Yet this teacher appeared to have remained unaffected, steeped in the seventeenth century and aloof to the whims of fashion. Thus, the young Fanny was obliged to stitch her long, narrow embroidery in a manner that was distinctly unfashionable and definitely out-of-step.

Although she has not yet been identified in any records, Fanny Drowne probably lived in Bristol County, Rhode Island, where several "Drown" families are recorded.[1]

NOTES:

1. *Federal Census, Rhode Island*, 1800. Girls around Fanny's age have been found in the families of Benjamin, Daniel, and Jonathan Drown.

13. ELIZABETH STINE (b. 1784?)
Philadelphia, Pennsylvania, 1793
Silk and twisted silk threads with crinkled silk floss
on linen (28 threads to the inch), quilled silk ribbon
with corner rosettes
Satin, queen, tent, outline, and cross-stitches
22 x 18 in. (55.9 x 45.7 cm)

Inscription: *Elizabeth Stine Her Work Made In The*
[number removed]*th/ Year of Her Age July 20th, 1793*

Schoolmistress: Mary Zeller

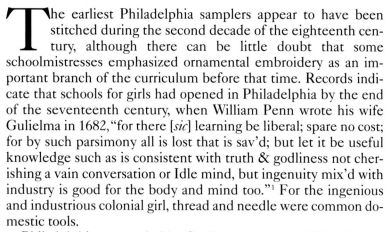

The earliest Philadelphia samplers appear to have been stitched during the second decade of the eighteenth century, although there can be little doubt that some schoolmistresses emphasized ornamental embroidery as an important branch of the curriculum before that time. Records indicate that schools for girls had opened in Philadelphia by the end of the seventeenth century, when William Penn wrote his wife Gulielma in 1682, "for there [*sic*] learning be liberal; spare no cost; for by such parsimony all is lost that is sav'd; but let it be useful knowledge such as is consistent with truth & godliness not cherishing a vain conversation or Idle mind, but ingenuity mix'd with industry is good for the body and mind too."[1] For the ingenious and industrious colonial girl, thread and needle were common domestic tools.

Philadelphia was settled by Quakers as early as 1683 and chartered as a city in 1701. The minutes of the Philadelphia Monthly Meeting of 1702 included the selection of the first recorded Quaker schoolmistress in the city, Olive Songhurst.[2] In May 1723, an advertisement in the *American Weekly Mercury* announced that a Mrs. Rodes would teach flourishing on muslin in "the most expeditious way."[3] It is, therefore, hardly a surprise to find diligent schoolmistresses well established in the city by 1727, the year Ann Marsh, age nine, worked her borderless, horizontal band sampler, inscribed with her teacher's name, Mary Ann Stanton.[4] She eventually became a schoolmistress herself and was responsible for the education of the daughters of many prominent Philadelphians.

Ann's embroidery is but one of a number of closely related samplers found to have originated in Philadelphia. These samplers were thought to represent the earliest documented group of needlework in this country, but the recent appearance of a narrowly bordered sampler worked by Anne Chase of Rhode Island bears the date 1721 and conforms to a newly recognized Newport group of sampler embroideries.[5]

Schools for Philadelphia girls increased notably after the middle of the century, culminating in the establishment of the Female Academy, a chartered institution, in 1792. By 1796, Anne Parrish, a benevolent Quaker, had opened Aimwell School for poor girls in Pewter Platter Alley, instructing her fifty pupils in "spelling, reading, writing, arithmetic, and sewing."[6]

The exquisite sampler worked by Elizabeth Stine represents a superb example of eighteenth-century Philadelphia sampler embroidery. It is characterized by the distinctively deep, pyramid-shaped lawn scattered with animals and figures in fashionable costumes. Part of the sky has been worked into a lavish basket of fruit, with grapevines swirling into the upper corners. A shaggy goat, a cow, a wellhouse with a yellow silk bucket, and a flock of insects also enter into the scene. A reclining stag—which first appeared on an engraving worked by Rosina Helena Furst of Nuremburg, Germany, in 1666[7]—has been prominently displayed. Enclosed within an undulating border on three sides of the rectangle, the sampler is surrounded by an edge of tightly quilled silk ribbon, each corner further embellished with rosettes of scarlet and cream.

By far the most mystifying and intriguing feature of these distinctive Philadelphia samplers is the unusual building depicted on a rise of green satin and tent-stitched lawn. Embellished with towers, spires, and weathervanes, this rust- and black-checkered castle is difficult to identify. In his *Guide to the Collection of Samplers and Embroideries at the National Museum of Wales*, F. G. Payne suggests that a similar, but more exaggerated, edifice of this style that is found on a nineteenth-century Welsh sampler may to some degree be compared with "such structures as Henry VIII's Palace of Nonsuch, which provided a favorite architectural motif for embroideries of an earlier period."[8] Today those visiting Hampton Court Palace in England might notice a resemblance.

Although this group of samplers was long thought by collectors to have originated in an unidentified school located near Burlington, New Jersey,[9] the recent appearance of a nearly identical sampler worked by Mary Snowden of Philadelphia bearing the name

13.

"M. Zeller" as instructress has allowed another piece of the sampler puzzle to fall into place. In this unexpected manner a talented schoolmistress and her school have been discovered.[10]

A needlework rendition of the Lamb of God, or Agnus Dei, has been identified as typical of Mary Zeller's instruction. Two of these ancient motifs are located at the base of the lawn on the sampler worked by Elizabeth Stine, and two are worked into the grassy slope of Mary Snowden's embroidery.[11]

Since Elizabeth Stine removed the threads giving her age, genealogical identification is difficult. The established custom of sending country girls to be educated in Philadelphia may have applied to Elizabeth, daughter of Elizabeth and Philip Stine of Bedminster Township, Bucks County, Pennsylvania. Born February 24, 1784, she would have worked this elegant sampler in her tenth year, that is, when she was nine. The Philadelphia directory for 1797 indicates that the widow of Philip Stine was living at 245 High Street.[12] Just a few doors away, Mary Zeller, "teacheress," could be found at 119 and 121 North Third Street. Records reveal that Mary Zeller kept her school for girls for at least a twenty-year span, from 1789 to 1808, instructing Philadelphia girls in the gentle art of ornamental needlework.[13]

NOTES:

1. Richard S. Dunn and Mary Maples Dunn, eds., *The Papers of William Penn*, vol. 2 (Philadelphia, PA: University of Pennsylvania Press, 1982), 269–277.
2. Woody, *History of Women's Education*, vol. 1: 199.
3. Ibid., 223.
4. The Marsh sampler is in a private collection; see Betty Ring, "Samplers and Pictorial Needlework at the Chester County Historical Society," *Antiques* (December 1984): 1423.
5. The location of Ann Chase's sampler is unknown; see ibid. See also Sotheby's, 5736, June 23, 1988, lot 320.
6. Woody, *History of Women's Education*, vol. 1: 202, 223, 230, 337.
7. Krueger, *Gallery of American Samplers*, 18.
8. F. G. Payne, *Guide to the Collection of Samplers and Embroideries* (Cardiff, Wales: National Museum of Wales and Press Board of the University of Wales, 1939), 32.
9. The location of Mary Snowden's sampler is unknown; see Bolton and Coe, *American Samplers*, opp. 260.
10. Sotheby's, New York, catalogue, *American Folk Art, Furniture and Related Decorative Arts*, 5156, January 27, 1984, lot 494. See also Ring, *American Needlework Treasures*, 40.
11. Ring, *American Needlework Treasures*, 40.
12. Rev. William John Hinke, *A History of the Tothickon Union Church, Bedminster Township, Bucks County, Pennsylvania* (Meadville, PA, 1925), 380.
13. The *Philadelphia City Directory*, 1797, lists a Jacob Zeller, bookbinder, at 119 and 121 North Third Street. He may have been Mary Zeller's husband. The *Federal Census, Philadelphia*, 1790, however, lists Mary Zeller as "Head of the Family" of three females, some of whom may have been boarding students registered in her house. In the *City Directory* of 1807, Mary Zeller, teacheress, is registered at 119 North Third Street; and Jacob, bookbinder, at 121.

Nineteenth Century

14. ANONYMOUS
Boxford, Massachusetts, c. 1804
Silk threads and crinkled silk floss on linen
(22 threads to the inch)
Eyelet, chain, outline, and cross-stitches
17½ x 14½ in. (43.4 x 36.8 cm)

Inscription: *Each pleasing art lends softness to the
mind/And with our studies are our lives refin'd/Those
polished arts have humaniz'd mankin*[d]/*Soften'd the
rude and calm'd the boistrou*[s] *mind.*

14.

This sampler is a superb example of a highly sophisticated design embraced by schoolmistresses in the vicinity of Essex County, Massachusetts, during the later decades of the eighteenth century. As can be seen here, the traditional colonial sampler slowly evolved into a highly decorative needlework exercise, emphasizing the fringe of the sampler by the addition of a wide, lavish border. Samplers belonging to this group exhibit a distinctive vine motif in the border, which is embellished with intricate multicolored flower and leaf patterns outlined with threads of a contrasting hue. This unusual pattern is found on numerous Essex samplers and adds an appealing element to the design.[1]

The somewhat timid green, cross-stitched garden visible on Elizabeth Cheever's 1736 sampler (fig. 1) has emerged into a fully developed landscape occupying a wide band across the base of the embroidery. The solidly worked hills are topped by distinctive pine trees. An unrelated vase has been worked into this handsome design. Decorated with a dainty gold-on-gold-toned geometric pattern edged with delicate loops of blue and white silk threads, the vase closely resembles the highly prized porcelain vases of the period and suggests a relationship with samplers worked during the same period in Canterbury, New Hampshire (fig. 8), as many of these feature a similar vase.

The unembroidered linen of the border of this sampler has been entirely worked in row upon row of white crinkled silk satin stitches, a technique that greatly enhances the character of the sampler, emphasizing the luster and sheen of the textile. This technique of covering entire portions of the exposed linen also appears on schoolgirl samplers worked in and around Salem as early as the 1750s. It is not surprising, therefore, that a sampler worked by Lucy Symonds in Boxford, 1796, described in *American Samplers*,[2] and the recently discovered sampler signed by Betsey Gould, inscribed "Boxford, 1804," identical in format, present tangible evidence of an as yet unidentified school for girls in the vicinity. We may assume that this anonymous embroidery was worked in the same academy and completed within the same

time frame as the Gould sampler.[3]

Although the samplermaker did not sign her work, she has inscribed it with groups of unrelated alphabet letters. Initials of this kind are often found on samplers influenced by Quaker instruction; this might include members of her family or schoolmates.

NOTES:

1. Krueger, *New England Samplers*, figs. 16, 18, 19. The recent appearance of a sampler worked by Abigail Brown, 1816, inscribed "Plymouth" (location unknown), has brought together a group of samplers stitched in a similar manner. Identified by the zigzag vine in the border, these samplers were further embellished with distinctive geometric motifs. Other related embroideries include pieces worked by Hannah Cutter (collection, Cooper-

Hewitt Museum of Design, Smithsonian Institution, New York, NY), Susanna Child of Watertown, MA (private collection, brought to my attention by Sheila Rideout), Lucy Lee Fessenden (location unknown; see *Antiques and Arts Weekly*, September 30, 1983, advertisement), and Lucy Barrett (collection, Concord Antiquarian Museum, MA). The introduction of this unusual border motif appears to have attracted schoolmistresses in surrounding towns, causing the cross-stitched, cubed vine pattern to become a characteristically regional pattern.

2. The location of Lucy Symond's sampler is unknown; see See Bolton and Coe, *American Samplers*, 78.

3. The location of Betsey Gould's sampler is unknown; see East Side House Settlement, New York, catalogue, *1986 Winter Antiques Show* (New York, NY: East Side House Settlement, 1986), advertisement of Marguerite Riordan, Stonington, CT.

15. BATHSHEBA COPELAND (1796–1842)
Northampton, Massachusetts, 1805
Silk threads and crinkled silk floss on linen
(26 threads to the inch)
Satin, couched satin, split, outline, and cross-stitches
13 x 13¼ in. (33.02 x 33.65 cm)

Inscription: *Then o divine benevolence be nigh/O teach me how to live & how to die Bathsheba/Copeland aged 9*

15.

Bathsheba Copeland's elegant sampler is as lustrous as a length of woven brocade. An exquisite sense of symmetry, achieved through placement, form, and variation of stitch, has been focused around a pictorial cartouche adorned with dainty scallops and ribbon bows. Framed by large vases of cross-stitched flowers, paired birds, pine trees, and familiar geometric shapes, the figure within the setting is balanced by a four-storied building, which may depict the school or academy where this inspired design was born.

The shimmering background has been achieved by long, floating, ivory-colored stitches of floss, which cover the unembroidered linen. This uncomplicated sewing technique was one that could be quickly mastered yet appears to have been seldom used by teachers of sampler stitchery. While some samplers have been found to be solidly embroidered with cross-stitches, such as that worked by Martha Avery (fig. 10), others made only occasional use of tent or satin stitches. Few, however, are known to be so fully embroidered with lengthy, uncouched silk floss and with such dramatic results as this one—with the possible exception of the

sampler worked by Louisa Plympton of Sudbury, Massachusetts (fig. 21).

In 1803, Emily Parsons of Northampton, Massachusetts,[1] worked a sampler identical to this one, portraying the same proper young woman wearing a bonnet within an oval setting. The ground of Emily's sampler has been worked in the same long-reaching, satin-stitch technique. Such evidence gives rise to the assumption that an as yet unidentified school existed in the vicinity of Northampton from at least 1803 to 1805. The shining image projected by these splendid pictorial samplers echoes the skillfully worked silk embroideries so popular in girls' academies of the Connecticut River Valley during the same period.[2]

Smith Copeland of Canterbury, Connecticut, and Polly Wetherbee were married in Boston by the Reverend Joseph Eckley on June 4, 1794. In 1800 they made their home in Hampshire County, Massachusetts. After 1823, they are shown to be established in Antwerp, New York, where Copeland worked as a shoemaker and innkeeper.[3]

Bathsheba Copeland, the oldest of their six children, was born in Northampton, Massachusetts, in 1796 and worked her sampler in 1805, the year she was nine. She remained unmarried and died in 1842.[4]

NOTES:

1. The Parsons sampler (Emily Parsons, 1794–1859), in the collection of the Northampton Historical Society, MA, was brought to my attention by Betty Ring, to whom I am most grateful. Another related sampler, worked by Sarah Wells in 1807 (private collection), has recently surfaced; see Sotheby's, New York, catalogue, *Important Americana*, 5968, January 24–27, 1990, lot 1397.
2. Needlework pictures emphasizing an oval central motif are known to have been worked at the school begun in 1804 by Abby Wright in South Hadley, MA (Betty Ring, "Needlework Pictures from Abby Wright's School in South Hadley, Massachusetts," *Antiques*, September 1986: 483–493.)
3. *Register of Publishments and Marriages in Boston: 1647 to 1799*, vol. 1646: 322. See also Alice Richardson Sloane, comp., *The Genealogy of the Lawrence Copeland Family of Braintree, Massachusetts* (Decorah, IA: Anundsen Publishing Company, 1983), 9. See also *Massachusetts Census*, 1800, comp. Laraine Welch, (Accelerated Indexing Systems, 1973), 254.
4. Sloane, *Genealogy of Lawrence Copeland*, 9.

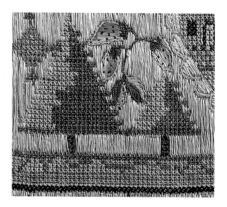

16. HARRIOT W. HILDRETH (b. 1796)
Haverhill, Massachusetts, 1807
Silk threads and crinkled silk floss on linen
(26 threads to the inch)
Outline, satin, tent, eyelet, and cross-stitches with
hem-stitching
12⅝ x 11¾ in. (32.07 x 29.84 cm)

Inscription: *Tis education forms the tender mind/Just as
the twig is bent the tree's inclin'd*
*HARRIOT W. HILDRETH wrought this in the 12
year/of her age 1807 HAVERHILL COUNTY ESSEX*

I n 1782, Reverend John Eliot of Boston wrote Reverend Jeremy Belknap in Dover, New Hampshire, expressing concern over the quality of education for the young women of Massachusetts:

> We don't pretend to teach ye female part of ye town anything more than dancing, or a little music perhaps, (and these accomplisht must necessarily be confined to a very few), except ye private schools for writing, which enables them to write a copy, sign their name, &, which they might not be able to do without such a priviledge, & with it I will venture to say that a lady is a rarity among us who can write a page of commonplace sentiment, the words being well spelt, & ye style & language kept up with purity & elegance.[1]

The attitude of Haverhill, Massachusetts, residents toward education was more enlightened, for as early as 1707 the dame school, a semi-public institution, was functioning as the first step in the education of young boys and girls. Traditionally, the dame schoolmistress would begin a simple stitching project, such as a small, uncomplicated alphabet sampler, for both sexes under her supervision.[2]

For at least seven years, between 1801 and 1808 (the dates inscribed on samplers belonging to the group represented by Harriot Hildreth's sampler), an anonymous embroidery mistress made use of a stunningly effective lozenge-shaped, geometric pattern that came to be identified with the most fashionable schools for girls in Haverhill.[3] The design, appearing on samplers worked in the area as early as the 1780s, was stitched in bands along the edges and often across the top of the alphabets, forming an inner border of vibrant color.[4]

The base of these samplers displays a pastoral frieze that can be traced to Boston-area needlework dating from the middle of the eighteenth century. These mounded gardens, with their petaled flowers neatly embedded within green silk folds, had for decades been favored by needlework teachers in the nearby towns that border the bays and important waterways of the north shore.

16.

The clue to the identification of this unknown academy for girls lies in the inscription that appears on each sampler in the group: "Haverhill County Essex." Other samplers with a similar format but lacking this distinctive arrangement of words were probably worked under another teacher's instruction.[5]

One of seven children, Harriot Warren Hildreth, born June 22, 1796, was the daughter of Dr. Samuel Hildreth and Abigail Bodwell, who had married in 1776.[6]

Bradford Academy, conveniently located in Bradford Township across the Merrimack River from Haverhill, was established in 1803 as a co-educational boarding and day school. The Hildreth children all attended; Harriot registered in 1810. A painting on satin fabric worked at the school by Harriot's older sister Nancy survives in the Bradford College collection, as does a profile of the sister done at the same time. Harriot, however, worked her sampler three years before becoming a student there.[7]

The Bradford College archives reveal worthwhile information regarding the education of young women in northeastern Massachusetts during the first years of the nineteenth century. Finding that the village schools offered only two hours of daily instruction for girls, the *Haverhill Observer*, April 27, 1803, announced that at Bradford young women would be "taught Reading, Writing, English Grammar, Arithmetic, Embroidery, and all other forms of Needlework together with Drawing and Painting."[8]

The first person hired to teach Bradford's female students was eighteen-year-old Hannah Swan of Charlestown. The trustees had been seeking "a reputable person well versed in the Science of Belles lettres, Embroidery, and all kinds of fine needle work," and clearly the young Hannah Swan was a wise appointment, for in November of 1803, when the first quarterly examination was held, the local paper reported: "The young ladies, under the care of Miss Swan, gave flattering proof of susceptible minds and refined taste. They exhibited such evidences of improvement in chirography, grammar, rhetoric, geography, composition painting, & embroidery as reflected the highest honor on their governess and themselves."[9]

Harriot Hildreth married Captain John Day of Danvers on May 27, 1821. It is possible they made their home in New York City, for evidence reveals that a Captain Day sailed from that port for many years.[10]

NOTES:

1. Jean Sarah Pond, *Bradford, A New England School (Bradford, A New England Academy)*, ed. Dale Mitchell (rev. ed., Bradford, MA, 1954), 13. Original quote from George Lyman Kittredge, *The Old Farmer and His Almanack* (Cambridge, MA, 1904), 229; by permission of the Harvard University Press. I am grateful to Sheila Rideout and Ann F. Powell, acting vice-president for college relations, Bradford College, for bringing this information to my attention.

2. Woody, *History of Women's Education*, vol. 1: 138.

3. Samplers related to this important group of embroideries include work done by Hannah Gale, 1801 (collection, Essex Institute, Salem, MA; see Marguerite Fawdry and Deborah Brown, *The Book of Samplers*, New York, NY: St. Martin's Press, 1980: 102); Mary Swett, 1808 (private collection); Mary Bradey, 1807 (private collection; see *Maine Antiques Digest*, August 1979: 29-C), and Harriot W. Hildreth, 1807 (illustrated here).

4. Ring, *American Needlework Treasures*, 12.

5. A strikingly similar sampler was worked by Mary Graves Kimball, 1808, aged ten (ex-Kapnek collection; see Krueger, *Gallery of American Samplers*, 45).

It is inscribed with the name of her instructress, "E. Plummers School." Mary's sampler shows a subtle change of format such as the inclusion of an urn as the central motif. In addition, the geometric border is measurably different in design, as is the outermost border of wavy flowers and vines. The absence of the words "County Essex" and the general style of this sampler suggest Elizabeth White Plummer accepted the format of Harriot Hildreth's embroidery as a regional style common to the town of Haverhill, but altered the patterns, and added variations of her own. Born August 2, 1789, Plummer kept a school in Haverhill in 1808 (see Krueger, *New England Samplers*, 172).

6. Dr. Samuel P. Hildreth, *Genealogical and Biographical Sketches of the Hildreth Family* (Marietta, OH, 1840), 302. Samuel Prescott Hildreth was Harriot Hildreth's brother.

7. The list of early students of Bradford Academy was printed on the occasion of the school's fiftieth anniversary in 1853. Harriot's name appears under the year 1810 on page 44. Much of this information came to me from Sheila Rideout in a letter addressed to her from the college by Ann F. Powell, September 11, 1985. The date of Charles's registration was sent to me by Ann Powell, October 8, 1985. I am grateful for their kind assistance.

8. Letter from Powell, October 1985.

9. Ibid.

10. *Vital Records of Haverhill, Massachusetts, to the End of the Year 1849*, vol. 2 (Topsfield, MA: Topsfield Historical Society, 1911), 166. See also John Lyman Porter, ed., *Second Publication of the Hildreth Family Association* (Hildreth Family Association, 1922), 28, 29.

17. LAURA MURDOCK (1804–1835)
Leominster, Massachusetts, 1816
Silk threads and crinkled silk floss on linen
(28 threads to the inch)
Satin, straight, rice, tent, and cross-stitches
17 x 16½ in. (43.1 x 41.9 cm)

Inscription: *How blest the maid, whom circling Years
improve,/Her God the object of her warmest love,/Whose
useful hours, successive as they glide,/The book, the
needle, and the pen divide,/Who sees her parents exult
with joy/And the fond tear stand sparkling in their eyes.
Wrought by Laura Murdock in her 12th/year
Leominster August 1816*

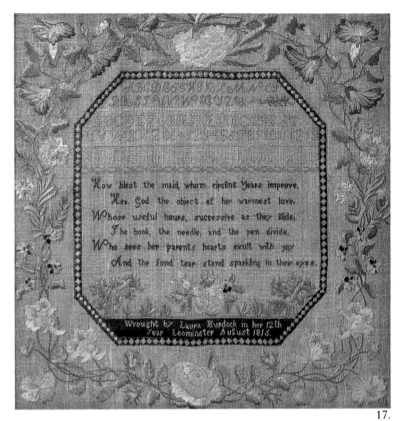

17.

The sampler worked by Laura Murdock is one of four known examples stitched under the direction of an unidentified schoolmistress who kept a school for girls in Leominster, Massachusetts, from at least 1806 to 1816.[1] Strikingly alike in format, these samplers display an uncommonly beautiful border and a center rectangle with canted corners, outlined with a strip of ivory-and-black satin stitches worked into diamonds. Three of the embroideries are inscribed with identical verses. Their inscriptions include the months of July or August, suggesting the mistress may have conducted her embroidery classes only during the summer.[2]

Reminiscent of samplers worked in Plymouth during the 1820s and 1830s (figs. 19, 20), the innovative slanting corners of the innermost square allow greater emphasis to be placed on the deepened border space. This area was then handsomely embroidered with naturalistic leaves, stems, and flowers. The framing border of Laura's sampler has been employed to introduce a charming array of twisting vines, cabbage roses, variegated morning glories, violets, and pansies.

A few carefully constructed details have faded, but close inspection reveals a pale bird with a long, sweeping tail, resting in one of the trees. Solidly embroidered black tent stitches form a band that delineates the inscription. This needlepointed strip, as it is called today, is a design technique that effectively uses color for emphasis within a given space.

Abel Murdock, a painter, and Tabitha Moore were married in Winchendon, Massachusetts, in 1799. Two of their eight children were born there; Laura was born on August 18, 1804, in Leominster.[3]

In 1827 she married Edward Snell of Boston, who was listed in the city directory of that year as a "chair maker." They had no children.[4]

Laura Murdock Snell died on July 13, 1835, in North Bridgewater, Worcester County, Massachusetts.[5]

NOTES:

1. The other known Leominster samplers are those worked by Martha Lincoln, 1806 (ex-Kapnek collection; see Krueger, *Gallery of American Samplers*, 42), Maria Butler, 1809 (location unknown; see Sack brochure, 26, October 1, 1974, item 43), and Eliza Johnson, 1809 (private collection). Maria Butler's sampler was brought to my attention by Betty Ring. I am grateful for her kind assistance.
2. The samplers of Maria Butler, Martha Lincoln, and Laura Murdock are inscribed with the same verse. Martha Lincoln's sampler was worked in July, 1806; Eliza Johnson and Maria Butler worked their samplers in July, 1809; and Laura Murdock, August, 1816. Details such as these help identify related samplers.
3. Joseph B. Murdock, *Murdock Genealogy* (Boston, MA: C.C. Goodspeed and Co., 1925), 49, 50.
4. *Vital Records of Leominster, Massachusetts, to the End of the year 1849* (Worcester, MA: Franklin P. Rice, 1911), 237. See also *Boston City Directory*, 1827 and 1830.
5. Family Record Archives, Family History Library of the Church of Jesus Christ of Latter-Day Saints, Salt Lake City, UT.

18. ELEANOR CAROLINE MALONE

Massachusetts, c.1820
Silk threads and crinkled silk floss on linen
(30 threads to the inch)
Eyelet, long, satin, chain, and cross-stitches
16¼ x 15¾ in. (41.2 x 40 cm)

Inscription: *O may I with myself agree/And never covet what i see/content me with an humble shade/My passions tam'd my wishes laid/
Wrought by/Eleanor Caroline Malone aged 8 years* [date removed]

18.

This remarkable sampler, worked by Eleanor Caroline Malone at the age of eight, was probably stitched in the vicinity of Essex County, Massachusetts. Sometime later in life, Eleanor was prompted by vanity to remove the date on her sampler. A large number of sampler embroideries underwent similar alterations as their makers grew to adulthood.

Eleanor's sampler has a finely stitched border of rosebuds and shaded leaves, with a woven basket of country flowers at the center top. A green field with a luxurious house and a large, strangely contoured tree dominate the foreground. The shape of the tree, though not the method of stitchery, is reminiscent of earlier samplers worked in Salem, as is the crinkled thread with which the sampler was stitched.

19. ELIZABETH DREW (b. 1810)

Plymouth, Massachusetts, 1824/1825
Silk threads and silk floss with paint, ink, and paper on linen (26 threads to the inch)
Split, four-sided, seed, eyelet, satin, straight, and cross-stitches with French knots
16½ x 17½ in. (41.9 x 44.4 cm)

Inscription: *Jesus permit thy gracious name to stand as the first efforts of an infants hand/And while her fingers oer this canvass move Engage her tender heart to seek thy/love With thy dear children let her share aparte And write thy name thyself upon/her heart*
Inscription on memorials: *Sacred to the memory/of/Charles Drew/Born January 11th 1821/Died December 2th 1821/Sacred to the memory/of/Charles S. Drew/Born September 30 1824/Died February 20 1825
Wrought by Elizabeth Drew Aged 13 AD 1824*

Elizabeth Drew's schoolmistress, yet to be identified, must be recognized as one of the most accomplished and talented of teachers, for this memorial sampler is a masterpiece. Fishing boats ride the painted waters of Plymouth Bay; the cove is ringed with trees embellished with aqua-tinted silken leaves. Poplars, four in a row, and paper epitaphs with delicate inscriptions lend perceptible depth to the landscape, the foreground of which has been worked in silvery blue silk that shifts and glows in the light.

An outstanding artist, Elizabeth's teacher guided her students to new aesthetic and technical levels. There are few American schoolgirl samplers combining the use of paint, stitches, ink, and paper on linen, and none so successfully as those executed under the instruction of this anonymous Plymouth schoolteacher.[1]

Samplers from Plymouth worked in this exceptionally stylish manner appear to have been created between 1813 and 1845. The earliest dated example is an 1813 sampler worked by Sarah Sturtevant.[2] In 1819 Betsey C. Battles stitched a needlework picture across the bottom of her embroidery that anticipated the elegant, painted style favored during the next decade.[3] Lucy Wadsworth's sampler (fig. 20), 1831, may have been worked under the same teacher, for comparison with Elizabeth's sampler reveals many similarities. The charming painted landscape has been omitted from the Wadsworth sampler.[4]

Each of these Plymouth pictorial embroideries exhibits an instantly recognizable format: a deep border embellished with full-blossomed China roses, twisting stems and leaves, buds, and small pansies. A distinctive inner border with canted corners encloses the verse and alphabet forms, which have been divided by thin rows of wavy vines and flowers. The samplers, almost invari-

19.

ably, combine both stitchery and paint.

Mary M. Davidson, in *Plimoth Colony Samplers*, describes the method of execution: "The alphabets, numbers and verses and signature were worked by counting threads. When this was finished the whole sampler was backed with a piece of soft cotton and the rest of the design was worked through both fabrics, following a drawn design."[5] In contrast, most American samplers are worked through homespun, with no backing or fabric added.

Elizabeth Drew's sampler is typical of the Plymouth school. Her embroidery is backed with a cotton fabric of medium weight with many of the heavily embroidered areas piercing through both textiles. The paint, apparently of an oil base, has been brushed on the linen with a fine, sure hand. Placement of the paint over some areas of stitchery implies the needlework was essentially completed before the brush was applied to the elaborate pictorial scene. This technique may be detected not only in the vivid indigo covering the willow trees but in the rust brown brush strokes found within the field of the border. There is evidence, however, that a final stitching was added after the painting to highlight the tree branches with leaves of aqua silk.

When studying these spectacular embroideries, we must pay homage to this unusual teacher. She was a dedicated, inventive painter—although probably not formally trained—who designed the pictures and painted the embellishments onto the beautiful samplers worked under her expert tutelage. Without question these scenes are too recognizable, too identical in execution, to doubt that the teacher was also the artist. No group of children, ranging in age from eight to fifteen years, could possibly duplicate her very sophisticated style of painting with such exact shading and such precise accuracy.

There is but one vital clue to her identity: she was either a member of the Friends, or, as a child, was instructed in a Quaker school, for many of the samplers ascribed to her school reveal two distinctly Quaker needlework characteristics: the boxy alphabet forms and the chain of ligatures worked across the extreme top of the canted cartouche. Ligatures—characters consisting of two or more letters united in the manner of printing type—appear on at least five of the known existing needlework samplers completed in Plymouth between 1813 and 1825.[6] Some samplers dating from the third decade of the nineteenth century, such as those worked by Sarah Stephens Lapham and Lucy Wadsworth (fig. 20), display neither an alphabet nor ligatures but in format appear to have been worked under the same supervision.[7]

Elizabeth Drew's sampler is an embroidered mourning sampler worked on linen, an uncommon form of schoolgirl art. The subject may have been recommended to her teacher by her par-

ents after the death of her infant brothers. Fragile paper epitaphs have been inscribed with ink in meticulous calligraphic lettering, still legible after more than 150 years. Applied to the sampler with fine black stitches, the paper has been pierced with blue silk-stitched leaves of the willow trees.

Elizabeth probably began her needlework before the summer of 1824, while she was still thirteen, completing it after February of 1825, the date of her second infant brother's death. School terms were often determined by the individual teacher and thus rather irregular. Elizabeth's attendance at her academy may well have been inconsistent and unmonitored, for, as we have learned, schooling for young girls was not generally considered of primary importance.

Born August 13, 1810, one of twelve children, Elizabeth Drew was the daughter of William Drew, Jr., and Sarah Holmes, who married in Plymouth in 1804.[8] In 1835, Elizabeth Drew and Isaac W. Proctor, a trader from Framingham, Middlesex County, were married. They had three children before Isaac's death in 1848.[9] Ten years later, Elizabeth married Thomas A. Walker, a United States land officer from Des Moines, Iowa.[10]

NOTES:

1. Mary M. Davidson, *Plimoth Colony Samplers*, (Marion, MA: The Channings, 1975), 34, 35, 40. Davidson theorizes that Maria de Verdier Turner, the European wife of Capt. Lothrop Turner of Plymouth, was the accomplished teacher who designed and guided many a young Plymouth girl in the art of embroidery. Maria Turner, however, left Plymouth for Boston after the death of her husband in 1824. Elizabeth Drew's sampler alone, bearing the dates of 1824 and 1825, would seem to refute this theory. Samplers showing the same technique and design format continued to be worked in Plymouth into the 1840s (Ring, *American Needlework Treasures*, 14, 15). Until additional documentation surfaces, it seems doubtful that Maria Turner was

this Plymouth schoolmistress.

2. The Sturtevant sampler is in a private collection; see Davidson, *Plimoth Colony Samplers*, 35, 37.

3. The Battles sampler, 1816 (private collection; see Skinner catalogue, Bolton Gallery, Bolton, MA, *Fine Americana*, 1146, March 21, 1987, lot 46), may be the only Plymouth sampler of this group yet to surface that displays a distinctive oval format rather than the familiar octagonal-shaped cartouche. All the other characteristics are present, such as ligatures, boxy alphabet forms, elaborate borders, and painted tableaux.

4. Another sampler of Plymouth origin related to this body of work is that worked by Susan Stephens Lapham, 1832 (collection, Philadelphia Museum of Art, PA; see Sarah B. Sherrill, "Current and Coming," *Antiques*, April 1979: 672). See also Ring, *American Needlework Treasures*, 14, 15. The samplers illustrated were worked by Marcia A. Harlow, 1822 (collection, Betty Ring); Mary A. Bradford, 1833 (collection, Betty Ring); and Betsy R. Churchill, 1835 (collection, Betty Ring).

5. Davidson, *Plimoth Colony Samplers*, 34.

6. Ring, *American Needlework Treasures*, 14, and Ring, "Samplers and Pictorial Needlework," 1425, 1426. See also Davidson, *Plimoth Colony Samplers*, 39. Samplers displaying ligatures and bold alphabets are: Sarah Sturtevant, 1813 (private collection); Betsey C. Battles, 1819 (private collection); Marcia Harlow, 1822 (collection, Betty Ring); Nancy Holmes, 1823 (private collection); and Elizabeth Drew, 1824–25 (illustrated here).

7. The Lapham sampler is in the collection of the Philadelphia Museum of Art, PA; see Sherrill, "Current and Coming," 672.

8. *International Genealogical Index*. See also *Vital Records of Plymouth, Massachusetts*, vol. 2: 60.

9. Thomas W. Baldwin, *Vital Records of Framingham, Massachusetts* (Boston, MA, 1911), 270. See also *Federal Census, Framingham; Massachusetts, Index to Births in Massachusetts, 1841–1850*, vol. 5: 40, and *Death Records, Framingham* (Family Record Archives, Family History Library of the Church of Jesus Christ of Latter-Day Saints, Salt Lake City, UT, microfilm).

10. *Marriage Records, Plymouth* (Public Library of Plymouth, MA, microfilm). Thanks to the kind assistance of Jean Medeiros of the Reference Department.

20.

20. LUCY WADSWORTH (1817–1881)
Plymouth, Massachusetts, 1831
Silk threads and crinkled silk floss on linen
(24 threads to the inch)
Satin, long and short, and cross-stitches
17 x 16½ in. (43.1 x 41.9 cm)

Inscription: *In youth improve the tender mind/Let virtue be with learning joined*
Wrought by Lucy Wadsworth/aged 13 years.
Plymouth/June 24th 1831

The sampler worked by Lucy Wadsworth displays many of the characteristics of the fine pictorial samplers known to have been worked in Plymouth. The basic design of the octagonal center panel seen in the sampler worked by Elizabeth Drew (fig. 19) has been retained, but it is far less sophisticated. Similar satin-stitched blossoms adorn each border corner, and thin rows of flowers remain from the pattern considered fashionable a decade before.

Betsey Ellis Hutchinson worked a sampler similar to Lucy's the same year.[1] Both have inscriptions that include the words "wrought by," making it probable that they attended the same boarding school. Neither of these embroideries, however, is embellished with an elegantly painted landscape—the trademark of Elizabeth Drew's teacher. Another school and schoolmistress may have been responsible for these two samplers, although it is clear that certain elements had become regionally popular.

After the death of his first wife, Dura Wadsworth, housewright, married Nabby Cushman in Duxbury, Massachusetts. Wadsworth, a Universalist, was known as a man of character who "paid bills 100 cents on the dollar." The first of their eight children was Lucy Abigail Wadsworth, born September 25, 1817.[2]

Lucy, or Abigail, as she came to be known, remained single throughout her life, living with her wealthy parents. She became a dressmaker and lived in Duxbury until her death on February 12, 1881.[3]

NOTES:

1. The Hutchinson sampler is in the collection of the Pilgrim Hall Museum, Plymouth, MA; see Davidson, *Plimoth Colony Samplers*, 47.
2. *Vital Records of Duxbury, Massachusetts, to the End of the Year 1850* (Boston, MA: New England Historical Genealogical Society, 1911), 182, 324. See also Horace Andrew Wadsworth, *Two Hundred and Fifty Years of the Wadsworth Family in America* (Lawrence, MA: Eagle Steam, 1883), 170.
3. *Death Records, Duxbury, Massachusetts*, 1880, 305. See also *Federal Census, Duxbury, Massachusetts*, 1880.

21. LOUISA H. PLYMPTON (b. 1812)
Middlesex County, Massachusetts, c. 1830
Silk threads and crinkled silk floss on linen
(34 threads to the inch)
Satin, tent, Gobelin, Roumanian, outline, and cross-stitches
15¼ x 16 in. (38.7 x 40.6 cm)

Inscription: *Louisa/bn/July 6 1806/Ebenr/bn/ July 4/1808/Louisa/bn/May 20/1812/Harriet/bn/Sept 29/1814/Fanny/ bn/Feb 24/1817/George/Bn/Nov 18/1828/Tho.R/Plympton/bn/Aug20/1782/ Elizabeth/ Plympton/ bn/Jan 28/ 1787 Family Record/Married Oct 2/1805/Louisa H Plympton*

22. LOUISA H. PLYMPTON (b. 1812)
Massachusetts, c. 1819
Silk threads on linen (24 threads to the inch)
Cross-stitches
7¼ x 12½ in. (18.4 x 31.8 cm)

Inscription: *Louisa H Plympton age* [date removed]

23. ADELINE L. BEARD (1833–1843)
Waltham, Massachusetts, 1840
Silk threads on linen (28 threads to the inch)
Cross-stitches with hem-stitching
11¾ x 8 in. (29.84 x 20.32 cm)

Inscription: *Adeline L. Beard/W ham. . .1840*

The folk artist in America has long shown a fondness for the tree of life as an expressive design form. This tree became a decorative motif much favored by stone carvers, painters, quilt and coverlet makers, and samplermakers, as well. During the colonial period, embroidered trees were depicted in a stilted, stylized manner. But in the newly formed republic a more naturalistic rendering of sturdy trunks, limbs, and fruit-filled branches emerged, replete with names and birth dates of family members.

This sampler stitched by Louisa Plympton is an exquisite example of the family tree design. The origin of the fruit motif to represent children that is seen here and in many other samplers remains a mystery. The double-heart at the base of the tree has been found on numerous watercolors from the end of the eighteenth century.[1] Imaginative schoolmistresses may have had access to the print from which this design originated, adapting it to classroom embroidery. Rebecca Wild's sampler (fig. 24), for example, is prominently decorated with an overlapping heart motif.

A family register watercolor painted by Rebecca Tufts

21.

22.

Fesseden between about 1810 and 1812 in a style similar to the Plympton family sampler has recently come to light. Inscribed "Mrs. Gill's Academy, West Cambridge," it is possibly the first tangible clue to the identity of at least one preceptress responsible for the tree-of-life embroideries worked in this area.[2] Louisa Plympton's teacher and the exact location of her school still remain unknown, but the design appears to have become a distinctively regional pattern that was employed by several Middlesex County samplermakers.[3] Peter Benes, in *Families and Children*, traces the use of this symbolic tree to three locations: eastern and central Middlesex County, Cape Ann in eastern Essex County, and coastal southeastern New England.[4]

Differing slightly in interpretation, these samplers are of two loosely related styles. One group is worked with an encompassing archway, or three-sided border, of thickly stitched, dark green leaves, while the other displays a delicately looped garland across the top, often tied with ribbon bows, and, frequently, decorative columns with elaborate plinths adorning the sides. The embroi-

deries date from about 1794 to 1833, with professional watercolorists employing the identical design during the same period.[5]

Long, uncouched stitches, resembling oyster-colored satin, cover the entire linen ground of Louisa's sampler, giving it a lustrous, opalescent sheen. The multicolored plumes have been directed to a point below the tree, adding another heart-shaped motif. Two unattached circles inscribed "Louisa, b. 1806," and "Fanny, b. 1817," separated from the branches, indicate that these children did not survive.

Louisa Holden Plympton was born on May 26, 1812, the date inscribed on her family record sampler (fig. 21). On an earlier sampler worked by Louisa, her age has been removed (fig. 22).

The daughter of Thomas Ruggles Plympton and Betsy Holden of East Sudbury, Massachusetts, Louisa married Josiah Beard of Waltham in 1832. They were the parents of Adeline Louisa Beard, who embroidered the marking sampler (fig. 23) inscribed "W ham. . .1840," revealing that she was attending needlework classes by the age of seven.[6]

NOTES:

1. Cynthia V. A. Schaffner and Susan Klein, *Folk Hearts, A Celebration of the Heart Motif in American Folk Art* (New York, NY: Alfred A. Knopf, 1984), 56, 57.
2. *Antiques* (April 1988): 760 (advertisement).
3. *Families and Children*, ed. Peter Benes (Dublin, NH: Dublin Seminar for New England Folklife, 1987), 91–129, fn. 21, 104. Benes presents the names of several candidates who may have been the schoolmistresses who instructed their needlework students in this specific and unusually decorative design. Among those thought to qualify are Bathsheba Whitman, who taught for a time at Sandwich Academy; Miss Bowers, who advertised a school for young ladies in Billerica during 1814 and 1815; the Misses M. & C. Stearns; and Mrs. Haswell of Charlestown.
4. Ibid., 103.
5. Ibid., checklist: 131–145. I am indebted to Sheila Rideout for bringing two of these related samplers to my attention.
6. *Vital Records of Sudbury, Massachusetts, to the End of the Year 1850* (Boston, MA: New England Historical Genealogical Society, 1903), 251. See also *Vital Records of Waltham, Massachusetts, to the End of the Year 1850* (Boston, MA: New England Historical Genealogical Society, 1904), 13, 205; and Levi B. Chase, *A Genealogy of and Historical Notices of the Family of Plympton in America* (Hartford, CT: Plympton Mfg. Co., 1884). Researched by Sheila Rideout.

23.

24. REBECCA J. WILD (1820–1899)
Charlestown, Massachusetts, 1831
Silk threads and crinkled silk floss on linen
(26 threads to the inch)
Satin, long and short, outline, and cross-stitches
17½ x 15½ in. (44.47 x 39.39 cm)

Inscription: *Elisha Wild/born Jan 3/ Caroline Healy/born June 4/1798/Married/Feb 26/1818 FAMILY RECORD/John F Wild bn Dec 23/1818/ Rebecca J Wild Bn Feb 21 1820/Caroline L Wild Bn Oct 13 1824/While I with care my work pursue/And to my book my mind apply/Ill keep my teachrs love in view/And guard my way with watch/ful eye/But most of all Ill mind that word/Which brings salvation from the Lord/Sacred to the Memory of Wrought by Rebecca J Wild/Charlestown Jan 1 1831/Aged 10 years*

For centuries, the heart-shaped motif has enchanted American artisans. Considered "a universal symbol of secular and religious love, courage, and friendship, hospitality, loyalty, and fidelity,"[1] the heart could be duplicated in two sweeping curves by even the most untrained artist. It decorates early American painted chests and other country furniture and has appeared in minute stitching on quilts, in garish colors on paper marriage and birth certificates, and in an endless variety of splendid folk art.

Since the eighteenth century, hearts—and the strawberry vine—have proved to be popular sampler motifs. Pennsylvania Germans delighted in embroidering samplers and decorating towels with a cross-stitched heart, frequently topping it with a crown. It is, in fact, a rare occasion when a Pennsylvania towel appears without a heart among its numerous patterns.[2]

The source of the arrangement of three overlapping hearts on Rebecca Wild's sampler presents a mystery in the world of sampler embroidery. The identical motif has been found on watercolor paintings in the same east-southeast section of Massachusetts as early as the last decade of the eighteenth century. Evidently, this enticing design found its way into popular use, inspired by an earlier print or engraving, which is yet to be discovered.[3]

Other samplers of identical format present ample evidence that a school for girls existed in Charlestown, Massachusetts, at least between 1824 and 1833.[4] Their unidentified schoolmistress was not a very creative artist. The linen is a jumble of unimaginative sampler patterns—a family record, a pictorial sampler with a yellow cross-stitched house, an alphabet marking sampler, and a

ABCDEFGHIJKLMNOPQ
RSTUVWXYZ · 1234567891011

ABCDEFGHIJKLMNOPQRSTUVWXYZ

abcdefghijklmnopqrstuvwxyz abcdefghijklmnopq

Elisha Wild
born Jan 3

Caroline Heath
born June 4
1798

F A M I L Y   R E C O R D

While I with care my work pursue
And to my book my mind apply
I keep my teachrs love in view
And guard my way with watch future
But most of all I'll mind that word
Which brings salvation from the Lord

Married
Feb 26
1818

John F Wild bn Dec 28 1818
Rebecca J Wild bn Feb 21 1820
Caroline L Wild bn Oct 13 1824

Wrought by Rebecca J Wild
Charlestown Jan 1835
Aged 10 years

Sacred
to the
Memory
of

mourning embroidery—all crowded into one. The violet-colored flowers adjacent to the hearts provide the only drama in the sampler. But the samplers are still enjoyable even when their artistic value is questionable.

Elisha Wild, a blacksmith, and Caroline Healy were married in 1818. Rebecca Wild, one of their four children, was born on February 21, 1820, as we know from her sampler.[5]

Rebecca Jane Wild married Moses Parker of Boston (d. 1855) in 1839. He was a blacksmith, like her father. Their only son, George Parker, was born on July 15, 1855.[6]

There appears to be no record of the date of Rebecca's second marriage, to Amasa Thayer of Braintree. The first mention of the name Rebecca J. Thayer is recorded in November 1869, when she formally requested guardianship of her son, George, a minor.[7]

Rebecca died May 19, 1899, in Braintree, Massachusetts.[8]

NOTES:

1. Schaffner and Klein, *Folk Hearts*, introduction.
2. Colby, *Samplers*, 175. See also Susan Burrows Swan, "Household Textiles," in *Arts of the Pennsylvania Germans*, ed. Catherine E. Hutchins (New York, NY: W. W. Norton, 1983), 226; Ellen J. Gehert, *This Is the Way I Pass My Time* (Birdsboro, PA: Pennsylvania German Society, 1985), 10, 59, 67, 69. I agree with Gehert, who declares that the embroidered towel is a folk phenomenon. However, it is difficult to imagine that Pennsylvanian-decorated towels are "not thought to have been worked under the influence of a schoolmistress" (p. 67). These embroidered towels are astonishingly similar to Pennsylvania German spot-motif samplers, and it would seem logical for a schoolmistress to require both a sampler and a towel to complete a girl's needlework instruction (p. 69). Concerning freehand drawings, Gehert writes, "Many young ladies drew freely onto their towel familiar objects, flowers, and birds" (the source of which is presumably "beyond recall," p. 67). Quite the opposite is true. An exact rendition of the leaping deer illustrated on the towel embroidered by Clary Hallman, 1841, can be found in sampler stitchery dating from the early years of the eighteenth century (Nancy Graves Cabot, "The Fishing Lady and Boston Common," in *Needlework: an Historical Survey*, ed. Betty Ring, New York, NY: Main Street Press, 1975), 48. Possibly further investigation into this puzzling situation might reveal a different conclusion.

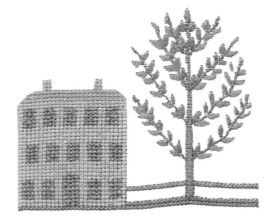

3. Gehert, *This Is the Way I Pass My Time*, 62, 63. Illustrated are excellent examples of the use of broadsides, book illustrations, and other printed material as inspiration for needlework patterns.
4. Eliza Ann Hunt worked an identical sampler in 1824 (collection, Cooper-Hewitt Museum of Design, Smithsonian Institution, New York, NY; see Schaffner and Klein, *Folk Hearts*, 42); Frances Howe worked hers in February 1827 (private collection; see Sotheby's, New York, catalogue, *Fine American Furniture and Related Decorative Arts*, 4590Y, April 29–May 1, 1981, lot 680); and Lucy Ann Williams worked her Charlestown sampler November 1830 (Sotheby's, 5156, January 27, 1984, lot 511). Rebecca Wild's sampler is dated 1831.
5. Edward Evarts Jackson, *Wild Genealogy* (excerpts from *Boston Evening Transcript*, Boston, MA: New England Historical Genealogical Society, 1905), 13. Dates given disagree with sampler dates, which are generally accepted as being more accurate. See also *Records of the First Congregational Church, Braintree, Massachusetts*, 1711–1762 and 1811–1859, copied by Abigail Phillips, Quincy Chapter, Daughters of the American Revolution (Wollaston, MA,1942), 115. These dates tally with the sampler dates. *Federal Census, Braintree, Massachusetts*, 1850, gives Elisha Wild's occupation as blacksmith. His real estate is valued at three thousand dollars.
6. A handwritten document in the Waldo C. Sprague Collection, American Department, New England Historical and Genealogical Society, Boston, MA, records the marriage of Rebecca Wild to Moses Parker. Moses Parker's death and occupation are registered in the *Death Records, Quincy*,1859, 166. The birth date for George Parker is included in the application for guardianship, Norfolk County Probate Court, November 25, 1869. *Petition, Citation and Decree for Guardianship of Minors*, vol. 123: 381.
7. *Probate Records, Norfolk County*, no. 18.046, filed January 9, 1866. Amasa Thayer's parents, Levi and Lilla Thayer, owned a parcel of land in Boston, on Market Square, held in life trust for their sons, Ira and Amasa. The record may be found in a trusteeship dated June 9, 1866, *Probate Records, Norfolk County, Will*, vol. 115: 927. In Amasa Thayer's will, June 9, 1866, his real property is valued at $14,915, including stores number 36, 38, and 40, Faneuil Hall, Boston. He left Rebecca the sum of $10, "together with what she may be entitled by the laws of the Commonwealth, had no will been made by me." See no. 21.860, Thayer, Amasa; will; filed March 24, 1880, Norfolk County, Town of Braintree.
8. *Probate Records, Norfolk County*, no. 33.516, filed May 3, 1898, allowed June 8, 1898, vol. 188: 419. Her death is recorded in vol. 494: 10.

25. ANN ELIZA GODDARD (1821–1834)
Probably Massachusetts, c. 1829
Silk threads on linen (24 threads to the inch)
Cross-stitches with hem-stitching
10½ x 10½ in. (26.6 x 26.6 cm)

Inscribed on paper insert: *Dear Ann Eliza let this be/A*
token of my love to thee
A E Goddard/April 14th 1834/Aged 12 ½ years

Ann Eliza Goddard died on April 14, 1834, at the age of twelve. Sometime after that date, a lock of her hair and her threaded needle were placed inside the frame of her unfinished marking sampler, along with her black and ivory silk brocade needlecase and a card, carefully inscribed in her memory.

Ann was probably the daughter of Benjamin Goddard and Dolly Tyler of Webster, Worcester County, Massachusetts.[1]

NOTES:

1. Family Record Archives, Family History Library of the Church of Jesus Christ of Latter-Day Saints, Salt Lake City, UT.

26. ELIZABETH BROWN
Probably Massachusetts, 1834
Twisted silk threads and crinkled silk floss on linen
(30 threads to the inch)
Split, tent, chain, queen, satin, and cross-stitches
17¾ x 21 in. (43.8 x 52.34 cm)

Inscription: *O hiLLs O vaLes whare I have strayd/O*
woods that rapt me in your shade/O scenes that I have
wandered over/O scenes I shaLL behoLd no more/I take
a Longe Last Lingering view/Adieu my native Land
adieu
Elizabeth Brown's Work 1834

Although Elizabeth Brown's schoolmistress remains anonymous, this sampler reveals a wealth of information about her. This talented teacher's venturesome design is delightfully colorful. The embroidery is framed by a bold, geometric border worked in vines, leafy stems, and large, open-faced flowers. Visually dramatic, this strong design element, probably indicative of her teaching approach, establishes the format. It presents a natural setting for the wedge-shaped platform at the center of the bottom that embraces a decorative basket of oversized roses.

This schoolmistress imaginatively inserted trees to fill the panels at each side, one a tree of ripening apples, the other delicately entwined with a vine of faded yellow silk grapes. Strawberry buds and sprightly birds embellish the border across the bottom.

Elizabeth's verse is enclosed within a dainty cartouche of flowered sprigs. To either side, handled urns—resembling blue-and-white patterned porcelain—have been embroidered. The stitches have been most skillfully executed.

As Elizabeth Brown's sampler is reminiscent of a group of large, floral-bordered samplers worked in northeastern Massachusetts near Newburyport, she may have attended an unidentified school for girls in that vicinity.

25.

26.

27. JANE ABBOT (1800–1880)
Peterborough, New Hampshire, 1811
Silk, twisted silk threads, and crinkled silk floss on
linen (36 threads to the inch)
Eyelet, straight, satin, and cross-stitches
15½ x 16 in. (39.3 x 40.6 cm)

Inscription: *Jesus permit thy gracious name to stand/As
the first efforts of an infants hand/And while her fingers
oer this canvass move/Engage her tender heart to seek thy
love/With thy dear children let her share a part/And write
thy name thyself, upon her heart*
*Wrought by Jane Abbot aged 10 years Peterborough Sept.
1811*

28. SALLY ABBOT (1806–1887)
Peterborough, New Hampshire, 1818
Silk threads and crinkled silk floss on linen
(34 threads to the inch)
Outline, eyelet, satin, and cross-stitches
16 in. square (40.64 square cm)

Inscription: *Youth the spring time of our years/Short the
rapid scene appears/Let's improve the fleeting
hours/Virtue's noblest fruits be ours*
Wrought by Sally Abbot aged 11 years. June 6th 1818

27.

The inscription on Jane Abbot's pictorial sampler is the single most popular verse to be found on American sampler embroidery. She has also stitched a charming four-bay house by working long-reaching stitches of creamy floss that have the look of overlapping, wooden planks. The elaborate front door has been embroidered with lengthy, herringbone stitches of twisted silk the color of beeswax. Prominent corner boards, often shown in sampler embroidery, and the tip of the roof have been meticulously outlined in thick loops of chain-stitching. The picturesque, green-gladed bourn beside the house may have reminded Jane of her own home, built by her father in a shallow ravine beside the Nubanusit River.[1]

Inside the green and beige sawtooth bands, another wider, three-sided border frames the sampler; it is decorated with cherry-tree twigs and fruit and a small cross-stitched basket of flowers at the top. In typical New Hampshire fashion, the birds in the small tree have been outlined in dark silk threads, as has the gaping knothole on the trunk of the thick shade tree. In 1811, Eliza Carter worked an identical tree on her sampler in the same classroom.[2]

Probably a student of the same instructor, Jane's sister Sally worked a sampler in Peterborough in 1818 (fig. 28). While Sally's embroidery does not appear to follow the exact format worked by

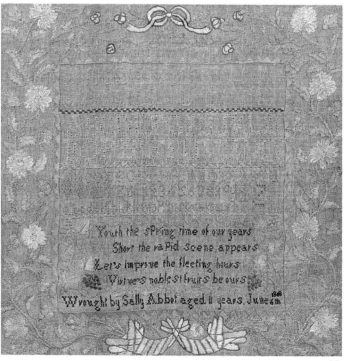

28.

her sister, it is similar. There is a comparable range of thread colors, and the alphabet lettering occurs in an identical sequence, with the eyelet capital letters being second in the orderly rows. In this instance, the flower-strewn border flows upward from cross-patterned cornucopias to an ivory, silk-ribbon bow and bowknots. Both these motifs have been outlined in threads of dark indigo silk—a hallmark of New Hampshire sampler embroideries.

Daniel and Sally Abbot lived in Peterborough, New Hampshire, with their four children in a house by the Nubanusit that has long since vanished. Jane Abbot was born on September 30, 1800, in Peterborough, and her sister Sally was born on November 3, 1806, in Newburyport.[3] Daniel Abbot was a cabinetmaker, librarian, and town clerk.[4]

Jane Abbot became the second wife of John Scott (1797–1846), after 1831. Also born in Peterborough, he had moved to Michigan and become an established pillar of Detroit society, as well as a political figure and successful builder. After the death of her husband, Jane was bequeathed an annuity of $250 to be paid "half yearly," while the balance of his vast estate reverted to his only surviving child, James.[5]

On May 6, 1830, when she was twenty-three, Sally Abbot married Jefferson Fletcher, a clothier in Peterborough. They were parents of two daughters and a son. About 1849, Jefferson moved the family to his place of birth, Westford, Massachusetts, where Sally's father and her sister Jane also made their home.[6]

Jane Abbot Scott died in 1880, and Sally Abbot Fletcher in 1887.[7]

NOTES:

1. Rev. Sebastian V. Ramge, *The Peterborough Meeting House and Common* (unpublished manuscript; St. Joseph's Priory, Peterborough, NH, c. 1970), 14. Ramge records that Daniel Abbot was an important builder and cabinetmaker in Peterborough, known to have assisted in the completion of the new meeting house. The house on the Nubanusit for many years served as his cabinet shop, chair factory, and residence. In 1813 he turned to the manufacture of cotton, forming the Eagle Factory with a few of his friends.
2. The Carter sampler is in a private collection; see Bolton and Coe, *American Samplers*, 136. See also Skinner catalogue, Bolton Gallery, Bolton, MA, *Fine Americana*, 1098, May 30, 1986, lot 144.
3. *Town Records, Peterborough, New Hampshire*, comp. Daniel Abbot, town clerk, 1815, vol. 1: 116.
4. Albert Smith, *History of the Town of Peterborough, Hillsborough County, New Hampshire* (Boston, MA: George H. Ellis, 1876), 5, 6, 199, 281.
5. Silas Farmer, *History of Detroit and Wayne County and Early Michigan* (reprint, Detroit, MI: Gale Research Company, 1969), 475. See also Clarence M. and M. Agnes Burton, eds., *History of Wayne County and the City of Detroit, Michigan*, vol. 2 (Chicago, IL, and Detroit, MI: S. J. Clarke Publishing Company, 1930), 1039–1041. See also George Abbot Morison, *History of Peterborough, New Hampshire*, vol. 1 (Ringe, NH: Richard R. Smith Publisher, Inc., 1954), map, 148.
6. Smith, *History of the Town of Peterborough*, 202. See also Morison, *History of Peterborough*, 562, and *Federal Census, Westford, Massachusetts*, 1850
7. Family Record Archives, Family History Library of the Church of Jesus Christ of Latter-Day Saints, Salt Lake City, UT.

29.

29. REBECCAH THOMAS (b. 1803)
Probably Jaffrey, New Hampshire, c. 1817 (incorrectly inscribed "1807")
Twisted silk threads, crinkled silk floss, and paint on fine linen, or tiffany (60 threads to the inch)
Satin, padded satin, herringbone, outline, tent, and cross-stitches with French knots
13 ½ x 15 ¼ in. (34.3 x 38.7 cm)

Inscription: *Rebeccah Thomas/ Born August 4th 1803 Now in the bloom of life/Would I desire to seek and find/That Pearl of greatest Price/Which is my Jesus Christ Wrought 1807*

The superb pictorial sampler worked by Rebeccah Thomas of Surry, New Hampshire, has been inscribed with the questionable date of 1807. This pale inscription, undoubtedly added at a later time, would mean that Rebeccah, born 1803, was an accomplished embroiderer by the age of four. Comparison with related samplers from this distinguished school, however, suggests a more reasonable date of about 1817, when Rebeccah was in her teens, or as she inscribes in her verse, "in the bloom of life."

The format of her sampler is extremely sophisticated. The variety of stitches and the use of thickly sewn, crinkled silk threads, alternating with a thinner silk twist, give an unusual and interesting depth to the picture. Placement of the hollows in the hills, and the rows of trees, give a sense of true perspective, often ignored in schoolgirl embroideries. Although the design was probably copied from a print or engraving, this unidentified teacher has been both inventive and skillful in transposing the picture from paper to linen and thread.

A woman in a cream-colored gown is shown wearing a silvery blue stole draped around her shoulders and a splendid high-crowned hat. Her face, hair, and decolletage have been expertly painted directly on the linen—the schoolmistress's task.

She is holding a looped garland of twisted flowers and leaves, which in color and form serves as a device to lead the viewer's eye from the tall shade tree, across the costumed figure, and directly into the pastoral landscape. A wavy border of naturalistic flowers and leaves circles the meadow, which has been outlined with a thin, silvery, sawtoothed border.

This elegant pictorial sampler is one of at least four samplers identified as having been worked in southern New Hampshire between 1817 and 1821. Laura Bowker, at the age of eleven, stitched an identical sampler in 1817, adorned with appliquéd, kidskin lambs and a woman with her face drawn on paper and pasted to the fabric.[1] Betsey Fay, at nineteen years, worked a similar sampler in 1818.[2] Nancy S. Perkins, aged fourteen, worked an exact duplicate, with a paper lady and prickworked, paper sheep on linen canvas in 1821.[3] These three samplermakers lived in Fitzwilliam, New Hampshire. Only Rebeccah came from Surry.

There is increasing circumstantial evidence to attribute their needlework instruction to a teacher keeping school in Fitzwilliam, but the town of Jaffrey is slowly gaining recognition, as it was once a thriving center for the decorative arts. It was in Jaffrey, for example, that Hannah Davis designed her beautiful wood and paper-covered bandboxes.[4] Samplers inscribed with the name of the town have begun to surface—such as the 1829 mourning sampler worked by Mary J. Perkins[5]—indicating an unusual number of schools for girls may have existed there during the second and third decades of the nineteenth century. Other sampler embroideries displaying similar characteristics are believed to have originated in these various academies (figs. 32, 33).[6]

The federal-style reverse-painted black glass matting with fine gilt lines and corner star motifs would have been more appropriate for a silk-on-silk embroidery than it is for Rebeccah's sampler. However, the sampler has been untouched since it was placed in the frame and backed with a *New York American and Journal* dated October 10, 1904.

Rebeccah Thomas, the daughter of Francis and Elizabeth Gregg, was the sixth of thirteen children. She was born in Ringe, New Hampshire, August 4, 1803.[7]

In 1827, Rebeccah married Seth Carpenter (1802–1843), a farmer. They were parents of three children.[8] After the death of her husband, she married William J. Griswold, an Englishman living in Surry, New Hampshire. In 1846, Griswold, involved in a fight, was found guilty of assault, fined two thousand dollars, and spent six months in jail. Records reveal he abandoned Rebeccah and by 1850 she was living in Westminster, Vermont, near two of her married children.[9] In 1877, Rebecca married David H. Maxfield; she was seventy-four years of age. She died after 1882 in Chester, Vermont.[10]

NOTES:

1. The location of the Bowker sampler is unknown; see Bolton and Coe, *American Samplers*, 130, opp. 146.

2. The Fay sampler is in a private collection; see Sotheby's, New York, catalogue, *Important Frakturs, Embroidered Pictures, Theorem Paintings, Cutwork Pictures, and Other American Folk Art: from the Collection of Edgar William and Bernice Chrysler Garbish*, part 3, 3692, November 12, 1974, lot 51.

3. Nancy Perkins's sampler is in the collection of the Museum of Art, Rhode Island School of Design, Providence; see Krueger, *New England Samplers*, fig. 69.

4. Hannah Davis (1784–1863) became famous for her decorated boxes. See Nina Fletcher Little, *Neat and Tidy: Boxes and Their Contents Used in Early American Households* (New York, NY: Dutton, 1980), 106, 107, 109, 112.

5. Mary Perkins's sampler is in a private collection; see *Antiques* (September 1982): 402, advertisement.

6. Krueger, *New England Samplers*, 77, 81. The towns of Jaffrey and Fitzwilliam, New Hampshire, are interwoven with the history of these exceptional samplers. I am indebted to Betty Ring for bringing the importance of the town of Jaffrey and the schoolgirl embroideries to my attention.

7. Frank Burnside Kingsbury, *History of the Town of Surry, Cheshire County, New Hampshire* (Surry, NH, 1925), 599. See also *Vital Records of New Hampshire for the Year 1803*.

8. Kingsbury, *History of the Town of Surry*, 325. See also Amos B. Carpenter, *A Genealogical History of the Rehoboth Branch of the Carpenter Family in America* (Amherst, MA, 1898), 398.

9. Kingsbury, *History of the Town of Surry*, 78, 119, 167.

10. *Vital Records of Vermont for the Year 1882*. Married in Chester by the Rev. Henry L. Sluck; recorded by the Town Clerk, Chris Robbins. David Maxfield is recorded as a married man when he died in November 1882.

30. ELIZABETH DORE (1809–1864)
Portsmouth, New Hampshire, 1822
Silk threads and crinkled silk floss on linen
(28 threads to the inch)
Satin and cross-stitches
15½ x 17¼ in. (39.3 x 43.8 cm)

Inscription: *Extract/The tear down childhood cheek that flow/Is like the dewdrop on the rose/When new the summer breeze comes by/And waves the bush the flower is dry/Three Golden Rules/Worthy the observation of every one/Do everything in its proper time/keep everything to its proper use/Put everything in its proper place Elizabeth Dore Aged 13 Portsmouth May 31 A.D. 1822*

Schoolmistress: probably E. Walden

In 1773, David McClure, a Portsmouth, New Hampshire, schoolmaster, wrote: "Opened school, consisting the first day of about 30 Misses. Afterward they increased to 70 or 80; so that I was obliged to divide the day between them and one half came in the forenoon and the other in the afternoon. They were from 7 to 20 years of age. I attended to them in reading, writing and arithmetic and geography principally. This is, I believe, the only female school (supported by the town) in New England, and is a wise and useful institution."[1] By the first quarter of the nineteenth century schools for girls in Portsmouth were well established and instruction in needlework and its various branches was diligently pursued.

The stylistic format of Elizabeth Dore's sampler—with its distinctive birdhouse and pyramid-shaped trees—was employed in this New Hampshire town as early as 1810, when Deborah Laighton embroidered her sampler with the name of her schoolmistress, Mary Ann Smith.[2] Many of the samplers worked in this format, such as that stitched in 1818 by Priscilla Hall Badger at Elizabeth S. Smith's school, were worked on a green linsey-woolsey fabric instead of the more common plain-weave linen.[3] Particular to this group is the inclusion of the month, day, and year that the sampler was embroidered.

The popularity of this pattern continued at least until 1835 when Martha Jane Fowler[4] stitched her sampler; the names of at least four schoolmistresses are inscribed on samplers of this style. For example, those worked between the years 1810 and 1822 name Mary Walden, E. Walden, Elizabeth S., and Mary Ann Smith. One would suspect that the two Smiths and two Waldens were related, although such evidence has yet to be confirmed.[5]

We may assume, however, that the two kindred samplers embellished with arcaded strawberry borders—the first worked by

30.

Elizabeth Dore, and the second by Adaline M. Ferguson, who named E. Walden as her schoolmistress—are products of the same classroom in 1822.[6]

Samplers worked in the characteristic Portsmouth tradition—with the understanding that students at other schools in this seaport town may have stitched samplers of a different sort—always gave prominence to a federal-style house, often in perspective. A picket fence forms a band of ribbing across the sampler, attaching house to barn. One bird is usually resting on the gatepost, and the birdhouse (with its own chimney) is on a tall pole high above the roofline of the barn. Another identifying feature is the depiction of trees: they are invariably arranged in odd numbers of one, three, or five, depending on the width of the sampler, and embroidered in a circular arrangement of cross-stitches. They shade the farmyard between the house and the barn.[7]

When reviewing this exceptional body of schoolgirl embroidery it becomes evident that, as with other embroidery patterns, this pleasing sampler style became a needlework tradition in Portsmouth, accepted by schoolmistresses and fashionable folk alike, for a period of at least thirty years, from 1810 to 1840.[8]

Although the Dore family is recorded as early as 1675 in Portsmouth Harbor, once called Strawbery Banke, the census of 1810 places John Dore and John Dore, Jr., in Somersworth, Strafford County, New Hampshire.[9] Elizabeth was born in 1809, to John Dore, Jr., and his wife, Elizabeth. The *Portsmouth City Directory* for 1821 reveals John Dore, a farmer, was living on Ham's Street, which ran from North Street to the Creek. Elizabeth Dore married Ezekiel Dyer, mariner, in 1829.[10] Ezekiel died at twenty-five in 1832. By 1834, Eliza Dyer, laundress, was living in a house at 20 Bridge Street with her widowed mother, Betsey, and her only child, Ezekiel.[11]

Eliza Dore Dyer died on March 17, 1864, at the age of fifty-five.[12]

NOTES:

1. Woody, *History of Women's Education*, vol. 1: 144.
2. The Laighton sampler is in a private collection; see Sotheby's, New York, catalogue, *The Theodore H. Kapnek Collection of American Samplers*, 4531Y, January 31, 1981, lot 67.
3. The Badger sampler is in a private collection; see Krueger, *New England Samplers*, 36.
4. The Fowler sampler is in the collection of Mr. and Mrs. Kent Willis; see Sotheby's, 4531Y, January 31, 1981, lot 147.
5. Mary Walden's name is inscribed on the sampler worked by Caroline Vaughan, 1818 (location unknown; see Krueger, *New England Samplers*, 37). Elizabeth S. Smith was Priscilla Hall Badger's schoolmistress during the same year (ibid., 36).
6. E. Walden's School is named on the 1822 sampler worked by Adaline M. Ferguson (collection, Betty Ring); see Ring, *American Needlework Treasures*, 19.
7. For another example, see the sampler worked by Martha Jane Fowler, 1822, Sotheby's, 4531Y, January 31, l981, lot 147.
8. Ibid., lot 67. See also Ring, *American Needlework Treasures*, 19. Ring gives 1818 as the beginning date, but Deborah Laighton's identical sampler was worked in 1810.
9. Correspondence with John LaBranche, September–October 1982, formerly of Strawbery Banke, who so kindly shared his research on Elizabeth Dore with me.
10. *Wentworth Genealogy*, 278. See also *Portsmouth Journal and Rockingham Gazette*, August 15, 1829. Researched by John LaBranche, to whom I am indebted.
11. *Portsmouth City Register and Directory*, 1834. Researched by John LaBranche. See also *Portsmouth City Register and Directory*, 1851. I wish to thank the librarians in the Portsmouth Public Library for their kindness in sharing various early publications with me.
12. *Portsmouth Town Records*, comp. John Eldridge Frost, vol. 2: 27. My thanks to librarians at the Portsmouth Public Library.

31. LUCY MUNROE
Probably New Hampshire, c. 1825
Silk threads and crinkled silk floss on linen
(23 threads to the inch)
Satin, padded satin, chain, split, back, and cross-
stitches with French knots and hem-stitching
17 x 13 in. (43.1 x 33 cm)

Inscription: *'Tis greatly wise to talk with our past
hours/And ask them what report they bore to Heav'n
Lucy Munroe aged 10 years*

This sampler worked by Lucy Munroe displays an unusual number and variety of complex stitches rarely seen on samplers worked at this late date. This fact alone suggests that it may have been stitched at an earlier time. Stylistically, the sampler appears to have originated in southern New Hampshire, for similar flower motifs can be found on the embroidery worked in Jaffrey, New Hampshire, by Dolly Yalding (fig. 33) in 1826.

The back-stitched outline of the basket of fruit that dominates the borderless design also implies a New Hampshire attribution. Not often found on samplers originating in other parts of New England, this dark outline, a skillful design technique, is effectively employed on the sampler motifs worked by Mehitable Foster in 1786 (fig. 8) and Sally Abbot in 1818 (fig. 28)—who were both from New Hampshire as well. The use of such contrasting outlines enhances the impact of these designs.

31.

32. MARY A. RICHARDS (1814–1873)
Jaffrey, New Hampshire, 1825
Silk threads and crinkled silk floss on linen
(24 threads to the inch)
Satin, padded satin, outline, and cross-stitches with
hem-stitching
19¾ x 19 in. (50.1 x 48.2 cm)

Inscription: *Family Record/Mr Luther A. Richards
born/sept. 26 1785/Miss Mary Page born/June 8
1794/Luther Richards & Mary Page married July 5
1813/Mary Adeline born Jan 1 181[4]/Roderick Streat
born June 22 18/15/Abijah born APril 10 Died APril
18/1817/Luther Abijah born APril 12 1818/Sarah Ann
born June 15 1820/Amanda born August 7 1822/
Harriet born Oct 1 1824/Huldah Hopkins born APril
13 ?/M When I this little Record see/I think how haPPy it
would be/If Pa and Ma should live to say/Our children
walk in wisdoms way/And when the Parting stroke is
come/And they and we are called home/May we all meet
in heaven above/And sing Redeeming grace & love
Mary A Richards AE 11 1825*

T he family record sampler flourished in private schools for
girls during the second quarter of the nineteenth century.
A surprising number of such samplers have recently surfaced, attesting to the increased popularity of this form of embroidery, particularly in northeastern Massachusetts, southern
New Hampshire, and around Portland, Maine. Prized for their
genealogical information, these embroideries have provided collectors with a precious art form that is distinctly American in concept.

Genealogical samplers worked earlier in the century, such as
those made by Louisa Plympton (fig. 21) in Middlesex County,
Massachusetts, and Mary Ann Goodrich (fig. 37) in Wethersfield,
Connecticut, were skillfully conceived but more pictorial in style.
With the exception of the exquisite Hanson sampler from Portland, Maine (fig. 35), family register embroideries worked during
the last years of the 1820s consisted primarily of a list of finely
cross-stitched inscriptions covering a central panel, which was
framed by a wide border of distinctive floral patterns. According-
ly, it is within these characteristic border motifs that comparisons
may be made and groups of related pieces assembled. Evidence
of this kind will eventually lead us to the identification of the
schoolmistresses and perhaps then to the location of the schoolrooms in which these remarkable samplers were made.

Mary Richards's sampler border, for example, is embellished
with specific flower shapes, such as the ivory and old-rose, full-
faced blossoms with carefully scalloped edges, small sprays of

dotted strawberries, and padded, bell-shaped flowers in bright
blue silk. Marianna Hornor, in *The Story of Samplers*, identifies an
identical sampler stitched by Sarah Blanchard "in Jaffrey, 1829."[1]
The flower-strewn borders on these two samplers are fundamen-
tally the same, which indicates that both girls attended the same,
as yet unidentified, school in Jaffrey, New Hampshire.[2]

A similar border appears on the sampler worked by Dolly Yalding of Alstead (fig. 33) in 1824. While the samplers are dissimilar
stylistically, such evidence indicates that these embroideries were
born in separate, but probably nearby schools. To this date, the
classrooms have not been located, although they were both, most
likely, found in Cheshire County, New Hampshire, in the vicinity of Jaffrey.

Although Mary's sampler is inscribed "1825," additional information has been added, including the birth date of her sister,
Huldah, born 1827, and of her brother, Mark—an unfinished
"M" on the sampler—born 1828. Empty space was customarily
left on genealogical samplers so that the maker could update vital
information, such as births and deaths, in the manner of the family Bible.

Mary Adeline Richards, the daughter of Mary Page and Luther
Abijah Richards of Waterbury, Connecticut, was born on January
1, 1814, in Westminster, Windham County, Vermont, the first of
thirteen children. She married Hobart Victory Welton in 1834 and
died in 1873.[3]

NOTES:

1. The Blanchard sampler is in the collection of the
Philadelphia Museum of Art, PA; see Marianna
Merritt Hornor, *The Story of Samplers* (Philadelphia,
PA: Philadelphia Museum of Art, 1971), 41.
  The relationship of these very distinctive border
flowers was brought to my attention by Betty Ring.
Her astute observation may lead to the attribution
of many New Hampshire samplers worked in the
first half of the nineteenth century to schoolmistresses active in the town of Jaffrey. I am indebted
to her for assistance.
2. Ibid., 41.
3. Family Record Archives, Family History Library
of the Church of Jesus Christ of Latter-Day Saints,
Salt Lake City, UT. Information regarding the
birth date of Mary Page is incorrect, according to
the sampler.

Family Record

June 81 784

sept 26 1785

Mr Luther A. Roichards born   Miss Mary Page born

Luther Roichards & Mary Page married July 5 1813

Mary Adeline born Jan 1 181   Rooderick Streat born June 22 18

1819
Abijah born April 10 Died April 18   Luther Abijah born April 12 1818

Sarah Ann born June 18 1820   Amanda born August 7 1822

Harriet born Oct 1 1824   Huldah Hopkins born April 13 181

M

When I this little Record see   And when the Parting stroke is com
I think how happy it would be   And they and we are called home
If Pa and Ma should live to say   May we all meet in heaven above
Our children walk in wledo's w   And sing Redeeming Grace & love

Mary A. Richards

33.

33. DOLLY YALDING (b. 1806)
Probably Jaffrey, New Hampshire, 1826
Silk, twisted silk threads, and crinkled silk floss on
sheer linen (80 threads to the inch)
Satin, outline, fly, bullion, running, and cross-stitches with French knots
16¾ x 14½ in. (42.5 x 36.8 cm)

Inscription: *Family Record/James Yalding was born
Mar 1st/1777. Hannah Parker was born Jan/19th
1777. They were married Oct 1st 1800./Perthenia F.
Yalding was born Aug 25th 1801/Louisa ann Yalding
was born July 18th 1804./Dolly Yalding was born Dec
9th 1806./Emily Yalding was born Dec 17th 1811/
Hannah Yalding was born June 17th 1813 and
died/Sept 30th 1813 Jonathan F Yalding was born
June/16th 1814 Lorra Yalding was born Nov 15th
1816/and died Sept 28th 1818 Lorra Yalding was/born
April 7th 1819 and died March 19th 1821/Hannah wife
of James Yalding/died Dec 29th 1824 AE 48.
Wrought by Dolly Yalding 1826*

Dolly Yalding was twenty years old when she inscribed the required names and dates inside the elliptically shaped enclosure of her genealogical sampler. Not often seen in family record embroideries, the oval format designed by Dolly's creative schoolmistress is effectively anchored by the green meadow embellished with sprightly flowers and grazing sheep.

Dolly's sampler bears an unmistakable, though imperfect, resemblance to the samplers worked by Mary Richards in 1825 (fig. 32) and Sarah Blanchard in 1829.[1] The border surrounding Dolly's sampler is adorned with the same flower motifs used by Sarah Blanchard in Jaffrey. Dolly Yalding also may have attended an academy for young women in Jaffrey, New Hampshire.

Clearly illustrated here is the custom of "carrying over" threads from word to word in the inscription. The sheer background of this sampler allows these black threads to be seen from the front, although this stitching technique is prevalent on most samplerwork. The knotting of silk from letter to letter would not have been tolerated by the frugal schoolmistress. Such an extravagance would consume endless amounts of precious silk thread.

Dolly Yalding was born in Concord, New Hampshire, to James Yalding, an innkeeper from South Carolina, and Hannah Parker.[2]

NOTES

1. The Blanchard sampler is in the collection of the Philadelphia Museum of Art, PA; see Hornor, *Story of Samplers*, 41.
2. *Concord Town Records, 1732–1820* (Concord, NH: The Republican Press Association, 1894), 537.

34. MARY O. FOLSOM (1815–1889)
Stratham, New Hampshire, 1827
Silk threads and crinkled silk floss on linen
(24 threads to the inch)
Gobelin, satin, and cross-stitches
16¾ x 12¼ in. (42.5 x 31.1 cm)

Inscription: *Mary O Folso/m aged 12 years*

Schoolmistresses: Abigail Rollins, Eliza S. Gilman,
Nancy Houg [or Hong?], E. A. Clark, and Elijah
Blake, instructor

34.

Mary Folsom's unfinished sampler is surrounded by a reversing strawberry vine border. The alphabets have been enclosed on three sides by a dazzling inner border of closely worked diamond motifs in an unusual combination of blue, white, and black crinkled silk threads.

Born in Exeter, New Hampshire, on May 17, 1815, Mary Olivia Folsom was the third of Peter Folsom and Hannah Pike Hook's eight children.[1] Their homestead of about sixty acres was located on the north side of the Plains Road, now called Stratham Heights Road, in Stratham.[2]

In a town meeting in March 1775, the residents of Stratham decided to "hire School Dams for each end of the town to larn' young children." The first female teacher recorded in the town, Mrs. Edward Taylor, the wife of Deacon Taylor, is listed five years later, in 1780.[3]

By the end of the first quarter of the nineteenth century—a period of tremendous expansion in the field of education for women—it was considered fashionable for the young women of Stratham to be sent to neighboring Exeter for schooling. However, the numerous rewards of merit presented to Mary Olivia (see below and page 84) suggest that she remained in Stratham for her schooling. For while William Perry notes in *Exeter in 1830* that a girls' academy existed in the town as early as 1818,[4] two of the surnames appearing on Mary's certificates of merit—(Nicholas) Rollins and (Levi) Clark—also appear on the report of the Stratham School Committee of the same year, making it almost certain that Mary's public school classroom was located in Stratham.[5]

These paper mementoes are of interest to us not only because they attest to her ability as a scholar, but because they are dated and reveal the names of several of her instructors. The earliest appears to be that of E. A. Clark, who wrote the date "Feb. 15, 1826," then changed it to read 1827. Five of these awards were signed by Eliza S. Gilman in 1826 and 1827, five by Abigail Rollins, one by Nancy Houg (or Hong?), and one by schoolmaster

Reward of merit presented to Mary Folsom by Abigail
Rollins, c. 1827

Elijah Blake, who placed his signature on the only example decorated with polychrome inks.[6] These signed certificates document that Mary Olivia Folsom attended school for a period of at least two years, from 1826 to 1827.

The presentation of these paper prizes was a common practice in New England schools. They were often painstakingly created by the teachers themselves,[7] although they could also be bought ready-made, lavishly embellished with allegorical scenes and decorative borders, with blank space left to insert both the student's and teacher's names. Many of Mary Olivia's merits were printed on the reverse side with verses of popular hymns. Only one of Mary's is handmade. It reads: "This may certify that Miss Mary Olivia Folsom/ is at the head of her class and by studious/ attention, merits the love of her friends and/ Instructresses./ Eliza S. Gilman/ July 9, 1826."

There is no evidence, however, that her sampler, worked in 1824, was accomplished while she attended the Stratham public school.

In 1839, Mary Olivia Folsom married John Paine Wingate, against his family's wishes. Their only child, Elias Paine, was born in April 1840, but died within six months. John, who had a reputation as a fast and reckless driver, died in a carriage accident a year later. Soon after his death, Mary Olivia became involved in a lawsuit with her husband's parents, who were eventually granted possession of her house. She returned to the farm of her childhood on Old Plains Road and in later years divided her time between Boston and Stratham, making her home with her unmarried siblings, Elizabeth and B. Frank, who was president of the National Granite State Bank of Exeter. Well liked and very astute, Mary was consulted throughout her life by her banker brother for business advice.[8] She was known to be "wise, thrifty, sensible, and a good housewife."[9] Mary Olivia Folsom Wingate died November 4, 1889.[10]

NOTES

1. Letter from descendant, Peter F. McFarlin, August 31, 1982. I am indebted to Peter McFarlin for lending original photographs of Mary Olivia and sharing a wealth of personal information about her life. I appreciate his kindness.
   See also Elizabeth Knowles, *Genealogy of the Folsom Family, 1638–1938* (Rutland, VT: Tuttle Publishing Co., 1938), 397.
2. McFarlin letter, 1982.
3. Charles B. Nelson, *History of Stratham, New Hampshire, 1631–1900* (privately published, no date), 204.
4. William G. Perry, *Exeter in 1830*, ed. Nancy C. Merrill (reprint, Hampton, NH: Peter E. Randall, 1972), 5.
5. Nelson, *History of Stratham*, 209.
6. This certificate is inscribed on the reverse, "Sold, wholesale and retail, by Geo. P. Daniels, Bookseller and Stationer, No. 5. Market-street, Providence, R.I." It appears to have been stamped with six colors, rather than painted. Others are imprinted "Sold by Munroe & Francis, 128 Washington Street."
7. Sandra Brant and Elissa Cullman, *Small Folk: A Celebration of Childhood in America* (New York, NY: Dutton, 1980), 108, 109.
8. McFarlin letter, 1982.
9. Ibid.
10. Ibid. Clipping of newspaper obituary dated November 4, 1889, enclosed with letter.

Left: Mary Olivia Wingate, 1864, Boston
Above: Reward of merit presented to Mary Folsom by Abigail Rollins, c. 1827

35. Probably JANE HANSON (1810–1886)
Portland, Maine, c. 1827
Silk thread, silk floss, and chenille threads with
pencil, ink, and paint on silk and linen
(28 threads to the inch)
Straight, four-sided, eyelet, diagonal, open chain,
couching, and cross-stitches with French knots
26 x 22 in. (66 x 55.8 cm)

Inscription: *GENEALOGY/ Timothy Hanson born
Augst 2nd 1776/Rebecca Hawkes born Nov 2nd
1775/Married May 1st 1800/PROGENY/Hannah
Hanson born Oct 14th 1800/Jonathan Hanson born
May 4th 1802/Fanny Hanson born April 27th
1804/Amos Hanson born July 7th 1806/Jane Hanson
born May 5th 1810/Emily Hanson born Sept 15th
1814/Mary Hanson born Augst 19th 1819*

Schoolmistress: Mary Rea (1787–1846)[1]

During the first years of the nineteenth century, large family record samplers became increasingly popular in local
schools for girls. In Portland, Maine, the style of this embroidered art grew from comparative simplicity to striking elegance, remaining a fashionable needle art from 1803 to the middle of the 1840s.[2]

Around 1819 the characteristic rose-vine border, which earlier
in the century had been worked in time-consuming queen stitches, came to be executed in closely worked satin stitches, resulting
in large, naturalistic, two-colored blossoms. Several buildings in
deep perspective were added to the landscape, and frequently a
monument was inserted for recording deaths in the family. The
word "Genealogy" began to replace the traditional alphabets and
verses, and a long list of family members with their dates of birth
appeared. Often, as in this sampler, vacant space on the linen was
available for including additional names.[3]

These changes brought about a great transition in the established format, introducing a style of elegance virtually unknown
in sampler embroidery of the period. The cross-stitched landscapes were transformed into elaborate works of textile art, highly decorative, richly painted, and, where the needle was applied,
thickly embroidered.

Recognized as one of the most spectacular of the surviving
Portland samplers, the Hanson/Hawkes genealogy is composed
of linen (backed with a sheet of muslin) and silk in an uncommon
form of sampler embroidery. A silk panel, extravagantly painted
and drawn upon, was appliquéd to the linen ground. The heavily
embroidered silk was outlined with black satin stitches when applied. The flower-strewn border of the Hanson sampler is embel-

GENEALOGY

Timothy Hanson born Aug^{st} 2nd 1776
Rebecca Hawkes born Nov 2nd 1775
Married May 1st 1800

PROGENY

Hannah Hanson born Oct 14th 1800
Jonathan Hanson born May 4th 1802
Fanny Hanson born April 27th 1804
Amos Hanson born July 7th 1806
Jane Hanson born May 6th 1810
Emily Hanson born Sept 15th 1814
Mary Hanson born Aug^{st} 19th 1819

35.

lished with vines of darkly colored green silk thread, arranged in such a dramatic fashion that the stems twine themselves toward the center rectangle, forming another border of recurring arcs.

These stunning Portland samplers, mourning pieces, and silk embroideries appear to fall into two closely related groups. The first, worked during the 1820s, may have been stitched at the school kept by Martha Merchant Mayo (c.1756–1831), who is recorded as having great "skill in exquisite needle-work."[4] Frequently worked on a silk grounding and painted in garish colors, these embroideries may be identified by the presence of a winged cherub often placed near their towering monuments.

The second group of these elaborately needleworked pieces from the coastal city may be recognized by their splendidly painted waterways and carefully drawn public buildings placed along the edge of the shore.[5] It is to this group that the Hanson genealogy belongs.

The watery estuary featured here is lined with trees of varying shades of green; the fields are depicted in French knots and satin stitches, with thick, velvety chenille threads used to work the trunks of the trees. These imaginative stitchery techniques, varied sewing threads, and intermixed stitches lend depth and perspective to an otherwise one-dimensional landscape. It is increasingly clear that during this period the emphasis on watercolor and other forms of paint embellishment took precedence over the ornamental embroidery of the past. Typical of related samplers, two unidentified white buildings have been drawn in pencil and black ink directly on the silk of this sampler, one a castle with a crenelated tower, the other a meeting house or church.[6]

Recent research by Betty Ring has uncovered the most promising candidate for the long sought-after schoolmistress of at least one of the two groups of silk embroideries—Mary Rea. The designer of the most elaborate family records and memorials executed in Portland, Mary Rea, the daughter of Dr. Caleb Rea, Jr., and Sarah White, kept a school for girls in Portland between 1823 and 1846. Advertising the opening of her school on March 18, 1823, in the *Eastern Argus*, she offered instruction in plain and ornamental needlework, the embroidering of genealogies, oil painting, and embroidering on satin, along with numerous academic classes.[7]

It is possible that Mary Rea drew and painted the ornate landscapes that distinguish her samplers from all others. However, the similarity of the rich pigmentation in both groups of Portland embroideries suggests that the same hand—perhaps that of a professional artist—painted both groups of samplers. A local painter may have been responsible for the wealth of painted scenes on fabric in the Portland area, for in general, artists are recognized by their use of color, as well as their painting technique.

This sampler was probably worked by Jane Hanson, who would have been seventeen in 1827, the approximate date of the embroidery. Most of the Portland schoolgirl embroiderers were in their teens.

One of seven children, Jane was the daughter of Timothy and Rebecca Hanson of Little Falls, Cumberland County, Maine. She married Isaac Woodford of Westbrook in 1831. They were the parents of one son, Henry. She was later married to C. Wesley Harding of Gorham. Jane Hanson Woodford Harding died October 25, 1886, aged seventy-six years.[8]

NOTES:

1. Betty Ring, "Samplers and Silk Embroideries of Portland, Maine," *Antiques* (September 1988): 520.
2. Ibid., frontispiece, opp. 493, 513. See also Krueger, *New England Samplers*, fig. 74.
3. Brant and Cullman, *Small Folk*, 56, 57. See also Krueger, *Gallery of American Samplers*, 58, 59, and Ring, "Samplers and Silk Embroideries," 512.
4. Ring, "Samplers and Silk Embroideries," 516.
5. Ibid., 523. Ring identifies the church buildings on these samplers as representing St. John's Episcopal Church in Providence, Rhode Island.
6. Ring, *American Needlework Treasures*, 17. The sampler attributed to Hannah Harding Smith, c. 1826 (collection, Betty Ring), also displays a painted and lavishly embroidered silk panel appliquéd to a linen ground, in the same manner as that worked by Jane Hanson.
7. Ring, "Samplers and Silk Embroideries," 519, 520.
8. Samuel Thomas Dole, *Windham in the Past*, (Auburn, ME, 1916), 417, 418. When, as in this instance, dates printed in historical and genealogical books do not agree with those inscribed on a sampler, the dates on the sampler are thought by those knowledgeable in the field to be the more accurate.

36.

36. LOUISA BRADLEY (1802–1880?)
Litchfield, Connecticut, c.1810
Silk threads on linen (34 threads to the inch)
Herringbone, eyelet, and cross-stitches
5½ x 13¼ in. (13.9 x 33.6 cm)

Inscription: *Phebe Stoddard/Accept this trifle from your niece/Louisa Bradley/Whose love for thee will never cease/Litchfield*

Louisa Bradley's simple marking sampler—a modest exercise in alphabet embroidery—is dedicated to her mother's sister, Phebe, who is beseeched to "accept this trifle." By these words, Louisa's early embroidered endeavor has become a presentation piece, a rather uncommon but delightful custom.[1]

Louisa may have received her embroidery instruction as a day student at Sally Pierce's Academy in Litchfield. This impressive school for girls began in the dining room of Pierce's house in 1792. By 1803, Pierce was conducting classes in a new building, teaching as many as 130 young ladies during the span of a year. "The fine accomplishments of music, dancing, singing and embroidery, of drawing and painting" were retained when the move was made from the smaller school, while classes in chemistry, astronomy, and botany supplemented history and geography.[2]

Louisa Bradley was born on July 29, 1802, to Lucy Stoddard and Joseph Bradley. She married Leonard Kenney in 1819 and is believed to have died on July 28, 1880.[3]

NOTES

1. George C. Woodruff, *A Genealogical Register of the Inhabitants of the Town of Litchfield, Connecticut* (Hartford, CT: Hartford Press, 1900), 20, 208, 209.
2. Alain C. White, *The History of the Town of Litchfield, Connecticut, 1720–1920* (Litchfield, CT: Litchfield Historical Society, 1920), 111–114.
  The influence of Sarah Pierce and her academy may be examined more thoroughly in two books by Emily Noyes Vanderpoel, *Chronicles of a Pioneer School from 1792 to 1833* (Cambridge: Cambridge University Press, 1903) and *More Chronicles of a Pioneer School* (New York, NY, 1927).
3. Woodruff, *Genealogical Register*, 20. See also Family Record Archives, Family History Library of the Church of Jesus Christ of Latter-Day Saints, Salt Lake City, UT. The date of Louisa's death was presented to the library undocumented by published information.

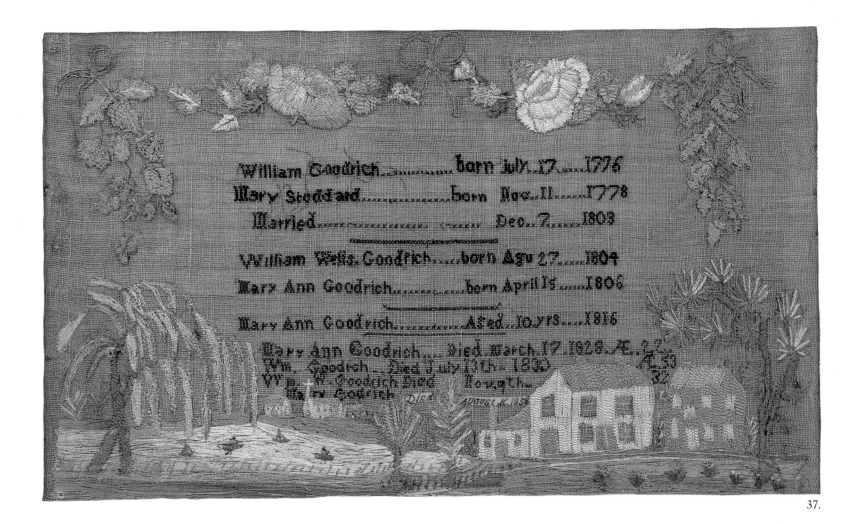

37. MARY ANN GOODRICH (1806–1828)
Wethersfield, Connecticut, 1816
Silk, twisted silk threads, and crinkled silk floss
with paper, on linen (20 threads to the inch)
Satin, couched satin, outline, and cross-stitches
11½ x 20 in. (29.2 x 50.8 cm)

Inscription: *William Goodrich.....born
july..17....1776/Mary Stoddard.....born Nov.
11....1778/Married......Dec. 7....1803/William Wells
Goodrich......born Aug 27...1804/Mary Ann
Goodrich......born April 15...1806/Mary Ann
Goodrich .....Aged..10. yrs...1816/*
[By another hand]: *Mary Ann Goodrich......
Died..March. 17.1828. AE. 22/Wm Goodrich..Died July
13th..1830 AE. 53/Wm. W. Goodrich Died
Nov.9th..32/Mary Goodrich...*[on paper] *Died August
16.1858....80*

By 1816, Wethersfield, one of the earliest settlements in Connecticut, was a thriving, prosperous town along a triangular stretch of the Connecticut River. A yellow-painted meeting house graced the town with a fine, high steeple, and pleasant houses, with carefully tended gardens, lined each thoroughfare.

The young girls of the neighborhood were instructed in the art of embroidery by an unidentified schoolmistress of exceptional ability. Her school was probably near the juncture of Sandy Lane and High Street, for a landownership map of the town, c. 1850, inscribed with surnames of the samplermakers indicates that many of them lived in this area.[1] Several similar pictorial samplers, dating from between 1804 and 1827, help to document that the school existed for at least twenty-three years.[2]

The sampler stitched by Mary Ann Goodrich is typical of this group, for it has been worked in the same format. A swag of flowers, draped like a lambrequin, spreads across the top of the linen and is characteristically caught in the center by a ribboned bow. Almost without exception, related embroideries depict similar buildings in a picturesque setting, often giving prominence to a wide rift of the Connecticut River, so vital to the town.

The foreground of Mary Ann's splendid embroidery pictures fishermen in their miniature boats afloat on the silken water, while in the distance the spired meeting house and the town take shape. A white silk house, with green-tinted windows and a roof worked in satin stitches the color of tarnished copper, is prominently displayed. As with at least half a dozen other family registers, a popular form of sampler embroidery in this Connecticut school between 1816 and 1821, Mary's sampler is lavishly adorned with the familiar garland of blossoms, leaves, and bowknots.[3]

Samplers from this region fall into two distinct categories. The earlier pieces are embellished with a thin, narrow loop of flowers, caught by a bouquet at center top, with no discernible ribbon or bow. Those of a later period, such as that worked by Mary Ann, reveal a more extravagant design. Probably influenced by the delicately elegant silk embroideries worked in nearby Hartford at the Misses Pattens' painting and embroidery school—which may be recognized by their heavy, gold-corded eagle, sequined bows, and lavishly draped blossoms—the full flowered, ribbon-tied garland made its appearance in Wethersfield, along with the characteristic townscapes that lend such captivating charm to the needlework.[4]

Such an abrupt change in format and composition is usually indicative of a change in instruction. In this instance, it would suggest that a different schoolmistress, perhaps in the same school, added a flair of her own to an already established regional needlework pattern. Because the surviving samplers are so similar to those attributed to the well-attended Patten school, where over four thousand students were educated over a span of forty years,[5] it is reasonable to assume that Mary Ann's schoolmistress received her education there. While the linen samplers lack the excessive decoration of the silk embroideries, there is unquestionably a relationship between these two schools of embroidery.

Mary Ann's genealogical sampler was additionally inscribed by at least two needleworkers. One was probably Mary Stoddard Goodrich, her mother, who on three separate occasions embroidered in the black silk threads of mourning the dates of death for Mary Ann; her husband, William; and her only son, William Wells Goodrich.

The later inscriptions, handwritten in ink on slips of paper,

were inserted following the established pattern sometime after 1856, when Mary Stoddard Goodrich died at the age of eighty. As inscribed on the sampler, Mary Ann Goodrich died on March 17, 1828, at the age of twenty-two.

NOTES:

1. Peter Benes, *Two Towns, Concord and Wethersfield: a Comparative Exhibition of Regional Culture 1635–1850*, vol. 1 (Concord, MA: Concord Antiquarian Museum, 1982), 6, 7, 128.
2. The sampler worked by Hope Mosely (private collection; see ibid., 90) is dated 1804, and the mourning sampler worked by Sarah Roberts Weeks (private collection; see ibid., 162) bears an 1827 date. Weeks, who married in 1829, has inscribed one part of the monument on her embroidery with the date of birth and death of her son, Charles Weeks Wiers, obviously a later addition.
3. Benes, *Two Towns*, 90, 91, 92, 153.
4. Ring, *American Needlework Treasures*, 80, 81. See also Suzanne L. Flynt, *Ornamental and Useful Accomplishments: Schoolgirl Education and Deerfield Academy 1800–1830* (Deerfield, MA: Memorial Hall Museum, 1988), 18, 19, 24. Suzanne Flynt theorizes that Deerfield Academy instructress Jerusha Williams, who attended the Patten school in Hartford as a young woman, taught her students the identical eagle and garland motifs, using the same corded-gilt threads and sequins so closely identified with the Patten school. It seems unreasonable to suggest that Williams would not have changed the patterns slightly or added some of her own creativity, given the opportunity (pp.17, 22).
   Ruth, Sarah, and Mary Patten kept a school in Hartford from 1785 until 1825. The elegant silk embroideries attributed to their instruction are today highly prized by collectors of antique needlework.
5. Elisabeth Donaghy Garrett, "American Samplers and Needlework Pictures in the DAR Museum, Part 1: 1739–1806," *Antiques* (February 1974): 82.

38. MARTHA PLATT (1815–1887)
Milford, Connecticut, 1827
Silk threads on linen (22 threads to the inch)
Eyelet, satin, buttonhole, outline, long and short,
and cross-stitches
16½ x 8 in. (41.9 x 20.3 cm)

Inscription: *Our life is ever on the wing/And death is
ever nigh/The moment when our lives begin/We all begin
to die*
Martha Platt s Wrought 1827 aged 12

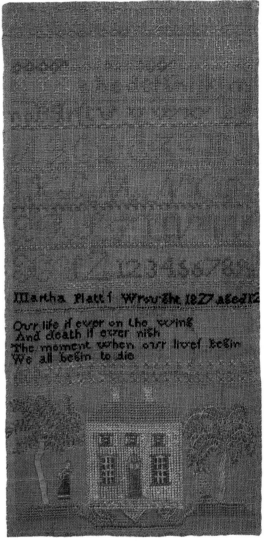

38.

The residents of Milford, Connecticut, which is situated on the Wepawaug River, along Long Island Sound, showed little concern for public education during the first few decades of the nineteenth century, depending instead on schooling by private means for those who could afford to pay.[1] An attempt was made in 1824 to hire Betsey Fowler of Ship Yard Lane at "8½ [dollars?]" a month (it is not known whether she accepted the offer). In 1836, schoolmistress Alma L. Williams billed Mr. Ford 14½ cents a week to educate his daughter, Elizabeth. The amount for an eight-week term was $1.16.[2]

While it is known that private schools for girls were available in Milford, many parents sent their daughters to be educated in more fashionable New Haven boarding schools. The long history of schooling in New Haven begins in 1651, with the dame school kept by Goodwife Wickham.[3]

Martha Platt may have studied needlework and ornamental embroidery in New Haven, for her sampler bears a certain similarity to a sampler worked by Lydia Church in 1791, at Mary Mansfield's New Haven school. Mansfield, who taught at least from 1791 to 1793, may have been responsible for the initial sampler design, which was then continued by another teacher.[4]

Martha's unbordered sampler displays a modest, and for the period straightforward, version of the central portion of that stitched by Lydia Church, which is lavishly embellished with a wide, solidly embroidered black border. Like Lydia, however, Martha has worked similarly branched trees, a house with two of the windows divided into twelve panes, a pedimented door pierced by two glazed inserts, a garden of flowers, and sprightly costumed figures.[5]

Although verging on the ordinary, Martha's sampler has been adorned with two of the most enchanting figures in American sampler embroidery. Each figure, meticulously endowed with human hair, holds a tiny nosegay of flowers. The figure to the left wears a fashionable blue, tent-stitched dress, scrupulously trimmed with pale ivory silk, while the figure at the right wears a dress with a soft blue bodice and a biscuit-colored skirt, worked

entirely in horizontal bands of buttonhole stitches. This unusual method of depicting a particular style of fashion—with thread, needle, and a minimum number of stitches—is technically extremely difficult. But Martha Platt succeeded in achieving graceful, properly proportioned figures and, most important, has created the effect of finely pleated, or gathered, tiers of fabric in one of the costumes. The very smallest of neatly worked slippers may be detected at the hemline of each dress.

Fancy needlework of the first and second quarters of the nineteenth century sometimes lacks a certain sophistication when compared to the fine examples taught by earlier, more demanding schoolmistresses. The rage for ornamental embroidery in schools for girls was diminishing by the middle of the century, to be supplanted by special classes in painting, drawing, and music. Thus an acceptance of greater simplicity in needlework may explain the missing border on Martha Platt's sampler, though her delightful sampler figures remain unsurpassed.

Born in Milford on October 28, 1815, to Nathan Platt and Sarah Fowler, Martha was the youngest of four children. Her family was among the first to settle in New Haven in the first half of the seventeenth century.[6]

The house in which Martha lived still remains on old East Town Street. Built in 1823, it was occupied by members of the Platt family for over 150 years.[7]

Sometime before 1841, Martha Platt married DeLuzerne Hubbell. They lived in a large white house on Clark Street in Milford. They had no children. Martha Platt Hubbell died April 26, 1887, and is buried in the Milford Center Cemetery.[8]

NOTES:

1. *History of Milford, Connecticut, 1639–1939* (State of Connecticut, Federal Writers' Project, 1939), 81.
2. *History of Milford*, 82. *Federal Census, Milford, Connecticut*, 1830, lists Betsey Fowler as a teacher.
3. Woody, *History of Women's Education*, vol. 1: 138.
4. Krueger, *New England Samplers*, 20, 145.
5. The Church sampler is in the collection of the Connecticut Historical Society, Hartford; see Bolton and Coe, *American Samplers*, opp. 324.
6. Susan Woodruff Abbot, comp., *Families of Early Milford, Connecticut*, ed. Jacquelyn L. Ricker (Baltimore, MD: Genealogical Publishing Co, Inc., 1979), 565. See also Charles Platt, Jr., *Platt Genealogy in America—From the Arrival of Richard Platt in New Haven, Connecticut, in 1638* (New Hope, PA, 1963), 98. See also Nathan Stowe, *Sixty Years' Recollections of Milford*, ed. Newton Harrison (rev. ed., Milford, CT, 1917), map between 92, 93. *Baptismal Records, Milford, Connecticut*, vol. 1 (First United Church of Christ, Milford, CT), 125. I am indebted to Richard Platt, Jr., and Caroline Platt Walsh, who corresponded with me from May through August 1982. Mr. Platt identified the location of Martha Platt's home and has shared many family remembrances. I appreciate his kind assistance.
7. Correspondence with Richard Platt, July 22, 1982.
8. Platt, *Platt Genealogy*, 98. See also *Connecticut Church Records*, vol. 2 (Connecticut State Library, Hartford), 37, 38. Martha Hubbell was admitted to the church in 1841; Platt letter of April 21, 1982. I have visited the cemetery in Milford to document the date of her death.

39. MARY STANTON (1814–1858)
Charlestown, Rhode Island, 1825
Silk threads on dark green linen
(24 threads to the inch)
Queen, chain, tent, rice, eyelet, satin, long-armed cross-, and cross-stitches
20½ x 17½ in. (52.1 x 44.5 cm)

Inscription: *Mary.Stanton s. Sampler made in the year. 1825/age 11 years . Ann.E.Mynard Instructor/Seize mortals seize the transient hour/Improve each moment as it flies/Lifes a short summer man a flower/He dies alas how soon he dies*

Schoolmistress: Ann E. Mynard

Blue houses on samplers such as that worked by Mary Stanton of Charlestown, Rhode Island, in 1825, reflect a local custom of painting bay houses in the Newport area. Mary has stitched an impressive, although now somewhat faded, blue building with five front windows and ornate, double-glazed doors, which are outlined with a row of sand-colored queen stitches.

The tent-stitched figure of a woman carrying a parasol is wearing an elegant gown with a stylish bustle. The gentleman accompanying her is suitably attired in a fashionable top hat. A broad-leafed tree shades the pair, but it also holds an alarmingly large blackbird. An equally impressive vase of dainty flowers balances the design. Having embroidered her sampler with alphabets, numbers and a verse, Mary was also obliged by her teacher, Ann E. Mynard, to stitch the vowels, *a, e, i, o, u,* and *y*. This sampler has been worked on green-dyed linen that greatly resembles linsey-woolsey.[1] While most samplers in North America were worked on plain even-weave linen or homespun, it is not uncommon to find schoolgirl embroideries dated between the years 1798 and 1832 stitched on a ground of linsey-woolsey fabric. The domestic cultivation of flax and the weaving of linen expanded with the need for greater independence from imported English wool. Linsey-woolsey was woven with a strong warp of linen threads; the horizontal weft was of a soft, warm wool. The result was a thrifty, practical fabric that could be produced locally or within the home. A plain wool or tammy background was not favored in this country for sampler embroidery, although a few examples may be found. Colored linen, such as that used by Mary, was also uncommon. Most frequently, plain linen was provided by the teacher.[2]

Mary Stanton's sampler was among those exhibited at the Rhode Island Historical Society, Providence, in 1920. This exhibition of 334 samplers reflected a growing interest in collecting American samplers in this country. While Mary's sampler appears

39.

to be totally unrelated in style to the superb eighteenth- and early nineteenth-century pictorial needlework of Providence, Newport, Warren, and Bristol, her embroidery is still regarded as being an historically important example of Rhode Island textile art.[3]

Mary Stanton was the daughter of Samuel Stanton and Elizabeth Reynolds of South Kingston, Rhode Island, who were married on April 11, 1799. He was town clerk of Charlestown for more than forty years. Mary, the last of their five children, was born on November 6, 1814, and was attending Ann Mynard's school by the time she was eleven.

Charlestown was originally settled as part of a land agreement between the Narragansett Indians and Roger Williams, the minister whose doctrines had so offended the magistrates that he was banished from the Massachusetts Bay Colony in 1635. He and his followers moved to Rhode Island to begin a grand experiment in religious freedom. Thomas Stanton, one of the new colony's first settlers, arrived in 1635. A century later, the town of Charlestown was formed, and it is on a portion of the Narragansett chief Ninigret's land that the Stanton house was built.[5]

In 1840, Mary Stanton married James Nichols Kenyon (d. 1895). They had two daughters. Mary Stanton Kenyon died on August 23, 1858, at the age of forty-four and is buried in a small cemetery on her family's property.[6]

NOTES:

1. Ring, *Let Virtue Be a Guide to Thee*, 59, 61.
2. Frances Little, *Early American Textiles* (New York, NY: Century Co., 1931), 19. See also Krueger, *Gallery of American Samplers*, 15, 16.
3. Ring, *Let Virtue Be a Guide to Thee*, 244.
4. William A. Stanton, *A Record, Genealogical, Biographical, Statistical, of Thomas Stanton of Connecticut and His Descendants: 1635–1891* (Albany, NY, no date), 435, 436.
5. William Franklin Tucker, *Historical Sketch of the Town of Charlestown, in Rhode Island, from 1636 to 1876* (Westerly, RI: Utter Printers, 1877), 9–18, 51. This book was brought to my attention by a clerk in the town hall, to whom I am exceedingly grateful. See also Ring, *Let Virtue Be a Guide to Thee*, 42. A handwritten genealogical history of the Stanton family accompanied the sampler. Dated January 8, 1982, Mary's descendant is unidentified.
6. Tucker, *Historical Sketch*, 51. See also Stanton, *Record*, 435. The descendant's letter gives 1840 as the year of Mary's marriage. Her date of death is on her gravestone, located in a corner of King Tom's Place, as the property is now known.

40. HANNAH WHITE (b. 1786)
Chester County, Pennsylvania, 1800
Silk threads on linen (38 threads to the inch)
Satin, queen, long-armed cross-, and cross-stitches
15½ x 11 in. (41.9 x 27.9 cm)

Inscription: *Rebecca White/Daughter of/John White and/Elizabeth was/born January/The 30th day/1785/Hannah White/was born Decem/ber The 19th/1786/William White was born Decem/ber The 10th 1789/In thy fair Book of life Divine/My God Inscribe my Name/There let it fill some humble/Place Beneath thy Slaugh/terd LAMB*
Hannah White/1800

Schoolmistress: possibly Elizabeth White (Hannah White's mother)

41. SIDNEY JEFFERIS (1790–1882)
Chester County, Pennsylvania, 1804
Silk threads on linen (28 threads to the inch)
Satin, queen, and cross-stitches
16 x 13 in. (40.6 x 33. cm)

Inscription: *My Parents Emmor Jefferis &/Rachel my Grand Parents/James Jefferis & Ann Samuel/Grubb & Rebecca/My Brothers & Sisters/Rebecca Cheyney/Ann James Phebe/Mary Elizabeth &/Samuel Jefferis./Sarah varnon/Be Christ my pattern/and my guide/His image may I bear/O may I tread his/sacret steps/And his bright glories share/Great God thy name be blestThy goodness be ador.d/My soul has been distress.d/But thou hast peace restor.d/E/W*
Sidney Jefferis s Work/aged fourteen Years/1804
Inscribed in ink on backboard: *The work of my great grandmother/Sydney Jefferis Way/1804/Laura C. Haines/Doylestown/Pa*

Schoolmistress: E W (possibly Elizabeth White)

The teaching traditions of Chester County, Pennsylvania, are reflected in the surviving needlework of the region. Young women of all faiths, including the predominant Quaker society, accomplished an astonishing array of exquisite sampler embroideries in this county. Formerly, this group of related samplers included work dating from 1804 to 1826; however, this recently discovered example, stitched by Hannah White in 1800, allows for an earlier attribution.

HANNAH WHITE
Hannah White, who probably worked in the vicinity of East

40.

symmetrical format with its characteristic baskets, urns, trees, paired birds, and cartouche remained intact. When Hannah Carter Carpenter and her cousin Lydia Carter worked their large samplers that year, a thin, geometric zigzag rather than the traditional reversing vine border surrounded the embroideries, and Lydia inscribed the initials "H. C." on hers.[4] Mary Graves inscribed Hannah G. [*sic*] Carpenter's name on her 1824 sampler as instructress.[5] As in other towns, students often eventually became teachers themselves.

If Elizabeth White kept a school for girls near East Bradford, Chester County, it is possible that she was responsible for the engaging sampler design, teaching it to her fourteen-year-old daughter, Hannah White. Modification of the original concept may have come about around 1811, when Hannah C. Carpenter worked her sampler and instructed her cousin Lydia Carter, perpetuating the stylish format that began with the new century by a schoolmistress whose initials were E. W.

SIDNEY JEFFERIS

The sampler worked by Sidney Jefferis (fig. 41), 1804, is strikingly similar in design to the ones stitched by Sarah Strode of East Bradford[6] and Lydia and Ann Jefferis in the the same year.[7] Lydia and Ann may have been cousins to Sidney. Beautifully stitched, duplicate patterns have been pleasingly arranged on each sampler, with a minimum of variation. Identical verses have been inscribed on Sarah and Sidney's samplers, and the same schoolmistress's initials, E. W., are prominently displayed on all three.

Until future research clarifies the relationship, Elizabeth White may indeed be considered the unidentified East Bradford schoolmistress, for among other distinguishing patterns, the engaging, blue-handled urns, with their bitter green, geometric embellishment, and the stylized tulip floral arrangement appearing on samplers worked by Sarah Strode and Sidney Jefferis conspicuously match those worked on Hannah White's embroidery. Evidence of this nature binds the embroiderers together, placing them under the same preceptress—whoever she may be.

One of nine children, Sidney was born on April 6, 1790, to Emmor Jefferis and Rachel Grubb of East Bradford Township.[8] The family was a member of the Society of Friends. Sidney married John R. Way (1776–1864), a farmer, in 1809 at Birmingham Meeting. The parents of three children, they lived in Avondale and London Grove, Chester County.[9]

Sidney Jefferis Way died in Oxford, Pennsylvania, in 1882.[10]

Bradford, where many of the samplermakers lived, remains untraced, but her sampler (fig. 40) may represent a prototype of this related group of sampler embroideries.

Three existing samplers, all dated 1804, worked by Sidney Jefferis (fig. 41); Lydia Jefferis,[2] probably a cousin; and Sarah Strode,[3] have been inscribed with the initials "E. W.," in honor of their schoolmistress. Although there is no evidence to support the theory, Elizabeth White may have been the unidentified instructress. Elizabeth was Hannah White's mother.

Most recognizable of the sampler patterns is the reversing tulip-band motif across the center. The same lovely color combination of rust, sea blue, green, and black prevails, with blocked units of lettering enclosing a verse and the names of family members. Only the oval cartouche suggests a regional Quaker influence. Neither John, Elizabeth White, nor their children have been found in Chester County Quaker records. By 1811, significant changes had occurred in this basic sampler design, but the

My Parents Emmor Jefferis &
Rachel my Grand Parents
James Jefferis & Ann Samuel
Grubb & Rebecca

My Brothers & Sisters
Rebecca Cheyney
Ann James Phebe
Mary Elizabeth &
Samuel Jefferis
Sarah varnon

Be Christ my pattern
and my guide
His image may I bear
O may I tread his
sacred steps
And his bright glories
share

E   W

Sidney Jefferis Work
aged fourteen Years
1804

Great God thy name be blest
Thy goodness be ador'd
My soul has been distress'd
But thou hast peace restor'd

41.

NOTES:

1. Ring, "Samplers and Pictorial Needlework,"
1431, 1432.
2. Lydia Jefferis's sampler is in the collection of the
Chester County Historical Society, West Chester,
PA; see Ring, "Samplers and Pictorial Needlework," 1426, 1433, f. 30.
3. The Strode sampler is in the collection of the
Chester County Historical Society, West Chester,
PA; see Ring, "Samplers and Pictorial Needlework," 1431.
4. Ibid., 1432.
5. Schiffer, *Historical Needlework of Pennsylvania*, 62.
See also Ring, "Samplers and Pictorial Needlework," 1432.
6. Ring, "Samplers and Pictorial Needlework,"
1431.
7. Both Jefferis samplers are in the collection of the
Chester County Historical Society, West Chester,
PA; see Ring, "Samplers and Pictorial Needlework," 1426, 1431, 1433, f. 30.
8. *Birth Records, Kennett Square Monthly Meeting,
Chester County, Pennsylvania*, 55. See also Gilbert
Cope, *Jefferis Family*, vol. 1 (loose-leaf notebook;
Chester County Historical Society, West Chester,
PA), 39, no. 1412. I am indebted to Betty Ring for
her research assistance.
9. D. Herbert Way, comp., *Descendants of Robert and
Hannah Hickman Way of Chester County, Pennsylvania*,
vol. 1 (1975), 134, 135. See also *Federal Census, London Grove Township, Pennsylvania*, 1850.
10. Ibid., 135.

"Fording the Susquehanna," c. 1825, aquatint by Strickland, J. L. Morton. Library of Congress, Washington, D. C.

42. BARBARA A. BANER (b. 1793)

Harrisburg, Pennsylvania, 1812
Silk threads and crinkled silk floss, hair, and paint
on sheer linen (60 threads to the inch), edged with
satin ribbon, overlaid with gilt and gold metallic
gimp
Long, short, split, filling, buttonhole, satin, outline,
and cross-stitches with French knots
17 x 15½ in. (43.1 x 39.3 cm)

Inscription: *Barbara A Baner a Daughter of
Joseph/and Esther Baner was Born in york M/arch the
20 in the year of our Lord 1793/and made this
Sampler in Harrisburgh in/Mrs Leah Meguier School
A.D. 1812/And must this body die this mortal frame/
decay and must those active limbs of/mine lie mouldring
in the clay. And there/for to remain until Christ doth
please to/come*

Schoolmistress: Leah Bratton Galligher Meguier
(1764–1830)

Barbara Baner's extravagant pictorial sampler (see page 2) is one of a group of important embroideries worked at Leah Meguier's school in Harrisburg, Pennsylvania. Samplers created under the instruction of Pennsylvania schoolmistresses in the Susquehanna Valley are considered to be among the most exquisite schoolgirl embroideries executed in the newly inde-pendent republic. Freedom of expression—encouraged by the prosperity of increasing westward migration and the patriotic fer-vor sweeping the land—found its way into the most common form of needlework, the sampler.

For a time a series of academies for the education of young girls stretched throughout the towns bordering the wide Susquehan-na, from Harrisburg to Lancaster. Many of the samplers from this area are inscribed with the names of the towns in which they were worked and the names of the schoolmistresses: Mary Walker, Mrs. Armstrong, Catherine Welchans, Mrs. Buchanan, Mary Reed—and Leah Galligher Meguier, whose exceptional academy in Harrisburg was school to many daughters of the local gentry.[1]

There are many similarities within this Pennsylvania group of samplers. Elements such as textile or background fabric—in this instance a sheer linen or muslin—types of silk thread, stitches and the placement of stitches, repetition of motifs, and a compa-rable format are all recognizable as being related to the region. Yet it is clear that no one instructress was entirely responsible for the development of the basic design, although this honor is often at-tributed to Leah Galligher of Lancaster (who later became Leah

Galligher Meguier).[2]

Leah Galligher conducted her school for the young women of Lancaster, at the north end of Queen Street, for at least five years from 1797 to 1802,[3] at which time she moved to Harrisburg, where her needlework instruction continued uninterrupted for at least another twenty-five years. The earliest sampler yet to be identified with her school is one worked by Anna Haverstick in 1798.[4]

The format of Anna's sampler was borrowed from patterns well established in southeastern Pennsylvania and Delaware by the middle of the eighteenth century, in which samplers displayed measured blocks of closely inscribed lettering.[5] Mary Webb of York, Pennsylvania, for example, worked a sampler in 1760 with a wide surrounding border, the center rectangle divided into nine squared units of alphabet forms, biblical inscriptions, the maker's name, date, and school.[6] Thirty years later, the sampler inscribed by Sarah Holsworth in Leah Galligher's Lancaster school mirrors this earlier style.[7]

Distinguished by their wide, compartmented borders composed of flower motifs, birds and baskets, and figures in miniature settings, Leah Galligher Meguier's designs fall roughly into two classifications. The earlier samplers are characterized by a center panel filled with minute, cross-stitched inscriptions. In later compositions, inscriptions are placed along the bottom of the panel, which has become highly pictorial and exceedingly ornamental. In both instances, samplers worked under her supervision have been skillfully stitched, the embroidery flawlessly executed. Long, uncouched satin and split stitches of silk floss have been worked directionally in a carefully controlled manner, following the shape of a garment, or the curve of a tree trunk, attaining a trompe l'oeil effect. As a result, figures and forms appear to be endowed with volume and shape, elements that are frequently absent from schoolgirl samplers, which tend to be flat and one-dimensional.[8]

It has been suggested that Barbara Baner's needlework is a mourning sampler. Mourning samplers, as opposed to silk mourning pictures, were generally worked on muslin or linen and are considered by collectors to be uncommon. Recognized by their conspicuous designs, they generally emphasize monuments with minutely inscribed epitaphs dedicated to the deceased, such as the samplers worked by Elizabeth Drew in 1823 (fig. 19) and Elizabeth Blyden in 1829 (fig. 65).[9]

Barbara Baner's needlework technique is impeccable. The central subject is a seated woman in an ivory-colored, Empire-style dress, holding a long, feathery fan, considered fashionable before parasols and umbrellas came into vogue: "Spreading like the train of a peacock, [it] was carried to keep off the sun as well as vivify the air."[10]

In her lap rests a cylindrical object with a domed lid and finial, which might represent a covered urn, although some have thought this object to be a birdcage, since there is an owl on the lawn at the tip of her blue silk slipper.[11]

Of far greater interest are two unusual and extraordinary motifs. Cutting across the lawn like a blade lies a long brown rifle with a curved wood stock. Also prominently placed is a silky, fur-tailed cap, worked in shades of fawn and black. The meaning of these uncommon but typically American objects is unknown. Do they symbolize the sweetheart of the maker? Possibly a lover who died in battle? Or are they purely decorative, lacking any symbolism? We must also consider that some needlework patterns may have had a highly personal meaning, known only to the needleworker and to her preceptress.

It is important to recognize that schoolmistresses traditionally relied on engravings and prints to supplement their needlework pattern repertoire. Memorial prints and neoclassical engravings, which placed great emphasis on allegorical figures in romantic settings, were readily available throughout the new republic. Other sources for needlework patterns were found in wallpaper designs and printed handkerchiefs, which were immensely popular during the federal period. Unquestionably, Leah Meguier modeled the design for Barbara's sampler on an engraving, although the exact one has yet to be discovered.

Meguier's highly developed form of pictorial sampler, with its wide, partitioned border, has been cleverly enhanced by an additional narrower border of twisting stems and flowers. This device serves to draw the viewer's eye directly into the pictorial panel, a masterful technique often employed by painters. Perhaps these exemplary samplers represent Meguier's interpretation of the more pictorial and demanding art of the fragile silk-on-silk embroideries and silk mourning pictures that were considered the height of fashion during the federal period. Samplers worked under Meguier's instruction were lavishly embellished with ornamental stitches, sequins, and people with painted faces and real hair. They were often completed by the addition of a colorful, wide, glossy satin ribbon. Barbara's sampler is edged with a green silk ribbon, which has been embellished with a narrow band of woven gold and metallic gimp. It is not surprising that Leah Galligher's exceptional sampler patterns set the style for those whose primary concern was to be fashionable.

The inscription on Barbara Baner's sampler reveals that she was born on March 20, 1793, the daughter of Joseph and Esther Baner, possibly in Newbury Township, York County, at the ances-

42.

tral home of John Bener, or Baner, and his wife, Barbara. Barbara Baner was one of four children. [12]

In 1794 brothers Joseph and Jacob Bener were members of the Pennsylvania militia. Between 1802 and 1805, Joseph, a "victualler," lived at 215 Second Street in Harrisburg—not far from schoolmistress Leah Meguier, who lived for a time on Second Street near State, where she kept her school for girls. The Bener family remained on the Harrisburg tax lists until 1809. [13]

Little else is known of Barbara Baner, who worked her beautiful sampler in Harrisburg at the age of nineteen. The verse, by Reverend Isaac Watts, so conspicuously lettered in black silk thread, expresses concern for her own mortality; we are left wondering about the mysterious Pennsylvania flintlock and the furskin cap of the frontiersman, so skillfully worked upon the muslin ground.

LEAH GALLIGHER MEGUIER

Leah and Rachel Bratton were twin daughters born to George and Sarah Bratton on May 23, 1764, near Wilmington, Delaware.

Leah married Francis Galligher in 1791 [14] and opened her classroom for the first time in May of 1797, soon after an advertisement in the *Lancaster Journal* on April 2 informed the public that she intended to teach "plain sewing, knitting and working of lace if required." Spelling and reading were also to be included in her curriculum. By 1802, Leah Galligher's marriage to Francis was dissolved, and in March of that year she moved to Harrisburg. [15] The recent appearance of a sampler worked by Mary Snodgrass dated 1802, "in Harrisburg," [16] attributed to Leah Galligher's instruction, makes it increasingly certain that she established a school for girls soon after her arrival.

Leah Galligher married Isaac Meguier (also, apparently, spelled Meguire, Maguire, and M'Guire), a shoemaker, sometime before 1807, for the sampler worked by Elizabeth Finney bears the inscription: ". . . made this sampler in Harrisburg in Mrs. Leah Meguier's School in the year of our Lord 1807." [17]

On May 22, 1813, the following advertisement appeared in the *Lancaster Journal:*

> Isaac Maguire, Boot & Shoemaker, respectfully acquaints his friends and customers, that he has removed to the new house of Mr. John Close, Locust Street, near to Doebler's Tavern Harrisburgh, where he will be happy to receive the commands and continued custom of his friends and others in his line. Mrs. Maguire will likewise continue her school as usual, in teaching all kinds of needle-work, music and the first rudiments of common education. She has room for a few more pupils.

If we are to consider the range of samplers worked at Leah Meguier's fashionable school for young women, the period of greatest achievement would seem to span the years after her move to Harrisburg, beginning in 1802 through 1812, when Barbara Baner and Catherine Boas [18] worked their exquisite samplers. High standards continued, however, for at least another thirteen years, as evidenced by the work of students Cassandanna Hetzell in 1823 and Ann E. Kelly in 1826. [19] Leah Bratton Galligher Meguier died on February 1, 1830. [20]

NOTES:

1. These schoolmistresses have given researchers a difficult puzzle to solve. "Mary Walker's School" is inscribed on Elizabeth Sansmich's sampler of 1803 (Hornor, *The Story of Samplers*, fig. 32); Fanny Rines's sampler of 1808 reveals that she attended "Mrs. Armstrong's School" (Bolton and Coe, *American Samplers*, opp. 268; see also Ring, *American Needlework Treasures*, 47); the name of Miss Welchans (who became Mrs. James Galbraith Buchanan) appears on samplers such as that worked by Mary Hamilton of Maytown in 1812 (Bolton and Coe, *American Samplers*, opp. 133; see also Ring, *American Needlework Treasures*, 46, 47). Mrs. Buchanan, formerly Miss Welchans, kept a school for young ladies in Marietta, Lancaster County, from at least 1823, when Ann Osborn worked her sampler (Sotheby's, 5156, January 27, 1984, lot 476), and Elizabeth Blanchard worked hers (*Antiques and the Arts Weekly*, March 6, 1987: 137), until 1826, the date inscribed on Mary Ann Lucy Gries's pictorial sampler (Ring, *American Needlework Treasures*, 46, 47). "Mary Reed's School" is inscribed on a sampler worked by Sophia Meyun in 1824 (Ring, *American Needlework Treasures*, 47).

2. The date of the opening of Leah Galligher's school is inscribed in the central panel of Sarah Holsworth's 1799 sampler. Included in this lengthy inscription is the date of birth of Rachel and Leah Bratton, twins; their baptismal date; their marriage dates; and their parents' birth dates. Research may document that Rachel Bratton Armstrong is the schoolmistress, Mrs. Armstrong (Margaret B. Schiffer, *Historical Needlework of Pennsylvania*, New York, NY: Charles Scribner's Sons, 1968: 41; see also Susan Burrows Swan, *A Winterthur Guide to American Needlework*, New York, NY: Crown, 1976: 16).

3. Franklin Ellis and Samuel Evans, *History of Lancaster County, Pennsylvania* (Philadelphia, PA, 1883), 404. "The first day of May 1797" is inscribed on Sarah Holsworth's sampler (Swan, *Winterthur Guide*, 16).

4. Anna Haverstick's sampler, in a private collection, was exhibited in "Decorative Arts of Lancaster County" in Lancaster, PA, at the Heritage Center; see *Antiques and Arts Weekly* (November 1, 1985): 84.

5. Schiffer, *Historical Needlework of Pennsylvania*, opp. 16.

6. The Webb sampler is in a private collection; see Bolton and Coe, *American Samplers*, opp. 55.

7. The Holsworth sampler is in a private collection; see Schiffer, *Historical Needlework of Pennsylvania*, 41.

8. There is a small, seemingly ordinary sampler worked by Susy A. Crider in 1801, which appears to employ the same exquisite sewing technique, giving shape and form to the delicate figure. Later, this same method was used to depict the figures on samplers of pictorial significance worked in Leah Galligher Meguier's school. While unidentified, apart from a Lancaster County attribution, this body of needlework may well have been a product of Meguier's instruction and served as a working model for those marvelous masterpieces that were to be executed later in Harrisburg. See Krueger, *Gallery of American Samplers*, 38.

9. Robert Bishop, consultant, *Quilts, Coverlets, Rugs and Samplers: Knopf Collector's Guides to American Antiques* (New York, NY: Alfred A. Knopf, 1982), 339.

10. Caulkins, *History of Norwich, Connecticut* (Chester, CT: Pequot Press, Society of the Founders of Norwich, CT, Inc., 1976), 335.

11. Elisabeth Donaghy Garrett, "The Theodore H. Kapnek Collection of American Samplers," *Antiques* (September 1978): 551.

12. *Memorandum, Will Book, York County*, vol. 227. See also *Inventory*, York County Court House, York, PA. See also Edwin Jaquett Sellers, *Genealogy of the Jaquett Family* (Philadelphia, PA, 1907), 157, 158. See also *The Pennsylvania Magazine of History and Biography*, vol. 13 (1889): 278.

John Bener was probably a descendant of the Swedish baron, Isaac Baner, who came to Pennsylvania around 1695 from New Castle, Delaware. Baron Isaac Baner died in November 1713, leaving his wife Maria and three children destitute. They are presumed to have returned to Sweden around 1727; however, the boys may have remained in Lancaster County, where they were apprenticed to a trade at an early age (Sellers, *Genealogy of the Jaquett Family*, 108).

The Bener family appears to have presented a problem to the scriveners of Pennsylvania. John Bener's 1774 inventory, for example, recorded in York County, is sprinkled with a seemingly casual and inconsistent spelling of the Bener name. In this same document, the often repeated Bener becomes Benner and then Beaner.

13. *Records of the Pennsylvania Militia, Cumberland County, Fourth Battalion*, 1790–1800 (Family History Library of the Church of Jesus Christ of Latter-Day Saints, Salt Lake City, UT, microfilm), 844, 565. See also *Federal Census, Harrisburg, Pennsylvania*, 1800 and 1810. See also *Grantee Index, Land Records, Dauphin County, Pennsylvania*, vol. N, no. 1: 520, dated April 14, 1802, recorded October 5, 1804. The property is described as a lot of ground bounded by Second Street on the East, Mary's Alley on the South, River's Alley on the West, and lot number 214 on the North, to become the new lot number 215. *Land Records, Dauphin County, Pennsylvania*, vol. O, no. 1: 239–242. See also *Tax Lists, Harrisburg*, 1792–1813. *Harrisburg City Directory*, 1839, places Isaac Meguier's residence at Second Street, Mulberry and Locust.

14. Sarah Holsworth's sampler inscription; see n. 2. See also *Grantor Index, Deed Book, New Castle County, Delaware*, vols. D, L, and M, nos. 3, 8. See also Schiffer, *Historical Needlework of Pennsylvania*, 41. The *Federal Census*, 1790 and 1810, shows Leah's father, George, Sr., and George Bratton, Jr., in Watertown, Mifflin County, Pennsylvania.

15. On March 8, 1802, a most peculiar document was recorded in the *Deed Book, Lancaster County*, vol. 1, no. 3: 40–44. This tripartite "Indenture," between Leah Galligher, Francis Galligher, and George Bratton, her brother, covers four closely inscribed pages. It represents a separation agreement which appears to have "dissolved the bands of Matrimony." This action brought about a notice in the March 10, 1802, *Intelligencer* by Francis Galligher: "Caution . . . whereas my wife Leah Galligher, alias Bratton, has absconded from my bed and board. . . ." The March 17 issue brought a response by George Bratton warning Francis Galligher to leave Leah alone or "his base and unmanly CHARACTER" will be made public. This, to all intents and purposes, appears to have ended the marriage of Francis and Leah Galligher. This article was brought to my attention by Susan Burrows Swan, to whom I am indebted.

16. The Snodgrass sampler is in the collection of Betty Ring; see Ring, *American Needlework Treasures*, 46.

17. Isaac M'Guire is on the tax list for Harrisburg 1806/1807 as a married man, while prior to this time he is recorded as being single.

The Finney sampler is in a private collection; see Schiffer, *Historical Needlework of Pennsylvania*, opp. 48. See also Krueger, *Gallery of American Samplers*, 91, n. 64.

18. The Boas sampler is in a private collection; see Sotheby's, New York, catalogue, *Important Americana*, 5810, January 26–29, 1989, lot 1101. The sampler worked by Catherine Boas makes use of the oval device and pictorial setting central to these exquisite samplers designed by their schoolmistress, Mrs. Meguier.

19. The Kelly and Hetzell samplers are in the collection of the Museum of the Daughters of the American Revolution, Washington, D.C.; see Garrett, *Arts of Independence*, 81.

20. Krueger, *Gallery of American Samplers*, 91, n. 64.

43. SARAH ANN BOYER (1807–1871)
Columbia, Pennsylvania, 1819
Silk threads, silk floss, and hair on linen
(28 threads to the inch)
Outline, buttonhole, satin, and cross-stitches
19¾ x 20¾ in. (50.1 x 52.7 cm)

Inscription: *Sarah Ann Boyer. . . 1819/Ever charming,*
ever new/When will the landscape tire/the view/
Sarah McCardell

Schoolmistress: Sarah McCardell (1791–1863)

In 1819, Sarah Ann Boyer of Conestoga, Pennsylvania, and Jane Hyland of Marietta, Pennsylvania,[1] attended a school for young ladies in Columbia kept by Sarah McCardell, whose name is carefully inscribed on the linen of the samplers they worked. The villages of Marietta, Conestoga, and Columbia, all in Lancaster County, overlap one another in the Susquehanna Valley near Pequea Creek, where shady oaks and slender historic houses still line the narrow streets.

Little is known of the early life of this accomplished schoolmistress, but the quality of the surviving needlework attests to her ability as an artist of exceptional merit. With sweeping pen, Sarah McCardell marked the linen for each child, creating samplers of great beauty. Although the Boyer and Hyland samplers are both known to have been worked under McCardell's instruction, it is evident that she made little effort to conform to a traditional format. It is as though she followed only her own whimsical imagination.

Each of these lavishly embroidered pictorial samplers depicts a balanced composition of an unidentified building and stylish fencing enclosures, furniture for the out-of-doors, flowers in baskets and empty baskets, lawns and swans, and young ladies with real hair. Either a bower of grape vines or intertwining leafy blossoms border the samplers within their stitched frame of large sawtooth satin stitches.

The female figures on both samplers are distinguished by their imperfectly shortened necks. They resemble a child's "handkerchief" doll, head gathered in the middle around a cotton wad and tied with a string. Certain similarities may also be detected in the manner in which the houses have been stitched. Both buildings feature a portico extending out to the left, and a round window of buttonhole stitches has been inset over the glazed, circular fanlight that enhances each sampler door. The endboards are outlined, and the foundations arranged in checkered squares. Architectural details such as these assist in identifying related bodies of needlework. Although Sarah McCardell, who by 1825 was Mrs. Joseph Shenk, remains unnamed on the sampler worked by Sarah Elizabeth Cooper,[2] this sampler resembles those worked by Sarah Ann Boyer and Jane Hyland, which makes it tempting to point to McCardell as the instructress of all three samplermakers.

In 1806, while attending Jefferson College at Canonsburg, Pennsylvania, Stephen Boyer married Sarah Ann Dunlap, daughter of Reverend James Dunlap, college president. The first of seven children, Sarah Ann Dunlap Boyer was born on September 18, 1807.[3]

From 1813 to 1823, Reverend Boyer was pastor of the Presbyterian Church in Columbia. During this time, Sarah Ann Boyer began attending classes conducted by schoolmistress Sarah McCardell.[4]

In 1823, Reverend Boyer accepted a position at the York County Academy. After the death of his wife, he married Mary Turner in 1827.[5]

In 1829, Sarah Ann Boyer married Reverend Alexander McCahon (1794–1873). Born in Ireland, McCahon was considered a "Presbyterian divine of great power." Soon after their marriage, Sarah Ann began to write regularly for a number of religious publications and New York weeklies. They became the parents of four children.[6]

Sarah Ann Boyer McCahon died in Reading, Pennsylvania, on October 7, 1871, at the age of sixty-four.[7]

SARAH McCARDELL SHENK

Sarah McCardell, the daughter of James Terrance McCardell (or McCardle), was born on June 17, 1791.[8] Probably, about 1820, she married Jacob Shenk, a widower with five children.[9] Their first child, Rachael, was born in 1821. In the summer of 1822, Jacob purchased from his parents a large tract of land adjoining Pequea Creek in the townships of Martick and Conestoga, for the astonishing sum of eight thousand dollars.[10]

They became the parents of six children, including one set of twins. It appears unlikely that Sarah McCardell Shenk continued to teach after marrying a wealthy man and beginning a family of her own.

Jacob died in 1843. Sarah McCardell Shenk died on December 28, 1863, at the age of seventy-two, leaving behind these intimate, fragile embroidered samplers, patterns of quite exceptional beauty.[11]

43.

NOTES:

1. The Hyland sampler is in the collection of the Chester County Historical Society, West Chester, PA; see Ring, "Samplers and Pictorial Needlework," 1433.

2. The Cooper sampler is in the collection of the Chester County Historical Society, West Chester, PA; see Schiffer, *Historical Needlework of Pennsylvania*, 72. I am indebted to Betty Ring for bringing the related details of this sampler to my attention.

3. Donald Arthur Boyer, *American Boyers*, vol. 1 (York, PA: Association of American Boyers, Inc., 1984), 641, 642.

4. Ibid., 642. See also *A History of the York County Academy* (York, PA: Trustees of the York County Academy and the Historical Society of York County, 1952), 88, 89.

5. Ibid., 88, 89. See also *York Recorder*, May 8, 1827.

6. Boyer, *American Boyers*, 642. In 1869, Sarah Ann Boyer began writing an unpublished genealogy of Gabriel Beyer, her immigrant ancestor. In 1984, it was in the possession of Mrs. Mary Bridenbaugh of Tarkio, MO, according to Donald Boyer.

7. Ibid.

8. *Records of Field Cemetery, Jacob Thomas Farm, Conestoga, Pennsylvania* (Historical Society of York, PA). The burial ground was "on the road from Conestoga Centre to Sickman's Mill."

9. This is based on information in a deed book (see n. 10), although the only recorded information regarding their marriage (see Family Record Archives, Family History Library of the Church of Jesus Christ of Latter-Day Saints, Salt Lake City, UT) seems to deny the fact.

10. *Deed Book, Land Records, Lancaster County*, vol. B, no. 5: 102–106. This records a deed transfer from "Sarah Shenk, daughter to Sarah Shenk, widow of Joseph Shenk," clearly establishing that Sarah Mc-Cardell Shenk was stepmother to Sarah Shenk.

11. *Records of Field Cemetery, John Hess Farm, Conestoga, Pennsylvania* (Historical Society of York, PA).

44.

44. MARY MITCHELL
Probably Pennsylvania, 1823
Silk threads on linen (26 threads to the inch)
Gobelin, slanted Gobelin, couched satin, padded satin, satin, straight, Smyrna, outline, four-sided, and cross-stitches
18¼ x 17¾ in. (46.3 x 45 cm)

Inscription: *Sweet are the lark's aspiring lays,/The buoyant clouds among:/But sweeter far the Savior's praise/In youth's devoted song*
Mary Mitchell's Work. 1823

This charming pictorial sampler was worked by Mary Mitchell somewhere in the mid-Atlantic states, probably Pennsylvania. Schoolmistresses in this area were known for designing elaborately designed sampler scenes featuring large buildings with wide, green fields in the foreground, such as that worked by Elizabeth Stine (fig. 13). Enclosed within a traditional strawberry border is an impressive, bright yellow public building with an arcaded cupola, capped by a globed weathervane and round gray clock. Dainty finials adorn the roofline, while high above the doors, just below the pediment's half-circle window, Mary has worked, in the smallest of black silk stitches, a puzzling inscription in what may be an embroidered version of Roman numerals.

Prominently positioned on the village green is a group of elaborately costumed women, men, and children, along with animals. Enormous Quaker-style flower motifs adorn the linen ground, quite out of proportion with the surrounding diminutive scene. Mary Mitchell's finely worked stitches have been cleverly enhanced with a shade of pink that seems to add a sparkle to this delightful sampler picture.

Long ago, damaged areas were mended with cotton threads, carefully woven through a brown paper bag.

45.

45. MARIA HYDE
Probably Pennsylvania, c. 1825
Silk threads on linen (42 threads to the inch)
Cross-stitches
6¾ in. square (17.1 cm square)

Inscription: *Maria Hyde/her Sampler*

Miniature marking samplers, such as the one worked by Maria Hyde, represented the first step in a child's needlework education. Often the only schooling a girl obtained was that offered by a widow, or single woman, in straitened economic circumstances. These dame schoolmistresses—or nursery teachers—taught both boys and girls from four to seven years of age. They were sometimes themselves uneducated; however, they were certain to have mastered the skill of plain sewing and knitting, and it was in this manner that these small and modest samplers came to be worked. In describing such teachers Thomas Woody quoted these classic lines:

> When a deaf poor patient widow sits
> And awes some twenty infants as she knits—
> Infants of humble, busy wives who pay
> Some trifling price for freedom through the day,
> At this good matron's hut the children meet
> Who thus becomes the mother of the street:
> Her room is small, they cannot widely stray;
> Her threshold high, they cannot run away:
> With bands of yarn she keeps offenders in,
> And to her gown the sturdiest can pin.[1]

Maria Hyde's diminutive sampler, complete with house, trees, and a narrow, heart-embellished border, is endearingly trimmed with a flat blue-green silk ribbon and a period frame. Stylistically, Maria's embroidery is typical of Pennsylvania samplers worked during the first quarter of the nineteenth century—and may have been made while Maria was attending a dame school.

NOTES:

1. Woody, *History of Women's Education*, vol. 1: 138, 140.

46. CAROLINE KROUSE (b. 1815)
Reading, Pennsylvania, 1826
Silk and twisted silk threads on linen
(30 threads to the inch), with a quilled, silk ribbon
border and corner rosettes
Satin, tent, queen, eyelet, and cross-stitches
18 x 17 in. (45.7 x 43.1 cm)

Inscription: *Protect Me Lord Amidst The Croud/From*
Ever'y Thought Thats Vain And Proud/And Raise My
Wondering Mind To See/How Good It Is To Trust In
Thee
Caroline Krouse Her Work 1826

46.

This exceptional sampler is typical of a group believed by historians to have been worked in Reading, Pennsylvania. Caroline's embroidery is identical in format to the sampler worked by Catherine Heister in 1786.[1] Both girls lived in Berks County. A third related sampler was stitched by Elizabeth Marx in 1802.[2] So similar, in fact, are these three embroideries that it is possible to attribute their instruction to the same unidentified schoolmistress who, it would seem, kept a school for girls near Reading for a period of at least forty years.

Two of the three embroideries have been elegantly set off with a frame of silk ribbon, each corner trimmed with a ribbon rosette. Traditionally, ribbon embellishment of this kind is found on samplers originating near Philadelphia and along the banks of the Delaware and Schuylkill rivers (figs. 13, 59).

Caroline's teacher was a skillful designer. Following the long-established custom of band motifs, she placed the most dramatic form, a wide strip of reversing vine, flowers, and buds, straight across the center of the linen. The equally deep band across the bottom of the center panel is also a distinctive element and balances the verse inscription. Individual flower designs are cleverly divided by geometric fountains of stitches, arranged in spiral-like pillars. Outlined in black or dark green threads for emphasis, the formal pattern here contrasts with the naturalistic blossoms in the band above. Executed in a variety of stitches, the sampler is an example of fine planning, as well as extraordinary technical expertise.

Caroline Krouse worked the sampler when she was eleven years old. She was born on April 28, 1815, the first of six children, to John and Elizabeth Krouse of Reading, Pennsylvania.[3] She was baptized Carolina Kraus on August 20, 1815. In the German Lutheran Church Records, her father's name was inscribed "Johan Kraus."[4]

NOTES:

1. The Heister sampler was in the Kapnek collection and is now in a private collection; see Krueger, *Gallery of American Samplers*, 28, 92.
2. The Marx sampler is in the collection of the National Museum of History and Technology (Smithsonian Institution), Washington, D.C.
3. *International Genealogical Index*. See also *Federal Census, Reading, Pennsylvania*, 1830.
4. *Records of the German Lutheran Church*, Reading, PA.

47. L. WITMER
Philadelphia, Pennsylvania, 1828
Silk threads on linen (24 threads to the inch), edged
with flat satin ribbon, double-glazed with paper
backing
Eyelet, queen, Gobelin, chain, tent, and cross-
stitches
17 inches square (43.1 cm square)

Inscription: *Stranger or friend, whoe'er thou be/That
gazest on Know you my doom/These tints shall fade, thus
beauty dies/But virtue lives beyond the tomb
L. Witmer/Philada/Wrought/1828*
Paper backing is inscribed:*Wrought/of Mrs. SG
Rapp's Seminary/SW corner of High & Eight Sts/
Philada*

Schoolmistress: Sarah G. Rapp

48. M. WITMER
Philadelphia, Pennsylvania, 1828
Silk threads on linen (24 threads to the inch), edged
with a flat satin ribbon, double-glazed with paper
backing
Eyelet, queen, Gobelin, chain, tent, and cross-
stitches
17 inches square (43.1 cm square)

Inscription: *While on my varied hues you gaze/And
fancy beauty glowing there/Reflect! All beauty is but
nought/Tis virtue that adorns the fair
M. Witmer/Philadela/Wrought/1828*
Paper backing is inscribed: *Wrought/at/Mrs SG
Rapp's/Seminary/S,W,corner of High & eight Sts*

Schoolmistress: Sarah G. Rapp

47.

48.

The Witmer sisters are an elusive pair, but their imaginative preceptress, Sarah G. Rapp of Philadelphia, devised an unusual stratagem to assure herself long-lasting recognition. By framing samplers worked under her instruction with glass, front and back, and inserting a calligraphic signature on the paper backing, she ensured that even twentieth-century admirers would remember her address. Indeed, as long as the sampler survived, so in a way would the clever teacher and her school for girls.

Sarah G. Rapp was hardly an inspired needlework designer, although she demanded perfection in execution. Conspicuously similar, the Witmer samplers are unimaginative and pedestrian in format, unlike the outstanding pictorial prototypes worked in countless other Philadelphia schools. They serve, instead, to establish Rapp's individual style, which appears resolutely impervious to the splendid creations being produced in the schools of her competitors.

There is one noticeable traditional pattern on these finely wrought linen squares: the double, entwined carnation border that became an integral element in Philadelphia sampler embroideries as early as the 1790s.[1] The softly colored frame of pink silk ribbon and the circular floral wreaths, encompassing the first initial of each Witmer child, are also familiar Pennsylvania sampler motifs.

Sarah Rapp points to the success of her school in an advertisement appearing in the *United States Gazette*, Philadelphia, on August 27, 1828:

> . . . Mrs. S. G. Rapp, grateful to her friends & the public for the liberal patronage hitherto received, informs them that the duties of her seminary were resumed on the 18th instant. The branches taught are reading, writing, arithmetic, english grammar, geography with the use of maps, ancient and modern history, composition and book keeping according to the most approved modern practice. Also, plain and ornamental needlework. . . .

Sarah Rapp

For over thirty years, Sarah Rapp, her husband Joseph, and their daughter Sarah kept a school for girls at various Philadelphia locations within the vicinity of Penn Square. The city directories reveal a pattern of constant relocation suggesting the need for larger, or perhaps smaller, quarters, as changing fortunes dictated. The Rapps began teaching on Eighth Street, moving through the years to Sixth, then Sansom (George), Tenth, Buttonwood, and Green streets.[2]

Sarah Rapp taught for one year after her husband's death in 1859.[3] By 1861 she had taken a house on Percy Street near Poplar and was engaged in the business of making paper boxes.[4]

These pasteboard boxes were extremely popular during the first half of the nineteenth century for storing various articles of women's apparel and other trinkets. Usually round or oval in shape, they were most often covered with handsomely designed lengths of block-printed wallpaper or stenciled paper of some colorful motif. Frequently, the boxes were manufactured by professional painters; however, after thirty-five years of instructing young ladies in sampler embroidery, ornamental needlework, and the increasingly popular art of drawing and watercolor painting, Sarah Rapp had served her apprenticeship and was adequately prepared to master the skill of covering paper boxes for the trade.[5]

The Witmer girls probably lived in or near Lancaster County, Pennsylvania, where the Witmer name can be found in early records.

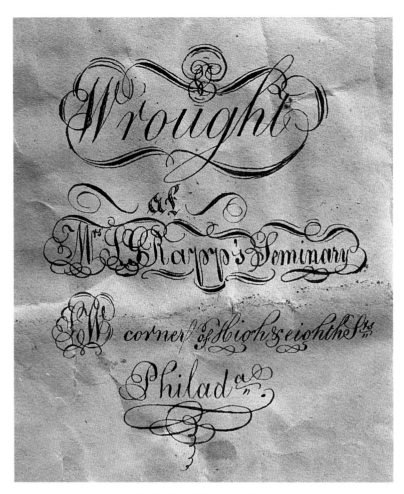

Inscription on paper inserted behind the Witmer samplers

NOTES:

1. Schiffer, *Historical Needlework of Pennsylvania*, 38. See also Ring, *American Needlework Treasures*, 39.
2. *Philadelphia City Directory*, 1819–1861.
3. *Board of Health Burial Records for Philadelphia, Pennsylvania* (Archives of the Historical Society of Pennsylvania, Philadelphia, microfilm), XR 499: 11. These records indicate that Joseph B. Rapp died on August 15, 1857, and was buried in the German Baptist Cemetery. Sarah A. Rapp, age 20 years, daughter of Joseph and Sarah, died of peritonitis on January 25, 1853.
4. *Philadelphia City Directory*, 1861.
5. Little, *Neat and Tidy*, 103.

49. BARBARA HUNSICKER (1805–1840)
Skippack, Pennsylvania, 1831
Silk threads on linen (34 threads to the inch)
Herringbone, queen, and cross-stitches
19 x 22¾ in. (48.2 x 57.7 cm)

Inscription: *BARBARA HUN/SICKER WAS/BORN THE 26/JUNE 18 AND FIVE/1805/THIS/IS/MADE FOR/THEM TO/SEE/THAT/LIVETH/AFTER/ME BDH 1831*

49.

In 1724, Valentine Hunsicker, Barbara's grandfather, built the first meeting house in Skippack, Bucks County, Pennsylvania, essentially a German-Mennonite community. The building was also frequently in use as a schoolroom for both boys and girls. The earliest specific reference to teaching in the community is in 1725, when the wife of Jacob Dubbs gathered the neighbors' children into her kitchen in the afternoon to teach them to read and write.[1] Christopher Dock, a pious Mennonite schoolmaster and writer, indicated that he accepted girls at his school. When receiving a new pupil, he wrote, "If it is a girl, I ask the girls, who among them will take care of this new child and teach it."[2]

The scattered format of Barbara Hunsicker's embroidery—more truly a sampler—was purposely designed to display, step by step, the method of stitching specific motifs. Incomplete designs worked at random across the linen clearly suggest that the stitcher was influenced by patterns prevalent in Pennsylvania-German needlework of the period. For instance, the castle in the upper left, with its tower, flying banner, and battlement, may be found in similar buildings embroidered on northern European samplers of the late eighteenth century.[3] The wreath, enclosing the mak-

er's initials and date, a custom prevalent in Quaker samplers, is also seen in Pennsylvania Fraktur and on embroidered towels and samplers stitched by the children of the closely knit Pennsylvania-German communities. The arrangement of the heart motifs originated in traditional German embroidery.[4] Identical plant motifs decorate a Pennsylvania sampler of 1813 worked by Elizabeth Coward.[5]

Barbara Hunsicker was twenty-six years of age when she worked this needlework sampler. And, while her work is atypical of the most prevalent form of Pennsylvania schoolgirl embroidery (for example, it is unstructured and lacks an ornamental border), it is nevertheless possible that even at that age she was still enrolled in needlework classes and may have been attending a boarding school.[6]

The second of eight children, Barbara Hunsicker was born in Skippack on June 18, 1805, to Isaac Hunsicker and Magdalena Cassel. Isaac, a farmer, accumulated valuable property in Perkioming and Skippack townships. Barbara, who remained unmarried, died on March 11, 1840, at the age of thirty-two.[7]

NOTES:

1. Henry A. Hunsicker, *A Genealogical History of the Hunsicker Family* (Philadelphia, PA: J. B. Lippincott Company, 1911), 17, 18. Hunsicker attests that the family was Mennonite even though many settlers joined the Quaker society. See also Woody, *History of Women's Education*, vol. 1: 210, 213.
2. Woody, *History of Women's Education*, vol. 1: 213.
3. M. G. A. Schipper-van Lottum, *Over Merklappen Gesproken* (Amsterdam: Wereldbibliotheek, 1980), 107.
4. Gehert, *This Is the Way I Pass My Time*, 171.
5. The Coward sampler is in a private collection; see Skinner catalogue, Hark Away, PA, *Hark Away, the Estate of Elisabeth T. Babcock*, 1100, November 15, 16, 1985, lot 146. See also *The Pennsylvania Germans: a Celebration of Their Arts: 1683–1850* (Philadelphia, PA: Philadelphia Museum of Art and the Henry Francis Dupont Winterthur Museum, 1982), ills. 104, 105.

I must take issue with the caption that accompanies these illustrations in which it is stated that "women learned sewing skills at home from their mothers or other relatives." Certainly there must have been many instances in which young girls were instructed in needlework within the home; however, overwhelming evidence indicates that only occasionally were educational studies limited to these circumstances. Far more documentation exists to support the fact that young girls were taught outside the home in all phases of their academic education, as well as the primary branch of needlework. Most certainly those families belonging to the Mennonite or Quaker societies, with their early emphasis on education for young women, have been seen to rely on preceptresses within the boarding school for more than the most elementary assignments for their daughters.
6. Ring, *Let Virtue Be a Guide to Thee*, 186, 203, 218. Ring quotes from Mary Remington's letter of 1813 wherein, at the age of twenty, she wrote she "was not adverse to the thought of attending school."
7. Hunsicker, *Hunsicker Family*, 20, 300. See also Hannah Benner Roach, *Montgomery County, Pennsylvania Families*, vol. G–M (Hannah Benner Roach Collection, Archives of the Historical Society of Pennsylvania, Philadelphia, PA, no date). In this document, Barbara's date of birth is given as October 24, 1807. Embroidered sampler dates are accepted as genealogically accurate. The Family Record Archives, Family History Library of the Church of Jesus Christ of Latter-Day Saints, Salt Lake City, UT, also give the October date. See also *Federal Census, Skippack, Pennsylvania*, 1850.

50. CATHARINE STAPE (b. 1821)
Pennsylvania, 1832
Silk, twisted silk threads, and crinkled silk floss on linen (28 threads to the inch)
Queen, satin, chain, tent, and cross-stitches
17¼ x 16¾ in. (43.8 x 42.5 cm)

Inscription: *Child of the summer charming/Roses No longer in confinement/Lie arise To light Thy form/Disclose Rival Tha spangle/of The Sky The rains are/Gone The Storms are ore/Winter retires to make/Thee Way Come lovely Strangers come/Catharine Stage Her/Samgler Worked in The 12th Year of her Age AG/1832./Do Thou O God/Direct my steps do Thou/direct my ways do thou/direct my every thoug/ht that i giv the gra/Barnerd/Stage/Julian Stape*

Household textiles were held in high esteem by the German-American families who settled in Pennsylvania. Domestic sewing exercises began with a sampler, embellished, inevitably, with heart-shaped motifs and paired birds of long-forgotten origin. Rarely framed, Germanic samplers were stored in drawers or chests, along with embroidered towels and linens, as evidence of a daughter's proficiency with the needle. Fortunately, this practice also protected them from harmful sunlight, which explains the clear colors of the silk and the fine condition of the linen so often found today.[1]

Although ornamental, or fancy, samplers were relatively uncommon, Catharine Stape's pictorial needlework, unlike Germanic spot motif samplers worked from paper charts, stylistically resembles a popular form of schoolgirl art found to have been worked in the vicinity of the Susquehanna River near Harrisburg. This group depicts "mile-high" figures in pictorial settings. These Lancaster County samplers share regional patterns, although they were not necessarily worked in the same schoolroom.[2]

Early in the nineteenth century, private schools for girls grew rapidly in Lancaster County. The Moravians, a German-American religious sect, established schools in Lititz and Bethlehem, which placed emphasis on needlework skills that came to be greatly admired.[3] In July 1775, Henry Bedinger of Shepherdstown, Virginia, wrote in his diary as he traveled north toward Boston that he saw in Bethlehem a "Nunnery consisting of about One Hundred and Thirty Young Women" in a large house, who "Do all Kinds of fine work, Make the finest of Lawn Cambrick, and Every Sort of finery that Can be Performed with Needles."[4] Other distinguished schools were kept by Leah Galligher Meguier (fig. 42), Catherine Welchans Buchanan, Rachael Bratton Armstrong, Mary Reed, and

Child of The Summer charming
Rose No longer in confinement
Liearise To Light Thy form
Disclose Rio al Tha Spangie

Of The Sky The rain sare
Gone The Storms ar tore
Winter retires to make
Thee Way Come lovely
Stranger scome

Catharine Stape Her
Samqler Worked in The
12th Year of her Age AG
1832 Do Thou O God
direct my steps do Thou
direct my ways do thou
direct my ever my thous
he that is my thoura

Barnerd
Stape

Julian Stape

50.

within an entire wall of windows. The tree of feathery branches shades a large figure of a woman in a peach-colored gown and a white silk bonnet. She carries a reticule and is walking a reluctant little dog. Dominating the sampler format are immense paired birds, worked in crinkled floss; they have been placed above the hearts that enclose the names of Catharine's parents.

One of six children, Catharine was born in 1821 to Bernard and Juliann (these are the spellings that appear in public documents, rather than the spellings used on the sampler) Stape of Washington, Lycoming County, Pennsylvania. By 1830, the family had moved to Maytown, East Donegal, Lancaster County, a village of twenty-five or thirty dwellings, stores, and taverns. They became members of the Maytown Lutheran Church. It was probably in Maytown that Catharine attended a private school for girls where she made this sampler.[7]

NOTES:

1. Catherine E. Hutchins, ed., *Arts of the Pennsylvania Germans* (New York, NY: W. W. Norton, 1983), 224, 226. See also Ring, *American Needlework Treasures*, 42.
2. Krueger, *Gallery of American Samplers*, 73. See also Ring, *American Needlework Treasures*, 48.
3. Hutchins, *Arts of the Pennsylvania Germans*, 222, 228.
4. Danske Dandridge, *Historic Shepherdstown* (Charlottesville, VA, 1910), 99.
5. Ring, *American Needlework Treasures*, 46, 47, 48. See also Bolton and Coe, *American Samplers*, opp. 133. The sampler illustrated was worked by Mary Hamilton in Maytown, 1812.
6. Schiffer, *Historical Needlework of Pennsylvania*, 12, 13. See also *The Pennsylvania Germans: a Celebration of their Arts*, 37, 38. The Stauffer sampler was in the Kapnek collection and is now in a private collection; see Krueger, *Gallery of American Samplers*, 72.
7. *Federal Census, Maytown, Pennsylvania*, 1810, 1820, and 1830. See also Thomas F. Gordon, *Gazetteer of the State of Pennsylvania* (Philadelphia, PA, 1832), 288. See also *Maytown Lutheran Church Records*, Maytown, PA. See also Family Record Archives, Family History Library of the Church of Jesus Christ of Latter-Day Saints, Salt Lake City, UT.

the yet to be located Mrs. Ross.[5]

The stitching and the spacing of the letters in the black silk inscriptions on Catharine's sampler suggests that English may have been her second language. For example, her execution of the letter *p* in the word *sampler* takes on the shape, though not the intention, of the letters *g* or *q*, spelling it *samgler* or *samqler*. Additionally, her surname, Stape, encircled within a leafy cartouche, and that of her father, Bernerd Stape, are spelled with the *p* reversed, thus *Stage*. Probably of German descent, she may not have had a fluent grasp of the English language. Many of the families who settled on the rich farming land around York and Lancaster counties lived within a relatively closed society, thus preserving their language and cultural heritage. Their churches and schools were designed to perpetuate the old world traditions of their ancestors. Occasionally a sampler will appear with inscriptions in both English and German, such as that worked by Mary Ann Stauffer of East Hempfield, Lancaster County.[6]

Catharine Stape's charming sampler is endowed with an amusing pictorial scene of a tiny building with a plain entrance set

Quaker Needlework

Members of the Society of Friends, or Quakers, who came to America from England were guided in their way of life by three basic principles: equality, simplicity, and peace. Maintaining a progressive attitude toward schools for girls—who were offered the same academic curriculum as the boys—they proceeded to establish a standard for women's education in this country that has persevered for over two hundred years.[1]

Comprehensive needlework classes, covering all phases of embroidery and sewing, from plain work to more skilled and accomplished embroidery techniques, were part of the regular curriculum. Instruction also included spinning, both flax and wool, and knitting. Quaker teachers, however, were expected to emphasize that which was consistent with established beliefs. As a result, in the early years, excessive ornamentation on needlework was discouraged.

After the 1780s, children not belonging to the Society were allowed to attend Quaker schools, receiving instruction consistent with the beliefs of that religious order. Tuition was free for those too poor to pay. Needlework became the mark of a sewing teacher's worth; the reputation of a school could depend on its students' embroidery skills. But the standards of plainness and simplicity remained the objectives of "a guarded education."[2]

Schools for girls existed in Philadelphia as early as 1724 and possibly before that time.[3] Many of these were kept by schoolmistresses who were members of the Society of Friends. Since few Quaker schools were advertised in the newspapers, identification of the school depends primarily on inscriptions found on surviving samplers. Although Quaker Meeting House records are readily available, schoolmistresses have rarely been identified as teachers. Needlework, therefore, has become a primary tool for researching education for women in America.

In the Chesapeake basin, where Quaker schools flourished, M. Smith opened a school in Baltimore in 1784, where girls were instructed in French and English along with "music, tambour, dresden, embroidery, plain and coloured needle work, mantua-making, millinery, and clear starching." While such frivolity might be considered inappropriate to strict Quaker parents, a break with tradition was in progress.[4]

By the first quarter of the nineteenth century, prompted, in part, by competition with the elaborate samplers and pictorial embroidery coming out of other academies and seminaries, Quaker schoolmistresses were compelled to teach a more fashionable approach to the needle arts. The rigid Meeting House standards began to fade. A growing attraction to more colorful expression prompted teachers to design more elegant examples for their students to stitch, resulting in the lavishly decorative Quak-

er pictorial samplers seen in private collections and museums today.

Plain samplers worked only in black silk thread (fig. 51) gave way to exquisitely executed silk embroideries depicting hemispherical maps,[5] silken globe samplers of paint and needlework (see page 113), and, by the 1820s, large, impressive samplers crowded with typical Quaker motifs, pictorial scenes, and figures in contemporary costumes (figs. 59, 60). Some were embellished with a finishing border of flat or gathered, serpentine-stitched (quilled) silk ribbon, each corner ornamented with a ruffled medallion. Often, these excessively decorative samplers were further enriched with wide, sumptuous frames, trimmed with raised corner-blocks. These beguiling marvels of Quaker needlework were certainly intended for display.

In many respects, Quaker samplers, and indeed those worked under Pennsylvania-German instruction, fall into a special classification of sampler embroidery. They share common patterns and a similar format, regardless of region of origin.

After 1800, Quaker samplers worked in Yorkshire, England, and the hundreds of unidentified American Quaker schools, from New York to Virginia, began to display designs that resembled one another. This trend in samplermaking contrasts markedly with that seen in all other recognized groups, which consist of regional sampler designs or distinctive patterns that may be at-

Portrait of Ann Trump Furnell and her daughter Lydia, watercolor, anonymous, English, c. 1815. Ann Furnell attended Ackworth School in England, from 1793 to 1797; samplers made by her and by her daughter are in the collection of Ackworth School, as is the needlework box seen in the painting. Ackworth School, Pontefract, West Yorkshire

"American Friends going to meeting in summer," engraving, anonymous, c. 1825. Illustrations such as this were copied by schoolmistresses for needlework patterns. Library of Congress, Washington, D.C.

tributed to a particular school or schoolmistress. It is, then, necessary, in identifying examples of Quaker embroidery, to note these similar characteristics, for they represent an important group of American needlework.[6]

First and foremost of these characteristics is the one distinctive alphabet style, deceptively modern in appearance, which appears on virtually all Quaker samplers. It consists of rather large, square, blocky letters with the *J*, *M*, and *Q*, in capital form, often falling below the thread-line of the linen (fig. 51). Another enduring pattern is the vine-and-leaf motif, which may have originated in Chester County, Pennsylvania. First introduced as a finely worked black wavy line (figs. 55, 56), in time this enclosure became a more colorful, profusely decorated cartouche, sprouting leafy sprays, flowers, and grapes, such as that depicted on Mary Lewis's sampler (fig. 59).[7]

Occasionally, these Quaker samplers, or those influenced by Quaker instruction, will display a narrow row of ligatures—characters uniting one or more letters—such as those worked across the top of the sampler stitched by Elizabeth Drew of Plymouth, Massachusetts (fig. 19). Most typically characteristic of the Quaker sampler, however, are the small floral sprays of lilies of the valley, roses, or tulips—in naturalistic arrangements—wreaths, half-medallion designs, paired birds, baskets of cross-stitched flowers, and a scattering of initials crowding the linen.[8]

NOTES:

1. Dean R. Esslinger, *Friends for Two Hundred Years, A History of Baltimore's Oldest School* (Baltimore, MD: Friends School of Baltimore, 1983), 7. See also Woody, *History of Women's Education*, vol. 1: 94, 95, 199, n. 82. See also Krueger, *Gallery of American Samplers*, 11, 12. Westtown School, Westtown, PA, has been accepting students since 1799 when twenty boys and twenty girls were enrolled (Helen G. Hole, *Westtown through the Years*, Westtown, PA: Westtown Alumni Association, 1942, 5).
2. Esslinger, *Friends for Two Hundred Years*, ix. The chronology lists 1784 as the first mention of a school in Baltimore Meeting records. The first Baltimore Quaker school for girls opened in 1816. Susan Yarnall of Thirdhaven, MD, was teacher to the girls. Yarnall attended Westtown School, enrolling the "fourth month" of 1810. *Catalogue of Westtown through the Ages: 1799–1945*, comps. Susanna Smedley and Anna Hartshorne Brown (Westtown, PA: Westtown Alumni Assoc., 1945), 30.
3. Sotheby's, 5736, June 23, 1988, lot 320.
4. Esslinger, *Friends for Two Hundred Years*, 15. See also Ring, "Samplers and Pictorial Needlework," 1424.
5. Brant and Cullman, *Small Folk*, 111. See also Swan, *American Needlework*, 20, 21.
6. Ring, "Samplers and Pictorial Needlework," 1425. This article identifies and discusses, for the first time, important patterns and motifs in Quaker embroideries and considers the Quaker influence in American sampler needlework.
7. Ibid., 1425.
8. Ibid., 1424.

Silk globe embroidered by a student at Westtown School, Chester County, Pennsylvania, ink and silk embroidery threads, 16 inches diameter (40.64 cm), c. 1815. Los Angeles County Museum of Art

51.

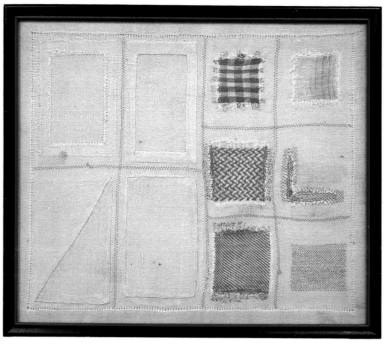

52.

51. MFH
Probably Pennsylvania, c. 1820
Silk threads on linen (28 threads to the inch)
Cross-stitches
16½ x 7¾ in. (41.9 x 19 cm)

Inscription: *MFH*

This Quaker marking sampler is characteristic of the first embroidery effort of a young schoolgirl. The four alphabets are worked in black and charcoal gray silk thread, stitched on coarsely woven homespun. Most distinctive is the third group from the top. This consists of square blocky letters, providing indication of Quaker instruction.[1]

NOTES:

1. Ring, *American Needlework Treasures*, 2, 3, 6.

52. MENDING AND DARNING SAMPLER
Possibly Delaware River Valley, c. 1800
Cotton threads on linen
(42 threads to the inch)
Plain sewing and darning weaves, with
hem-stitching
10¾ x 12¾ in. (27.3 x 32.3 cm)

The darning sampler was not commonly taught in American boarding schools for girls, except by Quaker teachers, who stressed practical domestic needle arts. This sampler, worked with cotton threads in a dashing shade of red, is probably an example of Quaker instruction. One of the earliest published illustrations of a darning sampler is inscribed "HCH 1790." It bears a certain resemblance to this sampler and may also be the product of Quaker instruction.[1]

NOTES:

1. Schiffer, *Historical Needlework of Pennsylvania*, 34.

53. ANN GIBSON (b. 1792)
Westtown School, Chester County, Pennsylvania,
1806
Silk threads and flax on linen
(40 threads to the inch)
Darning weaves and cross-stitches
8¼ in. square (20.9 cm square)

Inscription: *Ann Gibson/Weston School/1806*

Schoolmistress: Martha Barker or Martha Sharpless

54. ANN GIBSON (b. 1792)
Westtown School, Chester County, Pennsylvania,
1806
Silk threads on linen (28 threads to the inch)
Cross-stitches
5½ x 10½ in. (13.9 x 26.6 cm)

Inscription: *A Gibson/SG./MG/IG./AG*

Schoolmistress: Martha Barker or Martha Sharpless

53.

These two samplers were worked by Ann Gibson: the first, a practical darning sampler; the second, a plain, cross-stitched sampler depicting traditional, half-geometric motifs. Functional in design and modestly simple, these distinctive patterns are examples of Quaker schoolgirl needlework.[1]

When she was fourteen, Ann Gibson became a student at Westtown School, maintained by the Philadelphia Yearly Meeting of the Religious Society of Friends, in Chester County, Pennsylvania. She attended for one year,[2] during which she worked these schoolgirl embroideries, either under the instruction of Martha Barker, who taught sewing in the school from 1800 to 1808, or Martha Sharpless, sewing teacher from 1803 to 1809.[3]

Female students at Westtown School were instructed to do useful needlework and established forms of embroidery. Rebecca Jones, a needlework teacher in Philadelphia, brought back these tools of instruction from Ackworth School, Yorkshire, when she visited England as a member of the school committee in 1788. She greatly influenced the curriculum for sewing when Westtown was established in 1799, and became instrumental in guiding other American Quaker schools.[4]

Darning samplers were less common in America than in England and northern Europe. Many American Quaker schools, however, required their students to master the technique. Darning samplers worked at Westtown School are always signed and im-

printed with the name of the school. Frequently inscribed "Weston," other variations of the spelling of the school—"West-town" or "Westown"—might also be found. By the end of the nineteenth century the more precise "Westtown" was adopted.[5]

Plain sewing, and quite remarkably darning—a tremendously intricate exercise— became one of the first tasks for female students, whose education at Westtown varied little from that of the boys. It is recorded that "a piece twelve by eight inches must be so perfectly darned that the mending can scarcely be distinguished from the original material."[6]

Ann's darning sampler is consistent with similar patterns found in other Quaker examples. The repetition of identical darns, or weaves, suggests common, everyday household fabrics and domestic linens. She has worked a herringbone mend and several repeat diaper patterns, as well as a knitted darn, on her plain-weave linen ground. Almost without exception, Westtown darning samplers are worked with identical weaving designs.[7]

All of these patterned rectangles have been accomplished by "laying" threads on the surface of the linen ground, as opposed to removing threads or cutting holes. The desired effect of the woven patterns is achieved by threading the needle over one or several of these threads as designated by the weave, an extraordinarily difficult exercise. The needle thread, or darning material, used here is flax.

Geometric medallions and half medallions enjoyed great popularity in Quaker needlework classrooms from Ackworth School in England, as early as 1790, to Westtown School, as late as the 1820s.[8] These patterns are essentially a thread-counted arrangement of cross-stitches. Ann Gibson has worked her sampler in blue silk threads with two sets of initials, in the prescribed manner. A bird and one typical Quaker rose, in shades of green and peach, almost escape unnoticed.

Ann Gibson, born in 1792, was the daughter of Samuel and Mary Gibson of Kingsessing, Philadelpia. The records indicate that Samuel and his wife, Mary, received a certificate of membership from Haverford Monthly Meeting on March 26, 1790. In 1791, Mary was granted a certificate at another meeting house, the Southern District, Philadelphia.[9]

Ann Gibson married a man named Jackson, for as Ann Jackson in her father's will of 1836, she inherited three lots on Marsh Meadow and three thousand dollars of "my city loan at par value."[10]

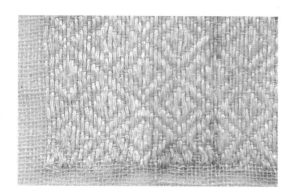

NOTES:

1. Ring, "Samplers and Pictorial Needlework," 1425, 1426.
2. Girls' entry book of Westtown School, no. 516, and letter from Mary Ann Wagner, July 21, 1987. Ms. Wagner has been extremely helpful in researching Ann Gibson, and I greatly appreciate her assistance. See also *Catalogue of Westtown through the Ages*, 19, 351.
3. Hole, *Westtown through the Years*, 384
4. Rebecca Mays, "Patterns of Belief," *The Westonian* (Spring 1985): 7. See also Ring, "Samplers and Pictorial Needlework," 1425.
5. Ring, "Samplers and Pictorial Needlework," 1428.
6. Hole, *Westtown through the Years*, 100.
7. Ring, *American Needlework Treasures*, 43.
8. Ring, "Samplers and Pictorial Needlework," 1427. See also Ring, *American Needlework Treasures*, 3.
9. *Census Index, Kingsessing Township, Philadelphia*, 1810. See also W. W. Hinshaw, *Encyclopedia of American Quaker Genealogy* (Baltimore, MD: Genealogical Publishing, Co., 1989), 531.
10. *Will Book, Salem County, New Jersey*, vol. 12, no. 177: 136.

54.

55.

56.

55. ESTHER TOMLINSON
Windsor, Berks County, Pennsylvania, 1807
Silk threads on linen (38 threads to the inch)
Outline, satin, and cross-stitches
10 x 11¾ in. (25.4 x 29.8 cm)

Inscription: *Windsor Township Berks C./Esther Tomlinson/1807*

56. HANNAH TOMLINSON (d. before 1825)
Windsor, Berks County, Pennsylvania
Silk threads on linen (42 threads to the inch)
Outline, satin, and cross-stitches
10 x 12 in. (25.4 x 30.4 cm)

Inscription: *Windsor Township Berks C./Hannah Tomlinson/1807*

The Tomlinson samplers represent a style of sampler embroidery particular to Quaker schools located near the Delaware River Valley. Their unidentified schoolmistress teaching in Windsor, Pennsylvania, may, as a student, have attended Westtown School in Chester County, for the distinctive black silk oval and vine-and-leaf format is thought to have originated at that school.[1]

In this instance, however, the absence of the characteristic boxy Quaker alphabet suggests that these examples were stitched in a local school, more influenced by Quaker design than by specific Quaker instruction. As has been noted, Quaker patterns inspired non-Quaker teachers, who often imitated the distinctive styles. These samplers may be the product of such a receptive schoolmistress.

The village of Windsor, established in 1752, borders on the Schuylkill River, north of Reading. Esther and Hannah were probably the daughters of John Tomlinson and Martha Wiley, who were married in 1777. Esther married Enoch Penrose on August 28, 1812.[2]

When John Tomlinson died in 1826, he listed his daughter, Esther Penrose, as wife of Enoch. There is no mention of Hannah, who probably died before the will was written in 1825.[3]

The condition of the samplers and the construction of the frames hints at further information about Hannah. Esther's sampler is in fine condition, and the frame is of an early period, while the sampler worked by Hannah looks as though it had been carelessly set aside in a trunk or drawer. There is evidence of staining and wear, although, at some stage, it was thoughtfully mended in an effort to preserve its historical value. The frame on this sampler is a twentieth-century construction. Even though these sisters attended the same school at the same time, it is apparent that one sampler was treated with special care, probably by the maker as a souvenir of her youth.

NOTES:

1. Ring, "Samplers and Pictorial Needlework," 1425, 1428. See also Ring, *American Needlework Treasures*, 43.
2. *Will Book, Berks County*, vol. 5 (Lightfoot Collection, Historical Society of Pennsylvania, Philadelphia), 559. Records indicate that John Tomlinson was "disowned" by the Friends before marriage. Martha Wiley was not a Quaker.
3. Ibid.

57. SARAH ELWELL (1814–1892)
Philadelphia, Pennsylvania, 1826
Silk threads on linen (32 threads to the inch)
Outline, straight, padded satin, queen, and cross-stitches
20½ x 15½ in. (52 x 17.1 cm)

Inscription: *Lord this I ask in faith sincere/The wisdom from above/To touch my heart with filial fear/And pure celestial/love/My selfish will in time subdue/And mortify my pride/And lend my youth a sacred clue/To find the crucified/Innocence is sweet/ SE HE CE Sarah/Elwell/Philadelphia/1826*

Among the faded penmanship exercises preserved in Hopewell Village archives is a list of twenty-four "anxious wishes" compiled by an unknown Pennsylvania schoolgirl. She wanted most of all to be independent, to be admired, and to be joined in matrimony, while to be in love was placed next to last. She desired to set the fashions, be happy, go to Europe, reign in all things, and be an ornament in society. At the very end was the wish to be wealthy. This extraordinary index reveals the expectations of a young girl in a remote nineteenth-century Pennsylvania village and provides a revealing glimpse of the culture that shaped her life in the tightly knit Hopewell community.[1]

It was into such an atmosphere that Sarah Elwell was born on August 17, 1814, the youngest of Samuel Elwell and Rachel Sheppard's seven children. Little is known of Sarah's early life in the village, except that she was orphaned before she was five.[2]

Hopewell, located in the valley of the Schuylkill, on the border of Berks and Chester counties, was dominated by the massive glowing furnace, the night-and-day operation of the creaking waterwheel, and the ever-present charcoal dust from the local ironworks. Samuel Elwell was apparently connected to the famous Hopewell Ironworks and Foundry, for land records indicate that the Elwell family owned sizeable tracts of land in Hopewell and Pittsgrove townships. As landowners, they would have been in a prestigious position in the community, both economically and socially.[3]

While some older children studied at home with tutors, there is evidence that a common school was established in Hopewell before 1804. After 1820, the school was presided over by a Sarah Brown, who received her fees in the form of subscriptions charged to individual pupils on the basis of attendance. There is no indication that Brown instructed the girls in any form of needlework. Such subscription teaching continued well into the 1840s.[4]

Pupils from all levels of Hopewell society began attending classes around the age of five; the ironmaster assumed responsibility for those families too poor to pay. Sessions were held in vacant houses, in the local boarding house, and at the Baptist church; the boys sat on one side of the room, the girls on the other.[5]

Upon graduation, the wealthier students were often sent to private boarding schools. Hopewell girls traditionally went to study at Mr. Price's school in West Chester or Mr. Hamilton's in Philadelphia,[6] occasionally progressing to Bristol College or Samuel Gummere's, both in Burlington, New Jersey. As genteel young ladies of fashion, they were instructed in dancing, riding, French, and Latin.[7]

Lord this I ask in faith sincere   My selfish will in time subdue
The wisdom from above   And mortify my pride
To touch my heart with filial fear   And lend my youth a sacred clue
And pure celestial   To find the crucified
love

Sarah
Elwell
Philadelphia
1826

Innocence is sweet

57.

Philadelphia, about fifty miles from Hopewell, was certainly considered the center of fashion, and it was there that Sarah Elwell was sent to boarding school.[8] As with many Philadelphia samplers, Sarah Elwell's embroidery is embellished with designs frequently associated with eastern Pennsylvania and the mid-Atlantic states. Such motifs as the ribbed fence and the deeply terraced lawn are reminiscent of samplers attributed to schools near Baltimore and the Delaware River Valley. The apple tree to the left of her beige silk house is an imaginative addition to this finely worked embroidery. But Quaker motifs also abound. The stylish wreath of flowers enclosing Sarah's name, the fine, precise letters of her boxy alphabet inscribing the verse and maxim, and the scattered initials representing fidelity to her siblings, Samuel, Hannah, and Christiana, are all identified as Quaker.[9]

Recently, two identical samplers have emerged that were unquestionably worked under the same instruction. One was stitched by Mary Florence in 1826, and the second by Isabella McDonald in 1829. The schoolmistress who designed the format for these charming samplers is still unknown. She may well be the woman who taught at the prestigious Hamilton School in Philadelphia, where many Hopewell girls were known to have completed their education.[10]

Sarah Elwell married Benjamin Crispin (1797–1877) in 1838. They had at least two children. Sarah died at the age of eighty-two.[11]

NOTES:

1. Joseph E. Walker, *Hopewell Village: the Dynamics of a Nineteenth-Century Iron-Making Community* (Philadelphia, PA: University of Pennsylvania Press, 1966), 329.
2. Elmer Garfield Van Name, *The Elwell Family, 17th- and 18th-Century Southern New Jersey* (Haddonfield, NJ, 1963), 25, 26.
3. Van Name, *Elwell Family*, 25.
4. National Park Service, pamphlet, *Hopewell Village* (Hopewell Village National Historic Site, PA). See also Walker, *Hopewell Village*, 347, 348, 381.
5. Walker, *Hopewell Village*, 351, 352, 353.
6. An advertisement in Poulson's *American Daily Advertiser*, March 27, 1815, has been brought to my attention by Betty Ring. It states that Hamilton Academy, in the village of Hamilton, one mile west of Philadelphia, was opening on the first day of April, with Ennion Williams as superintendent. This may have been the "Mr. Hamilton's school" to which Walker referred. Boarders were accepted in the "separate apartments of two adjoining houses," at a cost of $190 per year. Among the primary branches of instruction for girls was plain and ornamental needlework. I am indebted to Mrs. Ring for her kind assistance.
7. Walker, *Hopewell Village*, 355, 356, 357. See also letter from Elizabeth Barde to Sarah A. Brooke, February 12, 1837 (Hopewell Papers, Stokes Collection, Hopewell Village National Historic Site, PA). In 1830 and 1831, expenses for Caroline and Marie Brooke came to $112.49 for twenty-four weeks' schooling with Mr. Price.
8. Walker, *Hopewell Village*, 322, 356, 357.
9. Van Name, *Elwell Family*, 25, 26. While no date of death is recorded for Thomas and Martha Ann, the absence of their initials on Sarah Ann's sampler would suggest that they died before the sampler was worked in 1826.
10. The whereabouts of the sampler worked by Mary Florence is unknown. Isabella McDonald's sampler is illustrated in Sotheby's, New York, catalogue, *Fine Americana*, 4338, January 30–February 2, 1980, lot 1306. Once a part of the collection of Emma B. Hodge of Chicago, the McDonald sampler may have been exhibited at the Minneapolis Institute of Arts exhibition of the Hodge Collection, April 1921 (see *Bulletin of the Minneapolis Institute of Arts*, April 1921, vol. 10, no. 4: 25–28).
11. Van Name, *Elwell Family*, 26.

58.

58. ABIGAIL PASSMORE YARNALL
(1804–1882)
Edgemont, Pennsylvania, 1817
Silk, twisted silk threads, and crinkled silk floss on
linen (58 threads to the inch)
Satin, outline, bullion, eyelet, queen, and cross-
stitches
17 x 19 in. (43.1 x 48.2 cm)

Inscription: *Yet to thee my soul shall raise/Grateful vows
and solemn praise/And when ev'r'y blesing's flown/Love
thee for thyself alone/My parents/George Yarnall/Mary
Yarnall/ Naomi Yarnall/Ruth Yarnall/Abigail
Yarnall/William Yarnall
Abigail Passmore Yarnalls/Work 1817*

Abigail Yarnall's sampler, worked on a sheer linen, or tiffany, is characteristic of Quaker schoolgirl needlework and displays many of the Society's traditional motifs. Most evident is the pale beige silk alphabet, stitched across the top. While lacking the letter *J*, the tail of the letter *Q* falls below the baseline in the traditional manner. The chevron-like flowers above the grazing sheep are also found on the sampler worked by Sarah Elwell (fig. 57), who attended a Quaker school in Philadelphia.

Inscribed upon the fabric are the names of Abigail's parents, her sisters, and her brother. Closing her verse with "Love thee for thyself alone," she paraphrased Quaker ideology by emphasizing the importance of family and one's inner light.

Abigail Passmore Yarnall was born on Christmas Day, 1804, in Edgemont, Pennsylvania, one hundred years after her ancestors arrived in Delaware Bay aboard the *Bristol Comfort*. She was the third daughter of four children born to George Yarnall and Mary Howard.[1] The family may have lived in the gray fieldstone house still standing along Crum Creek, with its shimmering windowpanes, five bays across, built in 1720 by Philip Yarnall, Jr.

Abigail Yarnall married William Cox (b. 1805), a wealthy farmer, in 1841. She died childless at the age of seventy-seven on December 15, 1882.[2]

NOTES:

1. Harry H. Yarnell and Ruth Brookman Yarnell, *A Partial Genealogy of the Name Yarnall-Yarnell, 1683–1970* (privately published, no date) 1, 2, 370. The land ownership map (p. 5) shows the exact location of the Yarnall homestead. It was typical of the Quakers to build with stone rather than "English brick" or the local wood. Arriving in the New World, Francis Yarnall was obliged to pay three shillings as duty for "1 ¼ cwt. [hundredweight] shot; 3 dozen wool stockings; 40 ells English linen [an English ell measures approximately three feet, nine inches] and ¼ cwt. of gunpowder." Such evidence indicates the importance of textiles in the life of the early settlers.
2. Yarnell, *Partial Genealogy of the Name Yarnall-Yarnell*, 389. For additional genealogical information see Family Record Archives, Family History Library of the Church of Jesus Christ of Latter-Day Saints, Salt Lake City, UT. See also Rev. Henry Miller Cox, *The Cox Family in America* (New York, NY, 1912), 244.

59. MARY LEWIS

Chester County, Pennsylvania, 1824
Silk threads and crinkled silk floss on linen
(26 threads to the inch), with a quilled silk ribbon
trim and corner rosettes
Satin, tent, bullion, outline, and cross-stitches
20¼ x 21½ in. (51.4 x 54.6 cm)

Inscription: *This work perhaps my friends may
have/When I am in my silent grave/And which when e'er
they chance to see/May kind remembrance picture
me/While on the glowing canvas stands/The labor of my
youthful hands/ JC/MC/JL/PL/ NL/ML/EL/JL
Mary Lewis 1824*

59.

Mary Lewis, whose background has not yet been traced, worked this elaborate pictorial sampler in 1824, near Williston or Marple in Chester County, Pennsylvania, where the majority of these later, non-traditional Quaker embroideries are believed by researchers to have originated. This example represents a style of sampler embroidery that began in the area around 1820 and continued in popularity through the 1830s, a period when interest in delicate schoolgirl needlework was being supplanted by the more fashionable, heavy European woolwork.[1]

The vine-and-leaf motif of Mary's wreath enclosure is barely recognizable, yet its origin lies in the earlier, more severely formal pattern appearing on samplers worked by the Tomlinson sisters, 1807 (figs. 55, 56). By 1824, when this sampler was worked, the traditional Quaker design had become more decorative and elaborate through the addition of buds, flowers, birds, and twining grape vines.[2] A wide, undulating flowery border trims the top and sides of the sampler, while the base has been reserved for a well-defined pastoral setting of grassy mounds with a squirrel, playful sheep, and a large bird perched upon a platform.

The unusual arbor at the center bottom reveals a miniature landscape, a motif not found on other samplers of a similar style. The result of a particular schoolteacher's taste, this most recognizable design allows us to attribute at least four samplers to her school, or sphere of influence: those worked by Ann H. Vodges of Williston, 1823;[3] Alice Maris of Marple (c. 1824);[4] Hannah W. Haws (c. 1824);[5] and the unidentified daughter of Josiah and Mary Fawkes.[6]

Mary Lewis, Hannah Haws, and Ann H. Vodges may have attended embroidery classes together, for the verses inscribed on their samplers are very similar.[7]

Upon completion, Mary's sampler was finely stitched to a flat satin ribbon, which was, in turn, entirely hidden by the further embellishment of a glossy, quilled silk ribbon with corner rosettes, now of a faded, undeterminable hue. Lavishly framed, Mary Lewis's sampler was at one time both colorful and showy.

Closely related to embroideries worked under the instruction of Elizabeth Passmore, who kept a school for girls in East Goshen, this sampler format exemplifies a purely regional style.[8] Similar samplers continued to be worked for at least two decades in the towns of Chester County, influencing schoolmistresses and classroom instruction on both sides of the Delaware River. These densely patterned, superbly executed Quaker samplers mark the high point of elegant nineteenth-century schoolgirl embroidery in America.

NOTES:

1. Ring, "Samplers and Pictorial Needlework,"
1430.
2. Swan, *Plain and Fancy*, 65.
3. The Vodges sampler was in the Kapnek collection and is now in a private collection; see Krueger, *Gallery of American Samplers*, 62, 63, 91, 93.
4. The Maris sampler is in the collection of the Philadelphia Museum of Art, PA; see Hornor, *Story of Samplers*, fig. 38. See also Judith K. Grow and Elizabeth C. McGrail, *Creating Historic Samplers* (Princeton, NJ: Pyne Press, 1974), pl. 5. This sampler should be dated c.1824, rather than 1814. Samplers of this format have not yet been identified that bear such an early date.
5. The Haws sampler is in a private collection; see Sotheby's, New York, catalogue, *Property from the Collection of the Late Helen Janssen Wetzel, part 2*, H-3, Tulpehocken Farm, PA, October 2–4, 1980, lot 1939. I am greatly indebted to Blanche Moss for detailed information regarding this embroidery.
6. The Fawkes sampler is in a private collection; see Sotheby's, New York, catalogue, *Important American Furniture and Related Decorative Arts*, 4478Y, November 19–22, 1980, lot 1171.
7. This verse (see "Inscription") appeared on later Chester County samplers, which were similar, but even more lavish and elegant than their forerunners, for example, the sampler worked by Phebe Mode Hall, 1831, discussed in Ring, "Samplers and Pictorial Needlework," 1430. Phebe's sampler appears to be closely related to Mary Lewis's, although the window or arbor has been replaced by landscape foliage. See also Georgianna Brown Harbeson, *American Needlework* (New York, NY: Bonanza Books, 1938), opp. 52. The sampler, worked by Sarah H. James, 1820, names her instructress as "E. Passmore."
8. Ring, "Samplers and Pictorial Needlework," 1430.

60. ANN HOOTON

Gloucester County, New Jersey, 1812
Twisted silk threads and crinkled silk floss on linen
(28 threads to the inch)
Chain, tent, satin, split, outline, bullion, needle-
weaving, and cross-stitches
19 x 17 in. (48.2 x 43.1 cm)

Inscription: *Wrought by Ann Hootton Daughter of/William and Hannah Hooton 1812/E S*

Schoolmistress: E.S.

A distinctive group of samplers worked in classrooms on the New Jersey side of the Delaware River were embellished with a bewildering array of densely worked Quaker motifs. Samplers related to the piece stitched by Ann Hooton compose a cohesive body of extraordinary work, one that surpasses most sampler embroideries known to have a New Jersey provenance. Characteristic of this group is the terraced pictorial setting—with a detailed house or building, trees, and a farmyard of birds and animals—and the distinctive, undulating border. Surviving examples of this extravagant sampler format attest to its enduring popularity from the 1820s into the 1830s. In the recent past, textile historians have directed their attention to schoolmistresses of Burlington County, where more than a few of the young embroiderers have been found.

This sampler worked by Ann Hooton, who lived in Gloucester County in 1812, may be the earliest example of this New Jersey group. The sampler itself is replete with traditional Quaker motifs, but the border design is an unusual one.[1] Worked as a twisted ribbon, knotted with leaves, diminutive tulips, and buttonlike flower-shapes that punctuate the pattern, the border weaves around three sides of the sampler. Across the top, color and texture reverse with each turn, changing from solid green floss to beige, patterned with dots of rust-colored bullion knots. The uppermost corners are adorned with birds.

Border designs of similar samplers bearing later dates were worked in whirling waves of thin vines with leaf and flower decoration, such as that bordering the sampler worked by Martha Hooton—not related to Ann—in 1827.[2] One of the earliest examples was worked by Lydia Burroughs in 1814 at the Chesterfield School, a Quaker institution in New Jersey.[3] It is possible that Ann's charming border design was her schoolmistress's version of a developing regional pattern.

The most striking motif on Ann's sampler is the appearance of a seventeenth-century galleon, which would have been copied from a newspaper, broadside, or engraving, possibly during the

War of 1812 (see below). Sails are unfurled, flags fly in all directions, a lantern swings from a post above the high, jutting afterdeck. American samplers featuring sailing ships are uncommon, for reasons not yet fully understood, but this one is cleverly arranged within the cluttered format.[4]

Ann Hooton, born July 16, 1799, was the first of twelve children born to William and Hannah Kay Hooton of Haddonfield, Gloucester County, New Jersey.[5] Her maternal grandfather, Isaac Kay, was a leading citizen of the town.[6] Ann married Reuben Haines (b. 1796) of Waterford Township, in what is now Camden County. Their engagement was celebrated in the Quaker meeting house at Haddonfield in 1820.[7]

Little is known about the education of girls in Ann's small New Jersey village. Early in the eighteenth century, Jonathan Bolton and his wife, Hannah, kept a "family school" for the children of Haddonfield, for which they received forty acres of land for life. Hannah Bolton probably instructed girls in rudimentary embroidery stitches. By 1786, a Quaker school was well established in the town, "wherein English Grammar, the Mathematics, Geography, and the Latin and French languages (by a French nobleman) are, or may be taught."[8]

Girls were frequently sent to attend the fashionable Philadelphia schools, for needlework was the specialty of the private boarding-school teacher. But the sampler worked by Ann Hooton is characteristic of documented regional New Jersey patterns, suggesting this splendid embroidery was the product of a local school, stitched under the watchful eyes of an as yet unidentified Haddonfield schoolmistress, whose initials are E. S.

According to Quaker records, Reuben Haines was disowned by the Friends in 1856, and Ann Hooton Haines moved to the Upper Evesham Monthly Meeting in 1859.[9]

NOTES:

1. Ring, "Samplers and Pictorial Needlework," 1425, 1426.
2. Martha Hooton's sampler was in the Kapnek collection and is now in a private collection; see Krueger, *Gallery of American Samplers*, 69.
3. The location of the Burroughs sampler is unknown; see Bolton and Coe, *American Samplers*, opp. 304, 381. The Chesterfield School is recorded as dating from 1795 to 1821.
4. Ring, "Samplers and Silk Embroideries of Portland, Maine," 520. As an example of the custom, this engraving of a sailing vessel by James Akin, c. 1807, appears to have been copied in pencil, ink, and paint on Maine silk embroideries worked in Portland schools attended by local girls during the 1820s.
5. *Haddonfield Monthly Meeting Records of Birth and Deaths*, 1690–1820, 142.
6. *This Is Haddonfield* (Haddonfield, NJ: Historical Society of Haddonfield, NJ, 1963): 143.
7. *Haddonfield Monthly Meeting Records.* The document is signed, customarily, by the forty-four members in attendance.
8. *This Is Haddonfield*, 202, 203.
9. *Haddonfield Monthly Meeting Records.*

Masthead of the *Norwich Packet*, published by John Trumbull, 1787. The ship stitched on Ann Hooton's New Jersey sampler was based on an engraving similar to that which embellished Trumbull's Connecticut newspaper

60.

61.

61. HANNAH STEELMAN (b. 1824)
Squankum, New Jersey, 1834
Silk, twisted silk threads, and crinkled silk floss on linen (24 threads to the inch)
Queen, satin, outline, interlocking and slanted Gobelin, and cross-stitches
16½ x 17 in. (41.9 x 43.1 cm)

Inscription: *Tis religion that can give/Sweetest pleasures while we live/Tis religion must supply/Solid comforts when we die/IsGsH/sDsRI/SIBSLS/ Hannah Steelman Her Work Made/In the 11th year of Her Age/Wrought In Squankum October 1834*

Alongside a profusion of Quaker motifs, Hannah Steelman has inscribed an aphorism epitomizing the beliefs embraced by the Society of Friends. Her verse and signature have been stitched within a rectangular cartouche of Quaker flowers on angled stems, quite a change from the austere vine-and-leaf motif characteristic of early Quaker embroidery. The cornucopia, or curved vase design, appeared as early as 1802 on a sampler worked by Sarah Bye, at the Fallsington Boarding School, Bucks County, Pennsylvania,[1] as well as on a New Jersey sampler worked by Martha Hooton, 1827.[2]

Framed on three sides by a splendid queen-stitched strawberry border, the needleworked picture across the bottom is not typical of Quaker work. Little brown-stitched slippers may be observed just below each hemline of the fashionably garbed ladies. Two top-hatted gentlemen are posed beneath the stylized pine trees. The brick-styled house features an impressive green doorway and lavishly appointed windows, with as many as twenty-four panes, trimmed by thin satin-stitched shutters. Such a display of elegance hints at some wealth.

There was, indeed, an air of prosperity around Squankum Township at this time, which allowed for a higher standard of living than might be expected in a Quaker society. In 1830, at the head of the Squan River, a prized substance called marl was discovered whose trade resulted in the prosperity of many southern New Jersey landowners—of whom it was once said, the more land they owned the poorer they were.[3]

Settled primarily by Germans around 1758, Squankum was conveniently situated near little Squankum Creek in Gloucester County, on the Old Cape Road, which once cut through Cross Keys on a direct line to Cape May and the mouth of the Delaware. In the early years of the nineteenth century, Squankum was a village of two taverns and thirty-five houses, three stores, two blacksmith shops, and a thriving glass-house.[4]

Unquestionably, a Quaker schoolmistress prepared lessons for the young village girls attending her modest Squankum schoolroom, although many well-situated Squankum parents would have found it more fitting to send their daughters to Philadelphia boarding schools. It was this schoolteacher who selected, from the approved Quaker patterns, those motifs that appear on samplers such as the one worked by Hannah Steelman.

Although Hannah Steelman has not been located, research reveals numerous Quaker families with her surname living at the time near Egg Harbor in what is now Atlantic County. Squankum has been known as Williamstown since 1842.[5]

NOTES:

1. The Bye sampler is in a private collection; see Schiffer, *Historical Needlework of Pennsylvania*, 51.
2. Krueger, *Gallery of American Samplers*, 69. Martha Hooton's sampler (formerly in the Kapnek collection) was incorrectly identified as Canadian in Jean S. Remy, "A Collection of Rare Samplers," *The Delineator* (September 1903): 301. This article was brought to my attention by Carole Austin, to whom I am indebted.
3. Franklin Ellis, *History of Monmouth County, New Jersey* (Cottonport, NJ: Shrewsbury Historical Society, NJ, 1974), 648. Marl is a rich, earthy deposit of clay and calcium carbonate; it was much in demand by farmers trying to survive by working the flat lime-deficient soil of which most of southeastern New Jersey is composed.
4. Henry Charlton Beck, *More Forgotten Towns of Southern New Jersey* (reprint, New Brunswick, NJ, 1963), 37, 41, 43, 44.
5. Much to my dismay, I found there were two towns named Squankum in nineteenth-century New Jersey. Squankum Township, situated in Monmouth County, has vanished, with only an ancient Quaker burying ground left to verify its existence, and that shadowed all around by elevated turnpikes. The other Squankum, in Gloucester County, which concerns Hannah Steelman, was renamed Williamstown in 1842 when the mix-up of mail prompted the change. See Beck, *More Forgotten Towns*, 41, 45.

62. PHEBE BROWN SAYRE (b. 1812)
Newark, New Jersey, 1823
Silk and metal threads on linen
(26 threads to the inch)
Eyelet, chain, queen, and cross-stitches
19 x 13¼ in. (48.2 x 34.3 cm)

Inscription: *Phebe B Sayre's work aged 11 years*
September/20th/Newark 1823

P hebe Sayre's sampler was designed by a rather uninspired schoolmistress. The prosaic style, drawing heavily on traditionally popular needlework alphabet forms, is conspicuously similar to examples worked in hundreds of private boarding schools for girls along the eastern seaboard, from Maine to Virginia, during the first quarter of the nineteenth century.

The most common sampler pattern, the strawberry border, edges three sides of the sampler. Although the remaining strip of border design along the bottom consists of a more interesting double serpentine vine, the building, picket fencing, birds, and tree patterns are all reminiscent of samplers worked in the vicinity of the Delaware Valley. The hot-air balloon, however, is an unusual element.

A sampler worked in 1835 by Caroline Eliza Sayre of Newark has recently surfaced.[1] Although there is no evidence to substantiate the theory, the girls may have been related. While the format of the two samplers varies, the similar placement and design of the trees, fencing, and the two dogs within the pictorial scene may suggest a common bond. The same schoolmistress may have been responsible for tutoring both girls.

The youngest of five children, Phebe Brown Sayre was born in 1812, the daughter of Samuel Sayre and Rebecca Southwell of Newark, New Jersey. Her father, a mason, was a man of considerable wealth.[2]

After the death of her parents, Phebe lived with her sister, Joanna M. Murray, and Joanna's daughter, Mary Jane, until she married Charles Mattoon, March 26, 1857, when she was forty-five years of age.[3]

NOTES:

1. The Sayre sampler was in the Kapnek collection and is now in a private collection; see Krueger, *Gallery of American Samplers*, 79.
2. Thomas M. Banta, *The Sayre Family: Lineage of Thomas Sayre, a Founder of Southhampton* (New York, NY, 1901), 374. See also *Estate Records, Newark, New Jersey*, January 27, 1840.
3. *Federal Census, Newark, New Jersey*, 1850. See also *Marriage Records, Newark, New Jersey*, handwritten by Rev. J. B. Condit, Family History Library of the Church of the Church of Jesus Christ of Latter-Day Saints, Salt Lake City, UT. See also Banta, *Sayre Family*, 374.

62.

63.

Cumberland County, New Jersey, 1827
Silk, twisted silk threads, and crinkled silk floss on
linen (26 threads to the inch)
Satin, queen, outline, stem, and cross-stitches
16½ x 19½ in. (41.9 x 49.5 cm)

Inscription: *Ann W Dickinson/1827*

Readily identified by their conspicuous, uniformly shaped poplar trees, a specific group of samplers can be attributed to the southern section of New Jersey. A comparison of samplers known to have originated there reveals that a number of New Jersey schoolmistresses tended to include this specific tree motif in their embroidery designs.[1] Ann Dickinson's teacher has made use of this pattern in her stylish sampler format, placing one in the yard to the side and two crowding over the shingled roofline of the house, forming dark green wedges in the sky. This deliberate arrangement of rich green coloration begins at the terraced lawn, finds its way through the arched doorway and the closed and fastened window shutters, and peaks like a pyramid in the topmost *M* formed by the silhouette of the trees. It is an astonishingly effective, very dramatic device.

Uncluttered and stunningly pictorial in nature, Ann's sampler depicts a charming four-bay house, whose unsheathed windows disclose their finely delineated panes. Particular to this unidentified school is the bold geometry of the widely spaced strawberry border, in which the repeated use of deep-toned, green silk thread enhances the thick angular stems and leaf motifs. Stitched in this conspicuous manner, the vine-patterned border becomes an integral part of the total design, a daring concept rarely found in sampler embroidery. Fencing, trees, baskets of flowers, and isolated bouquets complete this exceptional embroidery.

Characteristic of a form of schoolgirl needlework now believed to have been stitched in the vicinity of Cumberland County, New Jersey, two samplers have recently surfaced that repeat the same distinctive pattern. The samplers are unquestionably related. One of them was worked in 1828, by Rhoda Mulford, of Cumberland County,[2] who kindly included family initials to assist in her identification. Rhoda's house displays similar, although not identical window treatment. In a somewhat whimsical display, some of the windows have been left open, while others are shuttered, thereby revealing the teacher-designer's delight in playing with the building's facade, and leaving a "behind the scenes" impression of subtle, unexpected amusement.

The second of these newly found samplers was worked by an unidentified child. This delightful embroidery belongs to the same school of work and was stitched during the same period, at the same New Jersey school, under the direction of the same, as yet unidentified, instructress. Three of the upper-story windows are shuttered, one open. Below, two are open and one is playfully left closed.[3]

Ann W. Dickinson is probably the same Ann Dickinson who married John Snitcher in Salem County, New Jersey, in 1834.[4]

NOTES:

1. Ring, *American Needlework Treasures*, 34.
2. The Mulford sampler is in a private collection; see Sotheby's, New York, catalogue, *Important American Furniture, Folk Art, Silver, Chinese Export Porcelain, Rugs*, 5282, January 31–February 2, 1985, lot 366. This sampler was researched by Sheila Rideout, placing the child in Cumberland County. See also *Maine Antiques Digest* (February 1986), advertisement.
3. The location of this sampler is unknown; see *Maine Antiques Digest* (June 1981), advertisement.
4. *Marriage Records, Salem County, New Jersey*, compiled by H. Stanley Craig (Merchantville, NJ, 1928), 169.

64. CHARLOTTE COATES BOYD (b. 1814)
Baltimore, Maryland, c. 1826
Silk threads and crinkled silk floss on linen
(28 threads to the inch)
Satin, padded satin, herringbone, and cross-stitches
16½ x 22½ in. (41.9 x 57.1 cm)

Inscription: *Charlotte Coates Boyd's Work Finished in
The Thirteenth Year of Her Age. A. D. [date removed]*

65. ELIZABETH BLYDEN (b. 1818, d. after
1860)
Baltimore, Maryland, 1829
Silk threads on linen (26 threads to the inch)
Long-armed cross-stitches and cross-stitches
21½ x 25 in. (54.6 x 38.1 cm)

Inscription: *A M/Sacred to/Adam Mewer/
S M/Sacred to/Sarah /Mewer
Elizabeth Blyden's work done in the 12th year
of her age. August 13th 1829. E. Baltimore.*

66. ELIZA PICKET (b. 1815)
Baltimore, Maryland, 1825
Silk threads on linen
21 x 18 in. (45.72 x 27.94 cm)
Chain, stem, tent, satin, and cross-stitches

Inscription: *Eliza Picket's work/done in the
11th year of her age* [1]

BALTIMORE

Lost at the late fire on McElderry's wharf, a square band box, covered
with bordering paper, containing a variety of articles, such as ruffs, pock-
et handkerchiefs, white muslin shawls—1 pink levantine fancy shawl, 1
lace handkerchief, seven or eight yards of English thread lace, different
patterns, and a few yards of edging, 1 handsome perfume box, covered
with red corded silk, ornamented and in the shape of a book, the ends
and front gilt, and a sampler with the owner's name worked in it. . . . [2]

Although there are few documented Southern samplers, the
number of schools for girls that advertised in Baltimore
newspapers between 1780 and 1825 suggests that a considerable range of educational institutions was available to daughters of the growing merchant class.

Many samplers worked in Baltimore academies still exist today, including rare examples of map samplers of the area and
marking samplers, inscribed with the name of the town. Such evidence suggests that schools for girls in this Chesapeake Bay city

were well attended, and needlework instruction was both competent and varied.[3]

Catharine Groombridge[4] (whose husband William was an accomplished landscape artist) kept a school in Baltimore from 1804
to about 1816, offering girls lessons in an astonishing array of needle arts: "marking, netting, tambour, artificial flowers, fillagree,
fancy baskets & plain, cloth, print, paper & shellwork with many
other accomplishments both useful and ornamental."[5]

Frequently, special teachers were hired in the fields of dancing,
languages, music, and sometimes riding. Often specific instruction, such as theorem (or stencil) painting, was the only subject offered, suggesting the emergence of specialized schooling. At 239
Baltimore Street, M. Carrick taught women in a "select domestic
sewing school" where classes were conducted for those who had
"finished their education, cutting and making Dresses and every
article of plain work necessary in a family would be offered."[6]

Enrollment in these academies was sizeable. Mrs. Groombridge informed the public on August 22, 1809, that in addition to
devoting herself full-time to teaching, she had acquired twelve assistants, "who are in every respect adequate to the branches of education they undertake to teach."[7] On the average, tuition for
most private schools came to two hundred dollars a year, one quarter in advance. Pupils at Mrs. Curle's and Mrs. Bowen's, as with
many other academies, were required to provide their own beds
and bedding.[8]

Rebecca and Harriet Rooker, who kept a school for girls in Baltimore for over twenty-nine years from 1808 to 1837—during
which time many of the important Baltimore samplers were
worked—advertised in 1810, apparently in response to criticism
from an unknown source, that the "number of their pupils is limited to one hundred and that ten persons will be regularly engaged in their instruction, five remaining in the house and the
others attending daily at stated hours."[9]

In 1809, Mrs. Decourt and Mrs. Baconais, who kept a school for
young women in Baltimore from 1807 to 1818, conducted exami-
nations of their various departments at the Assembly Rooms over
a period of several days.[10] Fierce competition motivated these determined ladies to place the following advertisement in 1811:

Madam Decourt & Baconais will open their Academy on Tuesday, 1st of
September and through the ensuing year invariably adhere to their old
system, both of discipline and instruction, that they may ensure the con-
tinuance of a liberal support by continuing to deserve it.
    Madam D. and B. assure their respected patrons that they have no in-
tention of giving up their business, and that the report to that effect so
constantly circulated during the last year was a vile and degrading false-
hood. The propagators of this shameful story are known, and should they

persist in their wickedness, they will assuredly be exposed.

In the pursuit of their business they have always courted a manly and generous competion [*sic*]; but they will never for a moment permit themselves to preside over any institution that must be indebted for its existence to mean solicitation or low and debasing intrigue.[11]

The most distinguished group of pictorial Baltimore samplers were large in size and visually dramatic. These spectacular samplers are marvelous works of regional embroidered art. The samplers of Charlotte Coates Boyd, c. 1826, and Elizabeth Blyden, 1829 (figs. 64, 65), are examples of this school of embroidery.[12]

During the two decades following 1821, one particular, and as yet unidentified, schoolmistress developed a stylish sampler format for her students that places work stitched under her instruction in a category quite unlike any other from this period.[13] The viewer can easily detect the guiding hand of the clever teacher. Boldly conceived, her design cuts across the lower third of the linen with a solid row of silk-embroidered fencing, dissecting it in the center with a black, two-leafed ornamental iron gate. She then opens up the wide walkway directly to the narrowing steps, which are generally endowed with black iron railings, and places the decorated doorway at the arrow's point. The designated buildings, many of which have been identified as specific homes or public buildings, stand firmly in place; the entire scene is enclosed within a wide flowering border.

Just as needlework design of that time borrowed freely from such other contemporary arts as prints and engravings, it was almost inevitable that samplermakers were drawn to the exceptionally fine painted furniture produced in Baltimore's cabinet shops. Of particular importance were the famous cabinetmakers, John and Hugh Finlay, who inspired this clever Baltimore school-

Detail of chair back, Baltimore, c. 1800, attributed to the cabinet shop of John and Hugh Finlay; painting of Rose Hill attributed to Francis Guy. Baltimore Museum of Art

mistress to include in her sampler designs landscapes virtually identical to those gracing the chairs and cabinets from their shop, which were probably painted by the renowned landscape painter Francis Guy (see above).[14]

Above all, it should not go unnoticed that many of the schools for girls in the city were, at one time or another, located on Gay Street, a most prestigious address at the center of a thriving cabinetmaking industry.[15]

It is important to note, however, that this body of exceptional Baltimore needlework reached its peak in popularity just as the fashion for similarly elaborate furniture was waning. It was not until at least 1819,[16] by which time production of lavishly painted furniture had diminished, that this unknown schoolmistress imitated the landscape designs appearing on these elegant, but no longer fashionable, pieces of furniture. Copying the original concept of depicting specific buildings or houses, this woman worked patterns that came to be accepted as fine needle art, and in textile circles are today recognized as the Baltimore Samplers.

CHARLOTTE COATES BOYD

The house depicted on the sampler worked by Charlotte Boyd (fig. 64) around 1826 is a duplicate of the one stitched on Sarah Wigart's sampler from the same year, which is identified on the back of the sampler as "St. Paul's Rectory, Baltimore."[17] The needleworked rendition is not an exact replica of the actual building on Cathedral and Saratoga streets, for the shape of the upper-story windows has been curved (see left). The two girls probably attended the same school, for their samplers were worked in a very similar format.

The green-shaded silk lawn of the Boyd sampler is adorned with charming ladies and animals, finely worked in padded satin

Detail of St. Paul's Rectory in painting by Thomas Ruckle (c. 1776–1853). Maryland Historical Society, Baltimore

64.

Detail of chair back, Baltimore, c. 1815. The palm tree to the right of this oriental scene is a familiar sampler motif. Private collection

stitches. The long-leafed palm tree, frequently found on samplers of the period, was probably inspired by oriental scenes found on eighteenth-century decorated wallpaper, porcelain, and contemporary Baltimore painted furniture (see above).

Charlotte Coates Boyd may have been the third daughter of Joseph and Elizabeth Boyd, who were married in 1800.[18] Joseph Boyd conducted business as a hatter at various addresses in Old Town, Baltimore. Charlotte Boyd married Lewis C. Jordan of Portsmouth, Virginia, in Norfolk on October 17, 1837.[19]

ELIZABETH BLYDEN

The building on Elizabeth Blyden's memorial sampler (fig. 65) has yet to be identified, although it may represent a naive version

Home of Robert Rose, Silver Lake, Pennsylvania, engraving, 1816. Baltimore schoolmistresses often borrowed images from engravings, such as this one, for their sampler designs. Library of Congress, Washington, D. C.

of the two-steepled First Presbyterian Church that dominated the skyline of Baltimore during the early years of the nineteenth century (see page 138); this church is prominently featured in several of Francis Guy's landscape paintings of the city.[20] The embroidered structure is certainly intended to represent a church, for there is a tiny bronze silk cross touching the lintel above the doors. No drawing or engraving has yet been found that shows a direct frontal view of the church, which in reality had two separate doorways, rather than one, and towers that stood to the side of the main building, not behind it. An identical sampler, stitched with wool strands rather than silk, was worked by Martha Jane Smith in 1839 (see page 138), adding to the puzzle.[21]

Elizabeth was one of two daughters born to John Blyden and Sarah Muir (whose first husband had died). Muir's family may once have lived on the Eastern Shore of Maryland.[22] The Blydens kept a tavern and grocery market in Fells Point, near the waterfront at Lancaster and Bond, and later at the Horse Market on Swan Street.[23] Elizabeth married John Malone, a farmer, in 1838.[24]

The couple lived with his aunt, Ann (or Nancy) Dorman, on her plantation on Maryland's Eastern Shore, with their six children. When Nancy Dorman died in 1850, John Malone was allowed lifetime use of the plantation. Upon his death it became the property of John Samuel, their oldest child.[25]

Sometime before 1870, Elizabeth and three of her children died, for their names have vanished from public records. In July of 1869, John Malone was sued for sixty-five dollars by Dr. Francis Marion Slemons of Salisbury.[26]

Elizabeth Blyden Malone is probably buried in the Banks/Malone Family Graveyard on the old plantation grounds close by Wicomico Creek, although there remains only one bleached wooden marker of the original six. It is inscribed "Mary L. Marthy Malone," probably Elizabeth's grandchild.[27]

ELIZA PICKET

The sampler stitched by Eliza Picket in Baltimore, 1825 (fig. 66), when she was ten years old, is the second of her two known needlework samplers.[28] This embroidery may hold the key to the identification of at least one of the schools where this unique style of Baltimore architectural sampler originated, for Eliza may have attended the Adelphi Academy on Gay Street in Baltimore.

Eliza Picket, born 1814, was probably the daughter of John and Elizabeth Rea Picket.[29] In 1823, they are shown in the *Baltimore City Directory* to be living on Gay Street, north of Orange alley. John was a merchant tailor and Eliza a milliner.

In the directories of 1824 and 1827, Elizabeth Picket, perhaps by then a widow, resided at 20 Gay Street.

65.

Detail of chair back, Baltimore, c. 1815, painted by John Barnhart in the cabinet shop of Thomas S. Renshaw, 37 South Gay Street. These lavishly gilded Baltimore chairs probably influenced the sampler designs of local schoolmistresses. Los Angeles County Museum of Art

Sampler worked by Martha Jane Smith, Baltimore, 1839, wool on linen. Maryland Historical Society, Baltimore

First Presbyterian Church, Baltimore, drawing by Benjamin Latrobe, 1832. Enoch Pratt Free Library, Baltimore

66.

Late in August of 1821, John W. Picket and Albert Picket advertised in the *Baltimore American,* announcing various academic subjects offered at their Adelphi School. The newly opened "Female Department" was to be located at 20 South Gay Street and the "Male Department" at 29 North Gay Street.

On August 28, they advertised for an instructress to teach the "ornamental" subjects; parents may have been put off by the "academic" subjects, preferring more fashionable, "polite accomplishments" for their daughters.

Within a week, on September 4, 1821, they proudly announced the engagement of an unidentified instructress, well-qualified to teach "various descriptions of needle-work."

This remarkable series of newspaper advertisements (see page 140) makes it possible to assume that this anonymous schoolmistress may have been the one responsible for the exceptional, almost unparalleled, sampler design that flourished for twenty years, from the 1820s to the 1840s. It was a style that at some point appears to have become a favorite locally, embraced by several Baltimore schoolmistresses and featuring buildings in the city.[30]

Until more solid evidence comes to light, it may be that Eliza Picket worked her sampler at the school on Gay Street, a school very likely conducted by a member of the family. Recent research reveals that around 1830 Albert and John Picket (although not Eliza's father, John W. Picket) kept a school for girls, the Cincinnati Female Institution, in Cincinnati, Ohio.[31]

It remains for future researchers to verify whether or not these characteristically unique Baltimore samplers, stitched over a span of two decades, were designed by the imaginative schoolmistress at the Adelphi School on Gay Street.

NOTES:

1. Bolton and Coe, *American Samplers*, 208, opp. 254.

2. *Baltimore American and Commercial Daily Advertiser*, July 19, 1822.

3. Betty Ring, "Maryland Map Samplers," in catalogue, *1986 Maryland Antiques Show*, (Baltimore: Maryland Historical Society, 1986), 105.

4. Columbia Academy, kept by Catharine Groombridge, is interesting to follow through newspaper advertisements and other sources. Between 1800 and 1804 she moved to Baltimore from Philadelphia, where she had kept a school for girls.

Her school opened in Baltimore in September of 1804. The Columbia Academy was originally located at the corner of East and Calvert. By 1809, she had hired twelve assistants, and in 1812, she moved to 18 Bank Street. In June of 1813, the school was at 24 North Gay, a street of schools for both boys and girls, and cabinetmakers (*Baltimore American*, August 31, 1807; August 22, 1809; August 27 1812; June 30, 1813).

After the death of her husband William—an English landscape painter who is frequently compared to his contemporary, Francis Guy—in 1811, Catharine Groombridge continued to appear in the city directories until 1815, conducting a young ladies' academy on Calvert Street opposite the Court House.

In *Four Late Eighteenth-Century Anglo-American Landscape Painters* (Worcester, MA: American Antiquarian Society, 1943), J. Hall Pleasants reveals a partial list of the inventory of William Groombridge's estate: three violins, a violoncello, two clarinets, three old piano-fortes, and music, valued at $235. These items were concluded to be for school use. Such documentation makes it clear that Groombridge's students were offered extensive musical instruction, as well as Spanish and Italian (*Baltimore American*, August 29, 1810), and ornamental needlework including the use of threads of gold and silver (*Baltimore American*, September 13, 1808).

Catharine Groombridge, an amateur painter, exhibited at least one work of art at the Second Exhibition at the Philadelphia Academy of Fine Arts in 1812. It is presumed that she closed the school in 1816, as she is no longer listed in the city directories after this year. She probably moved to Jamaica, where she lived until her death (Pleasants, *Four Late Eighteenth-Century Painters*, 32, 40). For a long while, I suspected that Groombridge was the schoolmistress responsible for the Baltimore Samplers.

5. Betty Ring, "Print Work: a Silk-Wrought Deception," in *1980 Theta Charity Antiques Show* (Houston, TX: Theta Charity, 1980), 10–15, fn. 2. Catharine Groombridge advertised in Philadelphia, October 13, 1800, that she would instruct print work in her school. Print work was an embroidery technique specifically designed to resemble the sepia tones of an engraving. Mrs. Ring aptly describes this needlework skill as that which so closely simulates an uncolored engraving as to be visually indistinguishable from ink upon paper, except under the closest scrutiny. Usually worked on silk or satin grounds, these finely wrought scenes declined in fashion about 1820. Apparently Baltimore school teachers were seldom required to instruct this tedious work, for print work rarely appears in advertisements there.

6. *Baltimore American*, August 17, 1821.

7. Ibid., August 22, 1809.

8. Ibid., August 16, 1811.

9. Ibid., August 18, 1810. See also Garrett, "American Samplers and Needlework Pictures, Part 2," 695, 699.

10. *Baltimore American*, July 18, 1807, and July 25, 1809. After Mr. Baconais's death in 1817, Madam Baconais conducted the school (*Baltimore American*, August 27, 1818).

11. Ibid., August 31, 1812.

12. This group of at least sixteen samplers includes those worked from 1820 to 1839: "Henrietta Gro . . a . . " (possibly Groverman, the daughter of Anthony and Henrietta W. Delius), c. 1820, private collection; "Baltimore Hospital" sampler, c. 1820, collection, Maryland Historical Society, Baltimore; Ann Marie Kreps, 1822, private collection (thanks to the Hampton National Historic Site, Towson, MD, for this information); Mary Ann Craft, 1822, collection, Museum of the Daughters of the American Revolution, Washington, D.C.; Mary Ann Kennedy, 1823 (private collection; see Bolton and Coe, *American Samplers*, 184); Mary Ann Armstrong, two Baltimore samplers, 1824 (private collections; see Bolton and Coe, *American Samplers*, 123); Ann Woodward, "House on Fayette Street" sampler, 1824 (private collection; see Bolton and Coe, *American Samplers*, 244); Eliza Picket, 1825 (private collection; see fig. 66 and Bolton and Coe, opp. 254); Sarah Ann Wigart, 1826 (collection, Maryland Historical Society, Baltimore); Martha Ann Cooper, 1826 (Bolton and Coe, *American Samplers*, 143); Mary Davis, 1826 (location unknown); Charlotte Coates Boyd, c. 1826 (fig. 64); Margaret Boyd, 1827, possibly related to Charlotte (private collection; see Bolton and Coe, *American Samplers*, 130); Elizabeth Blyden, 1829 (fig. 65); Martha Jane Smith, 1839 (collection, Maryland Historical Society, Baltimore); and Margaret Jane McGuire, "Maryland Hospital"

J. W. AND A. PICKETS'
SCHOOLS.
Female Department,
No. 20 SOUTH GAY-ST.
COURSE OF INSTRUCTION.
1. *Department of Language*—Spelling, Reading. English Grammar, Rhetoric, Composition, Moral Philosophy, &c.
2. *Geographical and Historical Department.*—Ancient and Modern Geography, Ancient and Modern History, Mapping, use of the Globes, &c.
3. *Mathematical Department.*—Arithmetic, Book-keeping, Geometry, &c.
4. *Department of Penmanship*—Plain and Ornamental writing.

An Instructress Wanted.
A LADY who is qualified to GOVERN, and to TEACH the ornamental branches IN PARTICULAR, is wanted in ADELPHI SCHOOL. No one need apply who does not wish a *permanent situation*; and who can produce the most *unquestionable* recommendations.

The Principals, considering themselves responsible to their friends and patrons for the fulfilment of Scholastic duties, are desirous of obtaining such help as will be satisfactory to their respective employers. The grand object in view is to adopt and pursue such modes of government and inculcation, as from experience have been found to be best calculated to ensure the greatest possible degree of mental and *moral* improvement, and thereby, secure to the youth under their charge, an equivalent for their time and money. Whoever may engage in Adelphi School, must delight in teaching "the young idea how to shoot," and be *attentive* and *industrious*. Apply at No. 20 South Gay street.
JOHN W. PICKET,
ALBERT PICKET.
au 29   eo1m

Above and opposite:
A series of advertisements published in the *Baltimore American and Commercial Daily Advertiser* by J. W. and A. Picket, in August and September of 1821: first announcing their academic curriculum and the opening of the "Female Department" of their Adelphi School; then advertising for a teacher of "ornamental subjects;" and then announcing the engagement of such a teacher

sampler, c. 1840 (private collection; see Ring, *American Needlework Treasures*, 87).

This impressive list of related Baltimore samplers was compiled with the kind assistance of Betty Ring. I am indebted to her for her information and suggestions.

13. Ring, *American Needlework Treasures*, 51.

14. Stiles Tuttle Colwill, *Francis Guy, 1760–1820* (Baltimore, MD: Museum and Library of Maryland History, Maryland Historical Society, 1981), 24. Colwill theorizes that Francis Guy, landscape painter of the period, worked for a short time in 1804 for the cabinetmakers Hugh and John Finlay, decorating chair crest rails, settees, and pier tables, examples of which may be seen today at the Baltimore Museum of Art and the Maryland Historical Society, Baltimore.

I believe that Mr. Colwill is correct in this assumption. It also seems likely that this unknown Baltimore schoolmistress was influenced by his work and applied it to her own.

15. Although most schools for girls neglected to include their addresses in the *Baltimore American* advertisements taken out between 1800 and 1830, it appears clear that most of the schoolrooms were clustered around the neighborhood of Gay Street and Frederick, Fayette, Saratoga, and Baltimore streets. Countless academies for both boys and girls were located in the area, such as the school of Mrs. Groombridge in 1813, Frederick Bassford's in 1817, the Moody school in 1819 and 1822, and the Adelphi Academy conducted by the Pickets in 1821.

16. William Voss Elder III, *Baltimore Painted Furniture: 1800–1840* (Baltimore, MD: Baltimore Museum of Art, 1972), 9, 15. See also Skinner catalogue, Bolton Gallery, Bolton, MA, 1305, January 13, 1990, lot 265. The sampler by Elizabeth Ireland (collection, Betty Ring) names Mrs. Lyman as teacher.

17. The Wigart sampler is in the collection of the Maryland Historical Society, Baltimore. A modern photograph of the rectory may be seen in John Dorsey and James D. Dilts, *A Guide to Baltimore Architecture* (Cambridge, MD: Tidewater Publishers, 1973), 40. See also Sotheby's, New York, catalogue, *Americana*, 4408, July 10 and 11, 1980, lot 455. A nineteenth-century painting by Thomas Ruckle of St. Peter's Catholic Church, Baltimore, includes a contemporary version of the rectory on the left.

18. Robert Barnes, *Maryland Marriages,1778–1800* (Baltimore, MD: Genealogical Pub. Co., 1978), 23. See also *Baltimore City Directory*, 1819–1830.

19. *Baltimore American*, October 31, 1837.

20. Colwill, *Francis Guy*, 49.

21. The Smith sampler is in the collection of the Maryland Historical Society, Baltimore; I am in-

A CARD.

J. W. & A. PICKET announce to their friends and the public, that they have engaged an INSTRUCTRESS who is well qualified to superintend not only the manners and morals of *female pupils*, but also their instruction in the various descriptions of needle-work.

In addition to the branches of English Literature, enumerated in a former advertisement, the FRENCH LANGUAGE will be taught, and strictly attended to, by a French gentleman, who is both competent and experienced.

Music, Drawing, &c. will also receive due attention.

Application to be made at No. 20 South Gay-street. se 4 T d1m

debted to Betty Ring for bringing this to my attention.

22. Robert Barnes, *Marriages and Deaths from Baltimore Newspapers, 1796–1816*, (Baltimore, MD: Genealogical Pub. Co., 1978), 29. See also *Baltimore American*, September 25, 1810. *Federal Census, Baltimore, Maryland*, 1830, reveals two daughters, ages ten and sixteen.

23. *Baltimore City Directory*, 1827, 1829.

24. *Princess Anne Herald*, September 4, 1838.

25. *Will Book, Princess Anne Court Records, Wicomico County, Maryland*: 5, 1837–1859.

26. *Federal Census, Upper Trappe, Maryland*, 1860. See also *No. 2 Folios, Princess Anne Court Records, Wicomico County, Maryland*, 1870, 253, 254. Recorded November 3, 1870, the case was brought against John D. Malone by Dr. Slemons on July 2, 1869. The amount in question was sixty-five dollars and must have been for medical services rendered to the Malone family. John Malone, having lost his wife and children through sickness, refused to pay their doctor. When Slemons won the case in court, it was settled by Malone's son, John Samuel Malone.

27. John E. Jacob, *Graveyards and Gravestones of Wicomico* (Salisbury, MD: Salisbury Advertiser, 1971), 1, 55. The use of wooden markers continued past the turn of the century, although few exist today. Some were carved of cedar or cypress.

28. Eliza Picket worked a six-alphabet sampler dated 1823 when she was nine years old, probably her first effort; see Bolton and Coe, *American Samplers*, 208.

29. Elizabeth Rea was the youngest daughter of George Rea of Baltimore; see Barnes, *Marriages and Deaths from Baltimore Newspapers, 1796–1816*, 254. See also Dielman File, Maryland Historical Society, Baltimore.

30. At least sixteen samplers of similar format have been identified as belonging to this body of work; see n. 12.

31. Sue Studebaker, *Ohio Samplers, Schoolgirl Embroideries, 1803–1850* (Lebanon, OH: Warren County Historical Society, 1988), 57.

67. MARY ANN ASBERY (b. 1805)
Probably Virginia, 1818
Wool and silk threads on linen
(3o threads to the inch)
Cross-stitches
18½ x 10¼ in. (47 x 26 cm)

Inscription: *Live Je us live and let it be |My life to die*
for love of thee|And grant my eyes one day to see|The sweet
reward of love in thee
Mary Ann Asberys|work|aged.|13|years|1818

During the eighteenth and early nineteenth centuries, a few wool embroidered samplers were worked in parts of Virginia, Kentucky, and Pennsylvania. The practice of embroidering with wool threads, however, was not common. Mary Ann Asbery's wool stitches have been embellished with small amounts of glossy silk that her schoolmistress would have provided.[1]

The embroidery patterns shown here, such as the flower basket and the twin wreaths enclosing her name and age, suggest a possible Quaker influence, although the winged cherub stitched above the date is not identified with Quaker needlework. The small ship and anchor imposed above the pictorial scene, an uncommon American motif, are reminiscent of English sampler embroidery. There is evidence that Mary Ann Asbery lived in Tazewell County, Virginia.[2] She may be the Mary Ann Asbery who, at the age of sixteen, married John Brooks on May 31, 1821.[3]

NOTES:

1. Krueger, *Gallery of American Samplers*, 16.
2. John Newton Harman, *Annals of Tazewell County, Virginia*, vol. 1 (Richmond, VA: W.C. Hill Printing Co., 1922), 67.
3. *Marriage Records, Tazewell County.* This information is courtesy Nellie White Bundy, director of the Historic Crab Orchard Museum and Pioneer Park, Inc., Tazewell, VA. I am grateful for her kind assistance.

67.

68. JANE LIKENS (1812–1880)
Shepherdstown, (West) Virginia, 1822
Silk threads on linen (26 threads to the inch)
Rice, chain, and cross-stitches
21½ x 16 in. (54.6 x 40.6 cm)

Inscription: *Virtues the chiefest beauty of the minb/The*
noblest ornament of human kinb/Virtues our safe guarb
anb our guibing star/That stirs up reason when our
senses err
Jane Likens is my/Name virginia is my/Station shepards
twon/Is my bwelling place &/Christ is my salvaio/n
Jane Likens workeb this inthe eleventh year/of her age
082-[last number removed]

Schoolmistress: probably Elizabeth Pierce

During the spring of 1822, Jane Likens of Virginia was diligently working her needle in and out of a crumpled linen square. At the same time, the *Farmer's Repository*, staunchly favoring education for both sexes, admonished parents to:

> Keep [their] children at school if possible, and take care not to find fault against the school master in their presence. Some people are always complaining of the school master or mistress. Let the school be ever so well kept they will be dissatisfied. If your children complain ten chances to one they are in the wrong and should you wish to injure them you cannot do it more effectually than to join with them against their master.[1]

Reminiscent of schoolgirl embroideries stitched throughout the colonies, Jane's sampler is based on the band patterns and deeply arcaded floral motifs of another age, enclosed within a traditional strawberry border. The terraced ground, fringed with an ascending row of pines, is topped by a brick Georgian house—a sampler format that may have originated in the Delaware River Valley. An early version of this style may be seen on Elizabeth Stine's Philadelphia sampler (fig. 13).

Jane Likens completed her designs and alphabets with a certain degree of precision. However, within the several lines of the verse and the inscriptions that follow, she reveals a difficulty in forming particular letters and spacing the words properly. In several instances, the letter *b* has been substituted for *d*, as in the words *mind* and *kind*. Following each of these, she has attempted to stitch, in black, a capital *J*, apparently to begin working the word *Jane*. One of these letters has been inscribed in reverse.

In addition, Jane has exhibited some confusion stitching the date, for she has inscribed in pale buff silk a zero instead of a one: 082-. The last number was removed in later years to disguise her

actual age, evidence that the samplermaker lived to maturity. An intermixing of the black silk threads with pale beige has made a portion of this strip virtually invisible.

Many of these miscalculations could be attributed to youthful fingers, or the lack of close supervision, for similar stitching errors are seen on an infinite number of American samplers. However, Jane's needlework betrays many of the classic symptoms of the learning disability called dyslexia. If such was the case, this suggests her embroidered sampler lettering was learned with frustration, and her difficulty reading would have shadowed her later years.

In spite of the dearth of southern schoolgirl samplers, schoolmistresses were apparently available to affluent parents. In local Jefferson County newspapers, teachers of private schools advertised a variety of needlework classes, academic subjects, and other polite accomplishments. Schools for children, probably young men, were well established by 1762, including German language schools. The earliest church records in Jefferson County were written in German.[2]

In the art of samplermaking, however, Jefferson County lagged behind its northern neighbors. In June 1778, Captain Alexander Dandridge of Jefferson County met young Sally Wister and her family, who lived along the Wissahickon Creek in Pennsylvania while the British occupied Philadelphia, admiring her sampler,

An early engraving of life in western Virginia. Library of Congress, Washington, D. C.

68.

which was in full view: "He wished I would teach the Virginians some of my needle wisdom," she wrote. "They were the laziest girls in the world." In typical schoolgirl fashion, Sally also described Dandridge: "His person [was] more elegantly formed than any I ever saw; tall and commanding, his features extremely pleasing."[3]

Although no specific female academy has yet been identified in Shepherdstown, where Jane Likens attended school, two other young girls, Elizabeth Towne and Lucretia C. Reynolds, inscribed the name of the town on their samplers, dated 1820 and 1822.[4] The absence of either surname on the 1820 census suggests that they may have been pupils of a boarding school in Shepherdstown.[5]

In September of 1811, the Charles Town Academy notified readers of the *Farmer's Repository* that they had "engaged a lady to instruct young ladies in needlework."[6] Mr. and Mrs. Peerce's Young Ladies' Academy of Charles Town, in 1813, offered all the useful branches of needlework and polite literature.

An obscure reference in Danske Dandridge's history of the region informs us that around 1791, John Pearce returned to teach school in Shepherdstown, "for a span of more than thirty years."[7] While it is evident the academy was actually located in Charles Town, Dandridge and other historical writers treat the two neighboring towns with a great degree of informality, as if they were one. It is also reasonable to assume that John Pearce and Mr. Peerce are one and the same.

Traditionally, as has been noted, schools tended to be impermanent. In this instance, it is possible that the school was moved to smaller, more satisfactory quarters, in the village of Shepherdstown, for by 1820, Elizabeth Peerce (or Pierce) was a widow. The census records that one boy and two girls under the age of ten were in residence at her home, probably boarding students. Such circumstantial evidence makes it reasonable to assume that schoolmistress Elizabeth Pierce instructed Jane Likens in the needle arts, and she may also have enlightened Elizabeth Towne and Lucretia Reynolds.[8]

Maria Jane Likens, born December 11, 1812, was the daughter of Thomas Likens and Mary Richardson. Sometime after 1815, they moved to neighboring Charles Town, where Thomas Likens, a prosperous shoemaker, became very active in the affairs of the Presbyterian Church. In 1820, there were twenty-two persons living under his protection.[9]

On June 19, 1836, Maria Jane married Thomas Alexander Moore (b.1803), a widower with a young son.[10] They became parents to six children. In 1840, Thomas Moore was appointed clerk of the court of Jefferson County, a position of great esteem, which he held until his death in 1889. It was in his courtroom that the insurgent John Brown was tried and found guilty of treason. During the Civil War, Thomas Moore, as clerk, was responsible for the removal of the most valuable papers and court records, taking them to Lexington in a horse-drawn wagon for safekeeping.[11]

Maria Jane Likens Moore died on May 5, 1880, at the age of sixty-eight.[12]

NOTES:

1. Farmer's notice in *Farmer's Repository, Charles Town,* February 19, 1823.
2. Danske Dandridge, *Historic Shepherdstown* (Charlottesville, VA: Michie Company, 1910), 53. See also *Journal of the Jefferson County Historical Society,* vol. 1 (December 1935): 28. Mose Hoge's school for boys opened in May of 1792. See also Betty Ring, "For Persons of Fortune Who Have Taste," *Journal of Early Southern Decorative Arts,* vol. 3, no. 2 (November 1977): 1–3. Ring discusses the puzzling absence of any recognizable body of Southern needlework, citing climate, an agrarian society, and the tutorial system of educating children as possible causes. The lack of competition within a classroom situation, as in New England for example, may explain the absence of Southern needlework.
3. Albert Cook Meyers, ed., *Sally Wister's Journal, 1777–1778* (Philadelphia, PA: Ferris and Leach, 1902), 159. See also Dandridge, *Historic Shepherdstown*, 313, 314. Sally Wister's sampler is in the collection of the Philadelphia Museum of Art, PA; see Ring, "Samplers and Pictorial Needlework," 1424.
4. Bolton and Coe, *American Samplers*, 213, 231.
5. *Journal of the Jefferson County Historical Society,* vol. 1 (December 1935): 29.
6. *Farmer's Repository*, October 4, 1811, and October 21, 1813. I am indebted to Frank Horton, former director of the Museum of Early Southern Decorative Arts, Winston-Salem, NC, for bringing this important newspaper advertisement (October 21) to my attention. It is the key to the puzzle.

The October 21 advertisement ends with the words "For further particulars enquire of Dr. Cramer, or of Mr. Peerce at the Academy." Dr. Samuel Cramer became Jane Likens's father-in-law. The use of Dr. Cramer (the town's most prominent physician) as a reference would have assured the respectability of Mr. and Mrs. Peerce. In the census of 1820, Dr. Cramer is shown to have three daughters under the age of ten, and three between the ages of ten and sixteen. These older girls were probably students of Mr. and Mrs. Peerce in 1813, in Charles Town. The younger children may have attended school with Jane in Shepherdstown.

The advertisement also proclaims that "needlework will be taught by Mrs. Peerce, to which she will add, if required painting in water, and body colors." A word here about the unusual reference to "body colors." In the *American Dictionary of the English Language* by Noah Webster, 1828, under the word "body," definition twelve, we find this explanation: "Among painters, colors bear a body, when they are capable of being ground so fine, and of being mixed so entirely with oil, as to seem only a very thin oil of the same color." With this in mind we can then interpret the advertisement to mean that Mrs. Peerce taught both watercolor and oil painting. This terminology, however, is unique. It is the only time I have seen it used in the hundreds of newspaper advertisements that I have studied in documenting this material.

7. Dandridge, *Historic Shepherdstown*, 340.

8. *Federal Census, Shepherdstown, Virginia, 1820*.

9. Maria Jane Likens Moore's date of birth and death are recorded on her gravestone in Edgehill Cemetery, Charles Town. The remains of Thomas Likens and Mary Richardson Likens were interred at the foot of their daughter's grave. According to the *Martinsburg Gazette*, April 20, 1843, Thomas was sixty-six years old when he died. His marker, incorrectly inscribed 1750, should more accurately read 1777.

The Likens property at 141 and 142 German Street, Shepherdstown, was brought to my attention by Jean A. Elliott, public-service librarian at Shepherd College, Shepherdstown, VA, in her letter dated August 14, 1975. I am indebted to Jean Elliott for her kind assistance.

It is difficult to determine the exact number of children in the Likens family; see *Federal Census, Charles Town, Virginia*, 1820, 1850. See also Millard Keshler Bushong, *Historic Jefferson County* (Boyce, VA: Carr Publishing Co., 1972), 117, 120, 216, 570, and 571. See also *Farmer's Repository*, February 21, 1821.

10. *Martinsburg Gazette*, July 7, 1836. I am indebted to the clerks, particularly Sarah Humston, in the Court House at Charles Town, WV, for their expert assistance, and to the late Rev. Lester Link, for helping me solve the problem of Jane's identification. Her name, Maria Jane Likens, had been changed to Maria Ann Likens when the records were copied long ago. It was Link who turned to the original documents to find the error.

11. *Martinsburg Gazette*, July 7, 1836. See also Bushong, *Historic Jefferson County*, 213. I am indebted to Ann Moore Cross, Jane's great-great-granddaughter, who recalled Jane's name as being pronounced "Mar-eye-a" rather than "Mar-ee-a" Jane.

Ann tracked me all over Jefferson County with fragments of information, for which I thank her.

12. Edgehill Cemetery, Charles Town, West Virginia.

69. MARTHA MULFORD (1796–1868)
New Carlisle, Clark County, Ohio, 1824
Silk threads on linen (26 threads to the inch)
Tent, outline, flame, queen, couched satin, and cross-stitches
17½ x 18 inches (44.4 x 45.7 cm)

Inscription: *Martha Mulford was born june first 1796 Ohio/1824*

Schoolmistress: Martha Meek Mulford

Unlike most samplers that represent schoolgirl embroideries, this rare, flawlessly stitched example was unquestionably worked as a model for use in schoolroom instruction. Its creator, Martha Mulford, was twenty-eight years old, married, and, as we learn from her handmade, carefully preserved arithmetic workbook, an intelligent and accomplished Ohio schoolmistress.[1]

Martha's unblemished, beautifully designed sampler is shown in its true, original colors. Never intended for framing or display, untouched by harmful rays of sunlight, this sampler was destined to be copied by her students. Quite remarkably, there is no permanent crease marring the linen, evidence that Martha's embroidery has been kept in flat, unfolded condition for over 150 years.

Clearly, Martha Mulford was herself knowledgeable in the intricacies of samplermaking, for this handsomely bordered example reflects the influence of childhood needlework instruction. Scattered across the linen are the paired birds, miniature floral designs, and a delicate, sprightly wreath—all traditional and readily recognizable Quaker motifs. Dominating the pictorial format are large, fluffy carnation sprigs, worked in mirror image, which appear to have their origin in the smaller flowers of similar shape favored by Quaker schoolmistresses working in the vicinity of the Delaware River Valley, such as those decorating the sampler worked by Abigail Passmore Yarnall (fig. 58).[2]

The brick red, five-bay house, with its ornamental fencing, ribbed gates, and green-shaded lawn adorned with sheep and birds, indicates the influence of needlework accomplished in schools for girls in New Jersey and Pennsylvania.[3] Related samplers of similar style are those worked by Elizabeth Stine, 1793

69.

(fig. 13), and Sarah Elwell, 1826 (fig. 57), both of Philadelphia, and Hannah Steelman of New Jersey, 1834 (fig. 61). Hannah's three-sided border makes use of queen-stitched strawberries, as does Martha's sampler.

Martha Mulford's sampler motifs chronicle the migration of sampler motifs from specific regions in the east to western parts of the new United States. Across overland trails and up the Ohio River, traditional embroidery patterns, along with other goods and services, were carried directly into the middle-western region of the country. In order to compete with the latest fashions, village schoolmistresses quickly adapted the patterns for schoolgirl needlework, just as they had in other sections of the country decades before. Recent research confirms that Quaker schools were established in Ohio as early as 1803.[4]

Clues of this nature allow us to speculate that either young Martha Meek attended a boarding school near Philadelphia, or that the Ohio schoolmistress who taught her embroidery, possibly a Quaker, may have once lived in that vicinity.

Martha Meek was born June 1, 1796, in North Bend, a river town in Hamilton County, Ohio.[5] She was one of two daughters born to John and Euphemi Meek or Meeks.[6] In 1830, the Meek family sold property in Clark County, Ohio, where they may have made their home.[7] There is, unfortunately, no record of Martha's marriage to Mulford.[8] It was, however, in the vicinity of New Carlisle that Martha Meek Mulford worked her sampler, kept a school for girls, and, on April 17, 1827, married David J. Cory.[9]

David's sister, Melissa Cory, born in Honey Creek, worked a modest alphabet sampler in 1825 when she was ten. It is possible Melissa worked her sampler under the instruction of schoolmistress Martha Mulford, for Honey Creek runs through New Carlisle, near Springfield. While the two embroideries have little in common, both samplers include the date of birth of the samplermaker, an infrequently stitched inscription.[10]

David Cory (b. 1801) was a very prominent judge, farmer, and dealer in real estate. After their marriage, Martha and David lived in Williams County, now part of Henry County, in Findlay Township where he owned some twenty-three hundred acres of land spreading across two counties. Cory was a "leading spirit in the projection, location and building of the Lake Erie & Western Railroad" and a member of the Methodist Church. In 1850, his real estate was valued at the enormous sum of sixty-two thousand dollars.[11]

Martha Meek Mulford Cory died on February 26, 1868, without issue.[12]

NOTES:

1. Martha Mulford's workbook is in my collection.
2. Ring, "Samplers and Pictorial Needlework," 1425–1427.
3. Ring, *American Needlework Treasures*, 38.
4. Studebaker, *Ohio Samplers*, 5, 6.
5. *Death Records, Hancock County, Ohio*, 1868, no. 86.
6. Martha Cory and her sister, Cynthia Edwards, were named in their father's will, presented for probate on June 8, 1833, Court of Clark County, Ohio.
7. *Deed Book, Clark County* G: 381, 382.
8. Marsh Mulford and Richard Mulford are recorded in *Federal Census, Cincinnati, Ohio*, 1817, and *Voters' Lists, Hamilton County, Ohio*, 1798 and 1799 (Cincinnati, OH: 1960), 49.
9. *A History of Hancock County, Ohio* (Chicago, IL: Warner, Beers and Co., 1886), 737. See also *Early Marriage Bonds of Ohio* (*Marriage Records, Clark County*, 1818–1865), copied by the Daughters of the American Revolution, compiled under the direction of Mrs. Stuart R. Bolin and Mrs. John S. Heaume, 161.
10. This sampler was brought to my attention by Gloria Allen, former director of the Museum of the Daughters of the American Revolution, Washington, D.C., to whom I am indebted. Documentation accompanying the sampler verifies that Melissa and David Cory were brother and sister. See also *History of Clark County, Ohio* (Chicago, IL: Warner, Beers and Co., 1881), 706.
11. D. B. Beardsley, *History of Hancock County, Ohio*, (Chicago, IL: Warner, Beers and Co., 1881): 311, 312. See also *Census Records, Findlay Township, Ohio*, 1850.

On a single page of paper, Martha Cory recorded their journey from Dayton, Ohio, to the Maumee and Lake Erie. With a team of horses, they followed Hull's Trail. "We were fifteen days on the road—or in the woods—for there was barely a road on the entire route," she wrote. Today it spans a distance of approximately eighty miles.
12 . Beardsley, *History of Hancock County*, 737. See also *Death Records, Hancock County, Ohio*, 1868, no. 86.

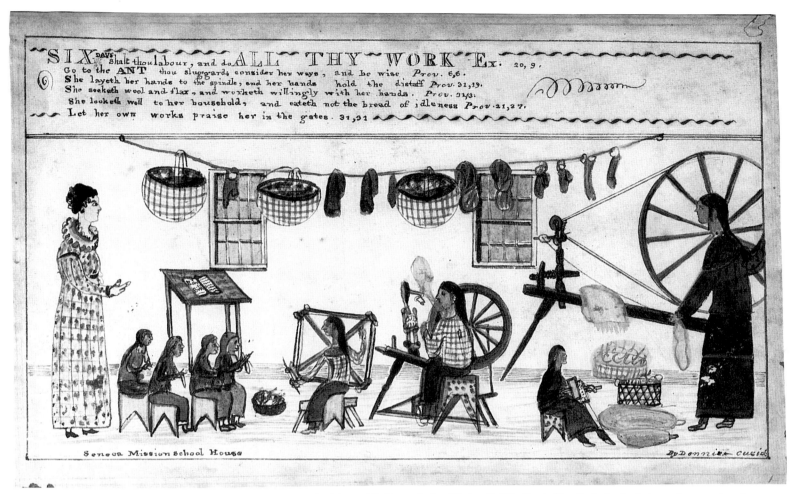

"Six days shalt thou labour and do all thy work," drawing by Dennis Cusick, c. 1827, Seneca Indian Mission, Buffalo Creek, New York. A schoolmistress instructs American Indian children in knitting, winding yarn, spinning flax, and carding and spinning wool. Sotheby's, New York

70. NANCY GRAVES (KU-TO-YI) (b. 1817)
Cherokee Mission, Dwight, Arkansas, 1828
Silk threads on linen (24 threads to the inch)
Cross-stitches
14 in. square (35.5 cm square)

Inscription: *Let western girls This sampler view/And viewing let them copy too/Learn well to mark the way thats/good/The path to glory and to God/ Whatsoever/thy hand finde/th to do do it with/thy might Eccl/Remember thy/Creator in the/days of thy/youth Eccl 12*
Wrought by/Nancy Graves/Cherokee Mission School Dwight/Arkansas july. 9./For Mr. Kingsbury. 1828.

Schoolmistress: missionary Ellen Stetsen (b. 1783)

As early samplers provide insight into the education for young girls of New England, so this rare sampler establishes without question the existence of schools for girls of American Indian heritage in the southwestern region of the young United States. Dated 1828, it was worked by Nancy Graves at the Cherokee Mission School in Dwight, Arkansas, making it the earliest surviving American Indian sampler yet to be identified.

The existence of Nancy's needlework allows us to focus on an aspect of women's education generally overlooked by historians, namely the mission school and missionary schoolmistress, who, in this instance, dedicated at least six years of her life to the welfare and instruction of young Cherokee girls.[1]

Through her relatively modest, though carefully worked, sam-

Dwight Mission, Arkansas, drawing by Asa Hitchcock, missionary, 1824. Houghton Library, Harvard University, Cambridge

pler, Nancy has issued a challenge to her western comrades, "Let western girls This sampler view/And viewing let them copy too."

Such was the intent, to promote this wholly foreign schoolgirl art from within a society more accustomed to an entirely different array of crafts. It is, in fact, rather astonishing that the art of inscribing alphabet letters with silk floss on a linen ground ever reached this geographically isolated part of the country.

Shortly before 1819, Tol-on-tus-ky,[2] chief of the Arkansas Cherokees, visited the well-established mission at Brainard, Georgia. He was immensely impressed by the accomplishments of the missionaries and determined that a settlement and school would vastly improve the lives of his own people, who lived on Illinois Bayou near present-day Russellville.[3]

Under the direction of the American Board of Commissioners for Foreign Missions, two ministers of the Congregational Church, Cephas Washburn, from Vermont, and Alfred Finney, his brother-in-law, accompanied by their wives and two young children, left their homes on November 19, 1819. Traveling by wagon, encountering illness and hardship, within a year they had selected a location for the mission, to be named Dwight,[4] and succeeded in opening the first school established in Arkansas Territory.[5]

The settlement grew rapidly, with a mill dam, grist mill, saw mill, and smokehouse. School instruction began long before the school buildings existed. The only accurate likeness that remains of the village was drawn by missionary Asa Hitchcock, in 1824 (see above).[6] The settlement was soon joined by two more competent missionaries, James Orr and Jacob Hitchcock of Massachusetts, and in December 1821, Ellen Stetson, Nancy Brown, and Asa Hitchcock arrived. It was Ellen Stetson who became the

schoolmistress, assuming the role of teacher and mother to the Indian girls committed to her care.[7] She was one of eleven children born to Thomas and Elizabeth Cook Stetson, of Kingston, Plymouth County, Massachusetts.[8]

The children were boarded within the compound, taught not only academic subjects but the religious principles of the missionaries. Washburn's plan was to prepare the minds of the children gradually so they would learn to be pleased with industrious habits and active life. By 1822, fifty children were enrolled in classes. Two years later, there were seventy-five or eighty-five students in the mission school, which had acquired a wide reputation for a high quality of instruction.[9] The plan for the education of girls included "spinning, weaving, sewing and the various kinds of labor in a well-regulated family."[10]

Before 1825, missionary teachers at Brainard had introduced marking on linen, that is, samplermaking, as an established branch of the educational program. The following letter was written by Nancy Taylor, one of fourteen students,[11] to an Indian mission pen pal:

Having been requested by my Teacher Miss Sawyer, I take my pen to address you. I have been informed that you were one of her scholars, & that you worked a sampler with a very fine border around it. I am learning to mark now, I have not finished marking yet.

I was born near Highwassee in a log cabbin, & the large tall trees shaded our dwelling. But now we live near the Chiccamogga river. There was some bushes. I went under them to cry. But mother would not take me home. And now I do not care about going home. Friday evening all the girls go to bathe. Where we go to bathe is a very pretty place. It is shady—Miss Sawyer sits on a log to see how we swim. The path which leads to the water where we go to bathe on the side is thick with berries. Saturday after washing and ironing and taking a little rest we four girls went to pick black berries for Miss Sawyer and our selvs.[12]

While reporting on the schools in the summer of 1827, Samuel Worcester wrote to Jeremiah Evarts in Brainard, indicating that a young woman described as being of "half blood" had been registered to enter Dwight Mission school, October 25, 1826. Her name was Ku-to-yi, or Nancy Graves. She was placed in the school's fifth class.[13]

Convinced that a teacher must possess boundless patience to be an instructor of "children of the forest," Washburn emphasized that teachers must be industrious, noting "every hour not usefully employed is simply thrown away."[14] Schoolmistress Ellen Stetson complied by preparing a remarkably detailed and historically important document, a personal characterization of each child under her tutelage (see page 153). At a time when such accounts were seldom recorded, she has listed the names of Nan-

Let western girls This sampler view
And viewing let them copy too
Learn well to mark the way that good
The path to glory and to God.

Wrought by
Nancy Graves
Cherokee Mission School Dwight
Arkansas July 9.

70.

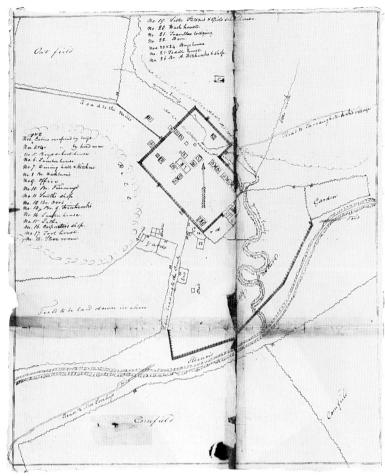

Plot plan of the Dwight Mission. Number 19 is described as the schoolhouse of Sister Ellen Stetson. Houghton Library, Harvard University, Cambridge

cy's classmates, their dispositions and personalities, ages, the length of time in attendance, and the particular curriculum offered each child. Faced, at times, with parental indifference and students who were naturally unaccustomed to the classroom setting, her impressions are nonetheless filled with hope and promise. The document contributes valuable information, previously unavailable, on these early mission schools.[15]

Sister Stetson writes that Nancy Graves was eleven years of age, attending classes half a day, studying reading, spelling, writing, and geography. She is described as being "a good scholar and very amiable. In many accounts the most promising girl in the school."

Little is known of Nancy Graves's ancestry, but an anonymous and meticulously detailed journal of the Dwight mission, now in the Houghton Library of Harvard University, reveals the existence of a Thomas Graves who was half-Cherokee and may have been Nancy's father. Described as "an infamous character," Graves was a Cherokee delegate and attended the treaty negotiations in Washington City when it was decided to relocate the tribe to new lands west of Fort Smith, Oklahoma.[16]

In order to compensate the tribe for their buildings, roads, and industriously cultivated land, it was necessary for Washburn to give an account of their value. In a letter to the Secretary of War, January 26, 1829, he described the school for girls as being two buildings, one, thirty by twenty-six feet, with four rooms, and a gallery occupied by the girls and the teacher, at $550, the other a framed house, twenty by twenty-four feet, accommodating the classroom, described as being well furnished, at $500. He sadly deplored the fact that the schools would have to close, recognizing that the dedicated work performed by the teaching staff would soon come to nought.[17]

It seems necessary to consider the circumstances surrounding the survival of the sampler itself. This, in fact, may be attributed to inspiration alone, for across the bottom of the needlework, in fading cross-stitches, Nancy was instructed to inscribe the words "For Mr. Kingsbury." With this inscription, the sampler became more than an alphabet sampler; it was transformed into a presentation piece—a gift bequeathed to Cyrus Kingsbury of Massachusetts, the first missionary to arrive in Brainard in 1816, and a man greatly admired by the Cherokee Nation.[18]

When the tribe was forced to move to Oklahoma, it seems possible the sampler was given to one of the retiring missionaries after the mission was abandoned. This token of affection for the beloved Mr. Kingsbury was then carefully glazed and framed— probably in Massachusetts.

We are exceedingly fortunate that this particular embroidery survived, for it gives us a rare opportunity to study an important, truly American schoolgirl sampler of great historic significance, from a region of our country where education for women has remained largely unexplored.

Detail of Sister Ellen Stetson's attendance list of Cherokee girls at the Dwight Mission School, 1827. She included the date the student enrolled, the number of months in attendance, and observations about the students. Nancy Graves is the second from the bottom. Houghton Library, Harvard University, Cambridge

NOTES:

1. Records reveal that Ellen Stetson arrived at Dwight in 1821; see Dorsey D. Jones, "Cephas Washburn and His Work in Arkansas," *Arkansas Historical Quarterly* vol. 3, no. 2 (Summer 1944): 131. The latest date recorded on the "teacher's report" appears to be 1827. It is possible that Stetson remained in Dwight, Arkansas, until the tribe, under a new treaty, moved to Fort Smith, Oklahoma, 1828; she may have traveled with them to the new settlement.

2. Tol-on-tus-ky is used in some references, Tahlontuskee in others.

3. John L. Ferguson and J. H. Atkinson, *Historic Arkansas* (Little Rock: Arkansas History Commission, 1966), 57–59.

4. Named in honor of Timothy Dwight, president of Yale University. Dwight deplored the neglect of female education, suggesting it was "high time that women should be considered less as pretty and more as rational and immortal beings" (Ring, *Let Virtue Be a Guide to Thee*, 7). He felt that children ought to be wise, virtuous, and useful. His strong opinions on education echoed those voiced in 1787 by Benjamin Rush of Philadelphia. Dwight died in 1817.

5. G. R. Turrentine, *Dwight Mission* (unpublished manuscript; Arkansas Valley Historical Papers, Russellville, April, 1962) no. 25: 2, 3. See also Jones, "Cephas Washburn," 127, 128.

Weak with fever, the missionaries arrived to find Chief Tol-on-tus-ky dead. They at first received a cool reception, but when the Indians understood the nature of their mission, they responded with great enthusiasm, and both missionaries were obliged to stand while each member of the tribe, including the women, greeted them and made them welcome. Turrentine suggests that this was the first PTA meeting ever held in Pope County.

6. Jones, "Cephas Washburn," 130, 132. See also Turrentine, *Dwight Mission*, 5.

7. Jones, "Cephas Washburn," 131. Schoolmistress Stetson's name appears under number nineteen on the Dwight plot map.

8. Family Archive Records, Family History Library of the Church of Jesus Christ of Latter-Day Saints, Salt Lake City, UT.

9. Jones, "Cephas Washburn," 130–133.

10. Ibid., 131.

11. *Dwight Mission Papers*, no. 349 (Houghton Library, Harvard University, Cambridge, MA). The girls named in the letter are Nancy Reece, Almira, Eleaner North, Sally Quaqua, Margaret McDonald, Catharine Spear, Mindwel W. Gould, Polly C. Quaqua, Lucy A. Campel, Sally Reece, Ann Busby, Lucy McPherson, and Lydia Huntly, along with the writer, Nancy Taylor.

12. Ibid. Miss Sawyer sent the letter to her superior, July 25, 1825, with the following notation: "I send this that you may see for yourself what the girls are doing at Brainard. The little girl, who wrote this is twelve years old—began to write last October."

13. *Dwight Mission Papers*, no. 349, and correspondence from Melanie Wisner, Houghton Library, Harvard University, February 28, 1984. I am indebted to Ms. Wisner for her dedicated assistance in interpreting these papers for the research on Nancy Graves.

14. Jones, "Cephas Washburn," 131, 132.

15. *Dwight Mission Papers*, no. 349.

16. John Lewis Ferguson, "William E. Woodruff and the Territory of Arkansas: 1819–1836" (unpublished manuscript; Oklahoma Historical Society, Oklahoma City, April 1960), 120, f. 20. Ferguson writes that Graves, who was part-Indian, murdered an Osage woman, with whom he was living, and her child in a "drunken frolick." Legally outside the jurisdiction of federal courts, he was released and compensated in the amount of twelve hundred dollars. "Bro. W.," whose impressions and travels are mentioned in the journal (possibly Samuel Worcester), divulges he had "free conversation with him [Graves] and that he has always been sorry for his crime and that he should not have committed [it] had he not been intoxicated."

On a hunting expedition with Graves and several other men one of his sons was captured and killed by members of the Osage tribe, who were recognized by impressions left by the unusually stitched soles of their moccasins. The bloodstained prints left little doubt that his son had been killed. The angry men were stilled by Graves's quiet words and judicious behavior.

17. Turrentine, "Dwight Mission," 7–9.

18. Jones, "Cephas Washburn," 125.

71. ABBIE ANN CARSWELL (b. 1845)
San Francisco, California, 1857
Silk threads on cotton or coarse linen, interwoven
with blue warp threads (26 threads to the inch)
Cross-stitches
5 x 14⅝ in. (12.7 x 44.7 cm)

Inscription: *Abbie Ann Carswell nine yrs/old. San
Francisco Cal. Union St./ Dec 4. 1857. To my
Grandma.*

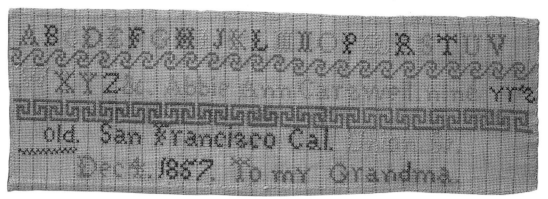

71.

By the middle of the nineteenth century, samplermaking was a lost art. Elegant pictorial stitchery on linen, the hallmark of the fashionable boarding school for girls, had become a thing of the past. Even hand sewing, or plain work, was losing ground to the increasingly popular sewing machine. Public schooling for women was widespread, and elementary education was now within reach of most levels of society, even in the far western regions of the United States.

This sampler worked by Abbie Ann Carswell in San Francisco in 1857 was part of her needlework instruction at the Union Street School, a public institution located near the intersection of Montgomery and Union streets. Abbie was taught by several public teachers, Lizzie and Kate Kennedy, Hannah Marks, Sarah Loring, L. H. Morgan, E. S. Comyns, and Elizabeth Turner. In1859, there were 231 children in attendance at the Union Street School, known as as a public or common school. Sewing was not listed as part of the curriculum.[1]

Abbie has dedicated her sampler to her grandmother, who probably did not live in California. Worked on coarse linen, it was woven with a blue warp thread at every tenth row. During this period canvas marked in this practical manner facilitated the counting of threads, a method used for working the colored, paper-charted, ornamental embroidery called Berlin Work. Stylishly fashionable, decorative and garishly colored, Berlin Work was most often stitched with commercially dyed wool threads.[2]

Abbie Ann Carswell, one of two daughters of John D. Carswell and Mary Ann Stewart, was born in Concord, New Hampshire, in 1845.[3] Sometime before 1860, John Carswell, a printer, moved his family to San Francisco, where Mary kept a boarding house at 20 Sansom, on Telegraph Hill, near the Union Street School.[4]

Abbie Ann Carswell married Herbert Baldwin of Sacramento on July 30, 1868, in the Green Street Chapel in San Francisco.[5]

NOTES:

1. *San Francisco Municipal Common School Report, 1859–1860, 64–66,* and *Common School Report, 1861–1862,* 205. With 980 registered students, the average daily attendance at Union School in 1861 was 510, "occasioned by the severe rains of our winter season and by the the very prevalent practice of parents retaining their children at home or in their places of business, to aid them in their work."
2. S. F. A. Caulfield and Blanche C. Saward, *The Dictionary of Needlework* (London: L. Upcott Gill, 1882), 89.
3. *Marriage Records, New Hampshire,* 1844. See also *Federal Census, Concord, New Hampshire,* 1850.
4. *San Francisco City Directory,* 1869. See also *Federal Census, San Francisco,* 1860.
5. *San Francisco Daily Evening Bulletin,* July 31, 1868, in the *Records of the Daughters of the American Revolution,* 169.

The Shakers

The Shakers are a religious sect who arrived in North America from England in 1774. Called by outsiders "the shakers," because of the dancing and shaking movements that were an integral part of their church ritual, they settled in communities across the United States, from New England to Kentucky. Isolating themselves from "the world," they vowed to practice unselfish cooperation, harmony, and simplicity.

All forms of their work emphasized utility, or function, rather than appearance. Desiring only the gratification of their labor, they shunned excessive ornamentation. Today their furnishings and textiles are appreciated for their meticulous craftsmanship, simple beauty, and plain, graceful forms.[1]

Each community was divided into families, which were named after points of the compass or numbers—such as North Family or First Family. There was total equality between the sexes. However, although their creed did not forbid marriage or require the separation of man and wife, the Shakers preferred celibacy. Separate but identical entrances were maintained in the white-painted, clapboard dwelling houses, which still stand today on vast green lawns—one leading to the women's quarters, the other to the men's.

Children were separately housed until they reached fourteen years of age; each was assigned a duty according to his or her age.

The quality of education was excellent. Girls attended classes during the summer and at other times worked in the laundry, helped in the kitchen, or served in the dining room of their assigned family. Boys received schooling during the three winter months, working in the fields or performing other tasks equal to their ability the rest of the year.[2]

Not all children, however, acquiesced willingly to this disciplined lifestyle. Harriet Martineau, who visited among several Shaker communities in the first half of the nineteenth century, recounts in *Society in America*, "One Sunday, when she [a young Shaker girl] was, I believe, about sixteen, she feigned illness, to avoid going to worship. When she believed everyone else gone, she jumped out of a low window, and upon the back of a pony which happened to be in the field. She rode round and round the enclosure, without saddle or bridle, and then re-entered the house."[3]

By the 1880s, the sampler had outlived its usefulness as an instrument of education in America. Academic studies became increasingly available to women, and needlework and painting accomplishments, no longer primary branches of education, were set aside. The Shakers, however, caring little for what went on in "the world," continued with the old ways. Linen, bedding, and clothing were still embroidered with numbers, or initials, although embroidery for the sake of ornamentation was deemed too fancy for their way of life.[4] Only a few Shaker samplers survive today—and these are highly prized by collectors—giving us a glimpse into the needlework requirements of this unusual, and at one time flourishing, society.[5]

The samplers worked by Calista Slack, c. 1826 (fig. 72), and Emily Tinkham, 1863 (fig. 73), are essentially small marking samplers. As with all Shaker samplers, these pieces share the same simplicity and plainness that prevailed within the confines of their isolated community life. The lives of the two girls, however, were to take entirely different directions.

Engraving of Shaker community from Frank Leslie's *Illustrated Newspaper*, September 13, 1873. Young women who lived among the Shakers, but were not yet members, were often assigned duties as waitresses, serving food in the family dining room. Library of Congress, Washington, D. C.

NOTES:

1. Edward Andrews, quoted in Karl Mang and Wend Fischer, *The Shakers: Life and Production of a Community in the Pioneering Days of America*, trans. Dawn Thompson (Munich: Die Neue Sammlung, 1974), 79.
2. June Sprigg, *By Shaker Hands* (New York, NY: Alfred A. Knopf, 1975), 19, and also correspondence with June Sprigg, October 29, 1982. I am indebted to Ms. Sprigg for her kind assistance.
    This information is also based on a conversation I had with Elderess Bertha, in Canterbury, New Hampshire, in the fall of 1982. Having visited this restored village, I was astonished to see the efficient, oversized washing machines and the innovative drying facilities devised to accommodate vast amounts of clothing. The laundry room was well-ventilated and lighted, making it a pleasant area in which to work.
3. Harriet Martineau, *Society in America*, vol. 2 (1837; reprint, New York, NY: AMX Press, 1966), 57, 61, 62.
4. Beverly Gordon, *Shaker Textile Arts* (Hanover, NH: University Press of New England and Merimack Valley Textile Museum and Shaker Community, 1980), 31, 94.
5. Undated letter from Robert F. W. Meader, librarian, Shaker Community, Inc., Hancock, Massachusetts. At the time this was written (1980), Meader knew of only thirty-five or forty Shaker samplers. Varying little from those produced by "the world," they were "severely plain, with no floriated borders (or extremely restrained ones), designed primarily to give the children practice in letters and figures, to enable them to mark linens used in the community—sheets, handkerchiefs, etc., together with a date or room number."

72.

72. CALISTA SLACK (1811–1867)
Enfield Shaker Community, New Hampshire,
c. 1826
Silk or cotton threads on linen (40 threads to the
inch)
Cross-stitches
8⅝ x 10½ in. (21.9 x 26.9 cm)

Inscription: *CALISTA.SLACK/BORN.SEPTEMBER
13YEAR1811/CAME.TO.ENFIELD.TO.
LIVE.MARCH.FEBRUARY.17TH.1826.CAME*

Born in 1811, in Plymouth, Vermont, Calista Slack joined the Shaker Community of Enfield, New Hampshire, in 1826, at the age of fifteen, becoming a member of the Second Family.[1]

In December 1833, at twenty-two, she was appointed to the Order of Family Deacon. By 1838, and for ten years thereafter, she was assistant to Eldress Nancy Allard. Assuming the title of Eldress, Calista Slack moved to the office of the North Family, June 28, 1864.[2]

She died March 11, 1867, at the age of fifty-five, having spent her adult life as a true believer in the Shaker Society.[3]

NOTES:

1. *Shaker Membership Card Index*, compiled by the Western Reserve Historical Society under the direction of Wallace H. Cathcart. Calista Slack is recorded in 1828 as being on the roll of Second Family, 1829, at the age of eighteen. Many other members of the Slack family are included on the sacred roll; a number of them signed it on the same day as Calista, May 5, 1843. Additional information typed by an unknown hand accompanied the sampler.
2. Note accompanying sampler.
3. Ibid.

73. EMILY TINKHAM (1848-1926)
Enfield Shaker Community, Connecticut, 1863
Silk or cotton threads on gauze
(42 threads to the inch), backed with plain
blue, glazed chintz
Cross-stitches
6¼ x 5 ½in. (16.5 x 13.3 cm)

Inscription: *Speak/Kindly/Emily Tinkham born/in
the year 1848/May 6 Now Aged 14/1863/I was brought
to th/is Society May 6 1856*

The sampler worked by Emily Tinkham is a form typical of Shaker schoolgirl needlework. It is plain and unadorned, and its colors are those most often employed for Shaker samplers, medium shades of red and blue. The loosely woven gauze of the finished sampler was attached to a backing of blue glazed-cotton chintz, a technique not commonly found in samplers of this type.[1] It remained unframed for over a century.

Emily Tinkham was the daughter of Seth and Elizabeth A. Tinkham (1827–1851), of Windsor Locks, Connecticut. Born May 8, 1848, she was brought to live in the Society just after her third birthday, following the death of her mother. It was a practice of the Shakers to refrain from recording genealogical data on "adopted" children, or those brought up within the community, except for dates of birth, death, and "belief," that is, the signing of the Covenant. Emily's name first appears in the census records of 1860, as a "house worker" in the Enfield Shaker Community, located north of Hartford, Connecticut.[2]

She did not choose to sign the sacred roll, or Covenant, when she reached adulthood. Instead, like many, she left the Shaker community when she reached maturity. In the summer of 1900, she was living in a boarding house on Chestnut Street in Hartford. The city directory of 1921 indicates that she worked as a chiropodist.[3]

Emily Tinkham, who remained unmarried, died in Hartford, September 2, 1926, and was buried in the Zion Hill Cemetery in an unmarked grave.[4]

NOTES:

1. Letter from Jean Anderson, librarian, The Shaker Museum, Old Chatham, New York, August 13, 1979, to whom I am indebted.
2. The birth certificate registered in Hartford, CT, gives Emily Tinkham's birth year and lists her parents as Seth and Elizabeth Tinkham, Windsor Locks. The death of her mother is recorded in Grove Cemetery at Windsor Locks, August 26, 1851, age 24 years. See also *Federal Census, Enfield Township, Connecticut,* 1860.
3. Information received from Robert F. W. Meader, librarian of the Shaker Community, Inc., Library, Hancock, MA, January 24, 1980. See also *Hartford City Directory,* 1921 and 1922. See also Martineau, *Society in America,* 57.
   Martineau observed, "I saw many a bright face within the prim cap-border, which bore a prophecy of a return to the world; and two of the boys stamped so vigorously in the dance, that it was impossible to imagine their feelings to be very devotional."
4. Date of death is recorded at the Public Health office, Hartford, CT. See also, Connecticut State Library, Hartford, records for dates and place of burial for both Emily and her mother, Elizabeth. I have visited Emily's grave site.

73.

Acknowledgments

It was a most precious gift, the opportunity to research and write this book; and it has given me extraordinary pleasure to pursue the puzzle pieces of the embroidered sampler, the samplermaker, and her schoolmistress. As it has consumed the past fourteen years of my life, many are curious to know how it all came about.

I began by researching the life of Jane Likens, who, in 1822, worked the first American sampler I hesitatingly purchased (see fig. 68). Her story nagged and bothered me until I set out to discover exactly who she was. I traveled to West Virginia, to Charles Town and Shepherdstown, scoured the nineteenth-century record books in the court house, visited the library and the cemetery, met nearly everyone in town, and marveled at the Shenandoah Valley that must be the most beautiful place on earth. Her great-great-granddaughter, Ann Moore Cross, joined in the chase, and the late Reverend Lester Link, a dear Southern gentleman, verified my conclusions. I found Jane all right. She is the one who is really responsible for this book, and I thank her for it.

I began working in the field of sampler embroidery and textiles soon after the completion of *Geometric Designs in Needlepoint* (1976). It brought me full circle from a course in textile identification at Western Michigan University, Kalamazoo, in 1938. Helen Dunham Humm Simon was responsible for my being there. Little did I suspect that I would, in time, have the privilege of associating as an equal with renowned collectors, prominent dealers, museum and university professionals, and scholarly amateurs, who deserve a better title.

Thanks to my husband, Jim, I have been able to travel and work in most of the major cities, and countless rural villages along the eastern seaboard, always searching the area where the samplermaker lived, meeting descendants, working in local libraries and historical societies. I've delved into many a dusty eighteenth-century ledger, losing myself in history as I read early wills and estate inventories. By studying the past, I learned the value of scholarship.

The idea for this book, and the exhibition it accompanies, was first suggested by Jean Taylor Federico, former Director of the Daughters of the American Revolution Museum, Washington, D.C., in 1978. I am grateful to Jean, who recognized my interest in documenting the young samplermaker and her schoolmistress, long before I realized it myself. As a fledgling collector, my education was shaped by Betty Ring. Thankfully, both women changed the direction of my life forever.

I have enjoyed laughter with kindred spirits along the way, including Davida Deutsch, Susan Burrows Swan, Dorothy McCoach, Joan Stephens, and Estelle Horowitz, who gave me my first sampler. And, I have fond memories of the late Theodore H. Kapnek, one of the foremost sampler collectors in America.

Dealers of antique textiles and folk art, patient with an apprentice, included: John Newcomer, Jackie Schneider, Sheila and Edwin Rideout, Amy Finkel, Carol and Stephen Huber, Joel and Kate Kopp, Stephen Score, and Rose Adams, to name a few. Nancy Druckman of Sotheby's, New York, and Louise Woodhead, formerly with Skinner's Gallery, Boston, deserve special appreciation for sharing information, guidance, and friendship.

I am indebted to the researchers who were primarily responsible for documenting the genealogical material. Elaine Justesen, and the late Betty French, scoured the vast Family History Library of the Church of Jesus Christ of Latter-Day Saints, Salt Lake City, Utah, on my behalf. Eva Slezak, specialist in Maryland history, worked on the Baltimore samplermakers. The late

Michael Berry and Gloria Allen frequently checked the records of Daughters of the American Revolution Library for verification of many of the samplermakers. Cherished London friends, Hugh and Betty Auger, kindly obtained valuable British material for me.

And, my husband, Jim Edmonds, who knows an early land record when he sees one, deserves a very special thanks.

I am grateful for the interest and encouragement of my sons, Jim and Chris, and their wives, Sue-Ellen and Diane. They always said, "Mom, it keeps you off the streets." And of course, it did.

Thanks are due to my dedicated friends, Ann Andriesse, Leda Hargrove, Phyllis Brinker, Lee Pierce Dreon, and Clydie Elliott, who listened patiently to my stories of samplermakers, schools for girls, and stitchery. Special appreciation is due the Sakimoto family at Aya's, in Long Beach, California, for their patient assistance in mounting and reframing most of the samplers. In addition, I am grateful to the descendants of the samplermakers who have graciously loaned photographs, maps, and documents.

My thanks to Blanche and Irwin Moss, for introducing me to Edward Maeder, curator of costumes and textiles at the Los Angeles County Museum of Art. Edward and associate curator Dale Gluckman have worked diligently to transform the concept of a sampler exhibition into an actuality. Gene Ogami is responsible for the beautiful photography. Mitch Tuchman, managing editor of publications, directed the original editing and guided the book toward publication, while simultaneously dispatching extravagantly complimentary remarks about the author's work. I am humbled by their confidence.

Museum Director, Earl A. Powell III, unhesitatingly encouraged the presentation of this, the first major sampler exhibition ever to be held on the West Coast. His understanding of the importance of the American sampler as an art form is rare in the museum world.

I owe a great deal to the librarians in this country, from Long Beach, California to Portsmouth, New Hampshire, and I thank them most sincerely for their tireless assistance. I also greatly appreciate the thoughtful copyediting of Jean Quayle and the patient production assistance of Michael Bertrand.

Finally, I would like to express a substantial measure of gratitude to Charles Miers and Sarah Burns of Rizzoli, who are largely responsible for the publication of this book.

M. J. E.

Selected Bibliography

Andrews, Edward. "The Community Industries of the Shakers," in *The Shakers: Life and Production of a Community in the Pioneering Days of America*, eds. Karl Mang and Wend Fischer. Munich, Germany: Die Neue Sammlung, 1974.

Ashton, Leigh. *Samplers*. London, England: The Medici Society, 1926.

Bank, Mirra. *Anonymous Was a Woman*. New York, NY: St. Martin's Press, 1979.

Benes, Peter. *Two Towns, Concord and Wethersfield: a Comparative Exhibition of Regional Culture*. Concord, MA: Concord Antiquarian Museum, 1982.

Bentley, William. *The Diary of William Bentley*, Salem, MA: Essex Institute. Reprint, Gloucester, MA: Peter Smith, 1962.

Bolton, Ethel Stanwood, and Eva Johnston Coe. *American Samplers*. Boston, MA: Massachusetts Society of the Colonial Dames of America, 1921.

Brant, Sandra, and Elissa Cullman. *Small Folk: a Celebration of Childhood in America*. New York, NY: E. P. Dutton/ Museum of American Folk Art, 1980.

Bushong, Millard K. *Historic Jefferson County*. Boyce, VA: Carr Publishing, 1972.

Cabot, Nancy Graves. "Engravings and Embroideries: the Sources of Some Designs in the Fishing Lady Pictures," *Antiques* (December 1941): 367.

————. "The Fishing Lady and Boston Common," *Antiques* (July 1941): 28–31.

Caulfield, S. F. A., and Blanche C. Saward. *The Dictionary of Needlework*. London, England: L. Upcott Gill, 1882.

Caulkins, Frances Manwaring. *History of Norwich, Connecticut*. Norwich, CT: Pequot Press, 1976.

Colby, Averil. *Samplers, Yesterday and Today*. London, England: B.T. Batsford, Ltd., 1964.

Colwill, Stiles Tuttle. *Francis Guy, 1760–1820*. Baltimore, MD: Museum and Library of Maryland History, Maryland Historical Society, 1981.

Cooper, Grace Rogers. *The Copp Family Textiles*. Washington, D. C.: The Smithsonian Institution Press, 1971.

Dandridge, Danske. *Historic Shepherdstown*. Charlottesville, VA, 1910.

Davidson, Mary M. *Plimoth Colony Samplers*. Marion, MA: The Channings, 1975.

Deutsch, Davida Tenenbaum, and Betty Ring. "Homage to Washington in Needlework and Prints," *Antiques* (February 1981): 402–419.

Deutsch, Davida Tenenbaum. "Samuel Folwell of Philadelphia: an Artist for the Needleworker," *Antiques* (February 1981): 420–423.

————. "Washington Memorial Prints," *Antiques* (February 1977): 324–331.

Dow, George Francis. *The Arts and Crafts in New England: 1704–1775: Gleanings from Boston Newspapers*. Topsfield, MA: The Wayside Press, 1927.

Earle, Alice Morse. *Diary of a Boston School Girl*. Boston, MA: Houghton, Mifflin and Company, 1894.

East Side House Settlement. *1986 Winter Antiques Show*. New York, NY: East Side Settlement House, 1986.

Edmonds, Mary Jaene. *Geometric Designs in Needlepoint*. Van Nostrand Reinhold. New York, NY: 1976.

Edwards, Joan. *The History of Embroidery*, vol. 5, *Sampler Making: 1540–1940*. Guildford, England: Bayford Books, 1983.

Elder, William Voss III. *Baltimore Painted Furniture, 1800–1840*. Baltimore, MD: Baltimore Museum of Art, 1972.

Embroidered Samplers in the Collection of the Cooper-Hewitt Museum, ed. Gillian Moss. Washington, D.C.: The Smithsonian Institution's National Museum of Design, 1984.

The Encyclopedia of Collectibles, vol. R–S. Alexandria, VA: Time-Life Books, 1980.

Esslinger, Dean R. *Friends for Two Hundred Years, A History of Baltimore's Oldest School*. Baltimore, MD: Friends School of Baltimore, 1983.

Gardiner, Dorothy. *English Girlhood at School: a Study of Women's Education through Twelve Centuries.* London, England: Oxford University Press, 1929.

Garrett, Elisabeth Donaghy. "American Samplers and Needlework Pictures in the DAR Museum, Part 1: 1739–1806," *Antiques* (February 1974): 356–364.

———. "American Samplers and Needlework Pictures in the DAR Museum, Part 2: 1806–1840," *Antiques* (April 1975): 688–701.

———. *The Arts of Independence.* Washington, D. C.: The National Society, Daughters of the American Revolution, 1985.

Gordon, Beverly. *Shaker Textile Arts.* Hanover, NH: University Press of New England, 1980.

The Great River: Art and Society of the Connecticut Valley, 1635–1820. Hartford, CT: The Wadsworth Atheneum, 1985.

Grow, Judith K., and Elizabeth C. McGrail. *Creating Historic Samplers.* Princeton, NJ: Pyne Press, 1974.

Harbeson, Georgianna Brown. *American Needlework.* New York, NY: Bonanza Books, 1938.

Hole, Helen G. *Westtown through the Years.* Westtown, PA: Westtown Alumni Association, 1942.

Hornor, Marianna Merritt. *The Story of Samplers.* Philadelphia, PA: Philadelphia Museum of Art, 1971.

Huish, Marcus B. *Samplers and Tapestry Embroideries.* London, England: Fine Art Society, 1900.

Hutchins, Catherine E., ed. *Arts of the Pennsylvania Germans.* New York, NY: W. W. Norton and Company, 1983.

Kemble, Frances Ann. *Records of a Girlhood.* New York, NY: Henry Holt and Company, 1884.

King, Donald. *Samplers: Victoria and Albert Museum.* London, England: Her Majesty's Stationery Office, 1960.

Knopf Collector's Guides to American Antiques: Quilts, Coverlets, Rugs and Samplers, ed. Robert Bishop. New York, NY: Alfred A. Knopf, Inc., 1982.

Krueger, Glee. *Gallery of American Samplers.* E. P. Dutton/Museum of American Folk Art. New York, NY: 1978.

———. *New England Samplers to 1840.* Sturbridge, MA: Old Sturbridge Village, 1978.

Lichten, Frances. *Folk Art of Rural Pennsylvania.* New York, NY: Charles Scribner's Sons, 1946.

Little, Frances. *Early American Textiles.* New York, NY: The Century Company, 1931.

Little, Nina Fletcher. *Neat and Tidy: Boxes and Their Contents Used in Early American Households.* New York, NY: E. P. Dutton, 1980.

Martineau, Harriet. *Society in America,* vol. 2. London, England: Saunders and Otley, 1837.

Nafie, Joan. *To the Beat of a Drum.* Norwich, CT: Old Town Press, 1975.

Palliser, Mrs. Bury. *History of Lace,* eds. M. Jourdain and Alice Dryden. Reprint, New York, NY: Dover Publications, Inc., 1984.

Parker, Rozsika. *The Subversive Stitch.* London, England: The Women's Press, 1984.

Payne, F.G. *Guide to the Collection of Samplers and Embroideries.* Cardiff, Wales: National Museum of Wales, 1939.

Penn, William. *The Papers of William Penn,* vol. 2, eds. Richard S. Dunn and Mary Maples Dunn. Philadelphia, PA: University of Pennsylvania Press, 1982.

The Pennsylvania Germans: a Celebration of Their Arts: 1683–1850. Philadelphia, PA: Philadelphia Museum of Art and the Henry Francis Dupont Winterthur Museum, 1982.

Perkins, Mary E. *Old Houses of the Ancient Town of Norwich, 1660–1800.* Norwich, CT, 1895.

Pike, Martha, and Janice Gray Armstrong. *A Time to Mourn: Expressions of Grief in Nineteenth-Century America.* Stony Brook, NY: The Museums at Stony Brook, 1980.

The Polite Lady; or, A Course of Female Education in a Series of Letters from a Mother to Her Daughter Philadelphia, PA: printed for Matthew Carey, 1798.

Power, Eileen. *Medieval English Nunneries.* Cambridge, England: Cambridge University Press, 1922.

Rettew, Gayle. *Behold the Labour of My Tender Age, Children and Their Samplers, 1780–1850.* Rochester, NY: Museum and Science Center, 1983.

Ring, Betty. *American Needlework Treasures.* New York, NY: E. P. Dutton/Museum of American Folk Art, 1987.

———. "For Persons of Fortune Who Have Taste," *Journal of Early Southern Decorative Arts,* vol. 3, no. 2 (November 1977): 1–23.

———. "Legacy of Samplers," in *1979 Antiques Show, Hospital of the University of Pennsylvania, Philadelphia.* Philadelphia, PA: Hospital of the University of Pennsylvania, 1979.

———. *Let Virtue Be a Guide to Thee: Needlework in the Education of Rhode Island Women, 1730–1830.* Providence, RI: Rhode Island Historical Society, 1983.

———. "Maryland Map Samplers," in *1986 Maryland Antiques Show and Sale.* Baltimore, MD, 1986: 105–109.

———, ed. *Needlework: an Historical Survey.* New York, NY: The Main Street Press, 1975.

———. "Needlework Pictures from Abby Wright's School in South Hadley, Massachusetts," *Antiques* (September 1986): 482–493.

———. "Print Work: a Silk-Wrought Deception," in *1980 Theta Charity Antiques Show.* Houston, TX: Theta Charity, 1980.

———. "Samplers and Pictorial Needlework at the Chester County Historical Society," *Antiques* (December 1984): 1423–1433.

Schaffner, Cynthia V.A. and Susan Klein. *Folk Hearts, A Celebration of the Heart Motif in American Folk Art.* New York, NY: Alfred A. Knopf, Inc., 1984.

Schiffer, Margaret B. *Historical Needlework of Pennsylvania.* New York, NY: Charles Scribner's Sons, 1968.

Schipper-Van Lottum, Bix. *Overmerklappen gesproken.* Amsterdam: Wereldbibliotheek, 1980.

Schorsch, Anita. *Images of Childhood: an Illustrated Social History*. New York, NY: Mayflower Books, Inc., 1979.

Sewall, Samuel. *The Diary of Samuel Sewall*, l674–1729, ed. M. Halsey Thomas. New York, NY: Farrar Straus and Giroux, n.d.

Smith, Frank. *Genealogical Gazetteer of England*. Baltimore, MD: Genealogical Publishing Co., 1968.

Southgate, Eliza. *A Girl's Life Eighty Years Ago: Selections from the Letters of Eliza Southgate Browne*. New York, NY: Charles Scribner's Sons, 1888.

Sprigg, June. *By Shaker Hands*. New York, NY: Alfred A. Knopf. Inc., 1975.

———. *Domestic Beings*. New York, NY: Alfred A. Knopf, Inc., 1984.

———. *Shaker Design*. New York, NY: Whitney Museum of American Art, 1986.

———. *Shaker Masterworks of Utilitarian Design Created between 1800 and 1875 by the Master Craftsmen and Craftswomen of America's Foremost Communal Religious Sect*. Katonah, NY: Katonah Gallery, 1983.

Swain, Margaret H. *Historical Needlework: a Study of Influences in Scotland and Northern England*. London, England: Barrie and Jenkins, 1970.

———. "Scottish Samplers: Names and Places," *Scottish Home and Country* (February 1980): 78–82.

Swan, Susan Burrows. *Plain and Fancy: American Women and Their Needlework, 1700–1850*. New York, NY: Holt, Rinehart and Winston, 1977.

———. *A Winterthur Guide to American Needlework*. New York, NY: Crown Publishers, Inc., 1976.

Vanderpoel, Emily Noyes. *Chronicles of a Pioneer School from 1792 to 1833, Being the History of Miss Sarah Pierce and Her Litchfield School*. Cambridge, MA: Harvard University Press, 1903.

———. *More Chronicles of a Pioneer School, Being Added History on the Litchfield Female Academy Kept by Miss Sarah Pierce and Her Nephew, John Pierce Brace*. Cambridge, MA: Harvard University Press, 1927.

Vinciolo, Federico *Les Singuliers et nouveaux portraicts*. Paris, France: Jean Leclerc, 1587. Reprint entitled *Renaissance Patterns for Lace and Embroidery*, ed. Eliza Ricci. New York, NY: Dover Publications, 1971.

Williams, Elsa S. *Bargello, Florentine Canvas Work*. New York, NY: Van Nostrand Reinhold, l967.

Wister, Sally. *Sally Wister's Journal, 1777–1778*, ed. Albert Cook Meyers. Philadelphia, PA: Ferris and Leach, 1902.

Woody, Thomas. *A History of Women's Education in the United States*. New York, NY: Octagon Books, 1974.

———. *Early Quaker Education in Pennsylvania*. New York, NY: Teachers College, Columbia University, 1920.

Index